Whitman

Whitman's Wild Children

Neeli Cherkovski

The Lapis Press

Venice   San Francisco

Published 1988 by The Lapis Press
Printed in the United States of America

George Scrivani first suggested that I write this book as a combination of personal reflection and literary criticism. His invaluable editorial assistance in the preparation of a final manuscript is deeply appreciated. Further editorial work was done by Raymond Foye who also provided much needed advice and information I could not have received elsewhere. Jan Butterfield of The Lapis Press has guided this book through all necessary stages. I wish to express my gratitude for her patience and understanding.

My appreciation to Michael Weiner, Gerald Nicosia, Les Ferriss, Harold Norse, Victor Di Suvero, Tim Paulson, John Mueller, and Aung Aung Taik for their encouragement, and to Charles Wehrenberg who led me into the computer age.

Earlier versions of some of these chapters appeared in *ACM (Another Chicago Magazine)*, *Los Angeles Times Magazine*, *Mirage*, and *ZYZZYVA*.

The title for my book is taken from Lawrence Ferlinghetti's *Populist Manifesto*.

The Lapis Press

589 N. Venice Blvd.
Venice CA 90291

1850 Union St., Suite 466
San Francisco CA 94123

ISBN 0-932499-57-0 Cloth
ISBN 0-932499-56-2 Paper

For Jessie Cabrera

Poets to Come

Poets to come! orators, singers, musicians to come!
Not to-day is to justify me, and answer what I am for;
But you, a new brood, native, athletic, continental, greater
    than before known,
Arouse! Arouse—for you must justify me—you must answer.

I myself but write one or two indicative words for the future,
I but advance a moment, only to wheel and hurry back in the
    darkness.

I am a man who, sauntering along, without fully stopping,
    turns a casual look upon you, and then averts his face,
Leaving it to you to prove and define it,
Expecting the main things from you.

Walt Whitman

Contents

Preface

Walt Whitman's ambition for *Leaves of Grass* was that it express his total being: "This is no book; who touches this, touches a man."

I hope that *Whitman's Wild Children* gives a living image of the poets I have chosen. Most were schooled outside formalist settings and understand the necessity of striking out on one's own, of breaking new ground. They adhered to the first rule for the Whitman tradition: taking to the open road both physically and spiritually.

Whitman embraced his Quaker upbringing and Ralph Waldo Emerson's writings: "We must find the world from within." Whitman's *Leaves of Grass*, written in 1855, was a declaration of independence from conventions; it stood as a living example of what a man might create on his own terms, listening to his own voice. As Whitman added to and subtracted from his epic poem, he never retreated from his original intention of disturbing and disrupting mundane, ordinary thought.

Leaves of Grass praised the individual's uniqueness and called for a renewed understanding of our commonality. Whitman's poem rings with interconnectedness, though he stood alone. He had no antecedents. His breakthrough became a floodgate: Jack London, Stephen Crane, Theodore Dreiser, Sherwood Anderson. Henry Miller wrote of Whitman: "I hardly think of him as a poet. Bard, yes, the Bard of the Future."

Since Whitman, the "writer as rebel" has become a tradition. Charles Bukowski is the most adamant among them in turning his back on academia. "Whores, hospitals, and jails, these are the universities of life from which I hold several degrees," he once wrote. "Call me 'Mister.'" When I first met him, he announced that he didn't own a dictionary. Years later, finding one hidden under the chair I sat in, he said, "Okay, kid, you found me out."

I met Bukowski when I was fifteen. What impressed me first was his sense of humor. He knew the power of the comic, and he understood the necessity of striking out on one's own, of breaking new ground. When I was twenty-three, I met Harold Norse; he has been both mentor and close friend. Allen Ginsberg has been important to me since 1957, when I began reading his works.

I started writing about Bukowski, Norse, and Ginsberg, three poets who have made the biggest impression on me. The experiences I had with them were rich, filled with humor and wit, trials and triumphs. After completing the three essays, I read them publicly. The response was positive, more so than with any of my previous prose works. I then decided to write about other poets, all of whom I knew well or with whom I felt a kinship beyond the literary. The project evolved into an intimate notebook about ten poets who helped define contemporary American literature.

Each of these ten poets has taken his own road. Each has had little to do with what was thought acceptable in mainstream American literature of the 1940s and 1950s. None have shied away from the use of the personal pronoun, nor do they labor under the influence of the avant-garde. They are all intensely American, and their rebellion is uniquely American in how they live and what they write. For many, their interest in pursuing the vocation of poet was strengthened by the McCarthy years and the great sleep of the Eisenhower decade.

Each of Whitman's wild children, with a few exceptions, has taken on the role of Bard, placing himself directly in line with Whitman. I like to think of Whitman happily looking down on this tribe of poets. Perhaps he would be envious, marveling at Norse's *Homo*; maybe a bit perplexed by Everson's intense struggle with Catholicism; clearly puzzled by Bukowski's hubris.

If I could take Whitman by the hand I would lead him to Land's End, where the continent meets the Pacific, and I would ask him for more songs. He might turn to me and proclaim from *Leaves of Grass*:

Walt Whitman, a kosmos, of Manhattan the son,
Turbulent, fleshy, sensual, eating, drinking and breeding,
No sentimentalist, no stander above men and women or apart from
   them,
No more modest than immodest.

Unscrew the locks from the doors!
Unscrew the doors themselves from the jambs!

Notes on a Dirty Old Man

the tragedy of the leaves

I awakened to dryness and the ferns were dead,
the potted plants yellow as corn;
my woman was gone
and the empty bottles like bled corpses
surrounded me with their uselessness;
the sun was still good, though,
and my landlady's note cracked in fine and
undemanding yellowness; what was needed now
was a good comedian, ancient style, a jester
with jokes upon absurd pain; pain is absurd
because it exists, nothing more;
I shaved carefully with an old razor
the man who had once been young and
said to have genius; but
that's the tragedy of the leaves,
the dead ferns, the dead plants;
and I walked into a dark hall
where the landlady stood
execrating and final,
sending me to hell,
waving her fat, sweaty arms
and screaming
screaming for rent
because the world had failed us
both.

Charles Bukowski
From *Burning in Water, Drowning in Flame*

Bukowski called. "I've got the blues, baby, the deep blues. Can you make it over?"

"Sure," I said. My apartment felt like a steam bath. Bad air hung over the city like a sheet of iron. Before leaving, I glanced over to the shelf holding Bukowski's works. I let those old titles, the ones printed on the book spines, tumble through me: *Run with the Hunted, Confessions of a Man Insane Enough to Live with Beasts, All the Assholes in the World and Mine, Crucifix in a Deathhand, Notes of a Dirty Old Man,* and *At Terror Street and Agony Way.* The poet's originality came through, even in his choice of titles. Looking westward from Los Angeles, he would not think of Japan and China across the wide expanse of the Pacific. His vision would stop at the Santa Monica Pier, where some old guy might be throwing his line into oily water while a cop beat on the head of a wino on a landing under the pilings, his badge illuminated in a glint of moonlight. In *the singular self,* one of his early poems, we are given the sea:

I have been unable to sleep,
and with my car above me
like a steel mother
I crawl down the cliffs,
breaking bits of rock
and being scratched by witless
and scrabby seaplants . . .

Don't expect a rhapsodic ode for the ocean to follow. What comes next is pure Bukowski. He is a man more used to fighting his way on and off the freeways of Los Angeles or standing in a liquor store line for a six-pack than baring his soul to the seashore:

the sea stinks
and makes flushing sounds
like a toilet
it is a bad place to die . . .

I left my apartment on Alta Loma, passing the landlord's front porch, but not before he called me over. I was in for another long rap.

"Good evening," the old man said. "My son is coming home from Vietnam. He is a very good boy. A good American boy. I got a postcard. People got a chance here."

I looked at my watch. Bukowski would be waiting. I wanted to break away, but the old man held firmly to my wrist. He squinted, making his prune-like face even more wizened.

"You come to Mykonos someday. We have windmills on my island just like the one I make here," he said, pointing to the miniature windmill in front of his court. It was made of concrete covered in stucco and painted a blazing white color. A little blue cupola sat on top.

"When my son come home, we drink together. Retsina from Greece. There is nothing like it here."

I insisted on leaving.

"You going to see that horrible man again? My Tom told me that your friend writes bad things in the newspaper, that anti-American paper. You watch out for him."

"Sure," I said, "I'll be careful."

I was reminded of the time I took Bukowski to a beer bar in San Bernardino where I hung out. We stood at the bar, drinking. Phil, the sad-faced owner, called me to the far end of the counter and whispered, "Look, I don't want no trouble. Finish your beer and get him out of here." Bukowski didn't have to say a thing. His face said it all.

Charles Bukowski. Henry Charles Bukowski. I drove to see him as stucco fell off the windmills of Mykonos. The sky was the same color as the face of the man dying in the window across from my place on Alta Loma. I paid sixty-five dollars a month to surround myself with death.

I passed Sunset Boulevard, heading east, passing the Hollywood Memorial Park, where I had snuck in one night to fall asleep on Tyrone Power's bench-like tomb, done in by cheap vodka. Then I took a turn north on Normandie, arriving at De Longpre, a street lined with huge palm trees that have been there since the days of Fatty Arbuckle. In the middle of the block sat an old Ukrainian Orthodox Church, its spires rising toward the sun, and across from it a low, pink building, Hollywood Rest Home, providing Bukowski plenty of opportunities to fantasize. He would say, "One day I might be sitting in one of those cold, sterile rooms, helpless. Then you can come in and dance around my body as I sit there trying to raise my arms."

I pulled up to his place, the first apartment in a shoddy court, rented from one Peter Krate, a short, bull-necked man who liked to drink with his famous tenant.

"He's in," Krate said, as he watered the thin strip of grass between the driveway and his units.

I stepped up to the porch and knocked. Bukowski called out, in that slow manner of speaking he had, "Hold on, baby, I'll be right there." A voice strong and resonant, not unlike that of Humphrey Bogart.

A few minutes later, the door opened and there he stood, Henry C. Bukowski. Hank. Beastbuk. The Outsider. Good time Charley. Charles. Never Chuck. That is one name he would always run from, quickly. He looked like an iguana, taking one step at a time, eyes leering from side to side. The only soft thing about him was his hands. He used to say, "Look at my hands, kid. See how delicate they are." He was old-time L. A. cool, slow to praise and slow to censure, yet quick on the rejoinder. His hair was carefully combed straight back; a casting director looking for a character in a screen adaptation of Raymond Chandler's *The Big Sleep* would not have to go further than Bukowski.

"Come on in, kid," he said, "I'm on the cross, tricked by mere horses. It was murder out there. Nothing was right. Even the grandstands lost their edge of glory and the once-beautiful ladies looked like subnormals."

I stepped into the cave-like front room filled with cheap furnishings. The most important item in the room, however, was the manual typewriter on a stand adjacent to the front door.

"Forget the track. At least you're making it with the writing," I said.

"If you call getting an invitation to submit poems to some mimeo magazine in east Dallas success, then I've really made it," he said. "These magazines appear out of nowhere. Any kid with fifty bucks can purchase a mimeograph and crank out forty pages filled with typos and call it a magazine. I mean, sometimes there's good stuff in these babies, but mostly . . ."

"But you have books out," I said.

"You do have a point there, kid. I can imagine some coed back East reading *Terror Street* and forming my name slowly on her lips, Bu . . . kow . . . ski, Bukowski. . . . But where the hell is she and where are the money boys, for Christ sake?"

He was in his bathrobe, a beer in hand. I saw a sheet of paper in the typewriter with a few lines typed out. He had been writing a poem when I knocked on the door. I felt a little guilty, but he was the one who had phoned.

"Grab a beer," he said. "When you get back in here from the kitchen, maybe you can tell me, when does the pain end? I want to know, when does it finally cease?"

"Jesus, Hank, you're supposed to have the answers . . ." I responded.

Bukowski worked for the U.S. Postal Service back then. It was a huge Spanish-style building, downtown, next to the old Union Depot where trains from the East came in. It bore the graceless American title, Terminal Annex Post Office.

"They got me on a treadmill," he said as I came back into the small living room, carefully avoiding the beer bottles scattered on the floor. "I stand there and sort these letters into their appropriate slots. What a dead-ass job. Me. Bukowski. Tough guy."

"You might make it someday with your prose," I said, "and then you can quit."

"I hope to hell I can, Neeli. By the way, they have openings for the upcoming Christmas season. I have pull down there. Do you want a job? Might do you some good. Look what it's done for me."

He always tried to make me suffer one way or another.

"Thanks, Hank. Some other time."

Rachmaninoff blared out of his cheap radio, against which a half-dozen books, all written by him, were propped.

Charles Bukowski was born on August 16, 1920, in Andernach, Germany, a small town on the Rhine River, the son of a German mother and an American GI father from Pasadena, California, who met his bride-to-be during the First World War. He was brought to Los Angeles at the age of three. His father held small-time jobs, and the family lived on the edges of the middle class. Speaking of the period, he said, "I remember the kids at school whose families had money. These kids would go on to the universities. All I looked forward to were shipping clerk jobs, road crews, and loading docks. Exactly where I ended up. Hell, I used to go down to Skid Row just to check on what the future held in store for me." The closest he ever came to big money was his one-year marriage in 1956 to Barbara Frye, a poet and heiress to a Texas fortune.

I first heard of Bukowski in 1960 from the poet Jory Sherman, who arrived in San Bernardino from San Francisco with crazy Beatnik stories. He had a packet of press clippings on his sixty-five unpaid parking tickets. He told me about a man in Los Angles named Charles Bukowski who had just published a chapbook of poetry, *Flower, Fist and Bestial Wail.* I liked the title. Sherman said, "He's not one of the Beats. This guy is totally his own man. Hardly anyone knows about him except a circle of writers who contribute to the small-press scene."

Bukowski was just over forty years of age. He had grown up in the Depression and World War II. The Beat scene bored him. Sherman kept promising to introduce me. Finally the day came when I was told that Bukowski would be coming to visit. I was fifteen and Bukowski was forty-two. When he arrived, I feigned sleep. He walked into my bedroom with my father who said, "Wake up. Bukowski is here." As I got out of bed, before me stood this large man with a ravaged face, broad shoulders, and deep, penetrating eyes.

"Okay, little Rimbaud. I heard you wanted to meet Bukowski," he said. Then he looked at the photos of some of my literary heroes on the wall and said, "Jesus, how come there are none of me?"

We went into the living room. I handed Bukowski a handmade book of poems I had written about him. He took one look at it, reading the first few lines, and threw it into the fireplace where my father had made a blazing fire.

I dove in after the book, managing to save it. Only the fringes were burned.

Bukowski took it from me, saying, "I'll read your little poem, but no one has ever written about me. I'm sorry, kid."

Fifteen minutes later he was in the kitchen trying to make love to my mother. "Come on, Clare," he said, "I'm more of a man than Sam. Let's make it."

Two years later, a small press in Florida published a collection called *Poems and Drawings*, followed in the same year by *Longshot Pomes for Broke Players*. I carried those books around everywhere. Occasionally I would call Bukowski. Having noticed that we appeared opposite one another in *Epos*, a little magazine, he said, "Hey, kid. Are you going to crowd me out of the journals?"

I thought of him as a weather vane of the human condition. He hadn't bought the Eisenhower decade, nor did the Kennedy cult of youth and glamor impress him much. In Bukowski's view, a blanket of doom lay over the country. In *the house*, he put it simply:

it seems people should stop working
and sit in small rooms
on second floors
under electric lights without shades;
it seems there is a lot to forget
and a lot not to do
and in drugstores, markets, bars,
the people are tired, they do not want
to move, and I stand there at night
and look through this house and the
house does not want to be built; . . .

I began picking up the literary journals and found Bukowski represented with increasing frequency. There was a tough edge to the poems I had never seen before. I felt the way he did. When I read him, it was as if he had pulled me over to his side from the rotting hulk of school and everything else that oppressed me. It wasn't so much what he said, but his attitude that crept up on me slowly. Unlike the Beat poets, his declamations were subtle. They were interwoven with storytelling in the classic sense of the word. I loved the deliberate misspelling I found in the title of *Longshot Pomes for Broke Players*. Another book from those years, *Run with the Hunted*, he signed, "For Neeli Cherry. I hope I have awakened some of your young sleep, Charles Bukowski." Next to it was a picture of a man smoking a cigarette with a p.s. beneath: "God, you should have heard some of Franky Roosevelt's fireside chats."

When I was fifteen I edited a poetry magazine called *The Black Cat Review*. Bukowski sent me a packet of poems, and I chose *New York as I Remember It and I Guess It Hasn't Changed* for my first issue. The poem remains one of his only sustained comments, in poetry, on an American city other than Los Angeles. I liked the earthiness of such lines as "but its hates are real: you can smell them on the sweet subways / of morning; / but at least give them this: everyman does not dream himself king / as in L.A. where even hamburgers try for / glamour in the pan." In the biographical note accompanying his poem I wrote: "Bukowski is widely publ. in literary journals and has three books of poetry to his credit. Hates the word 'stars' in poems. Lives in L.A. and on occasion drops over to San Bernardino to keep this youthful editor from getting his needed sleep." On the following page I printed a poem of my own called *This one Bukowski threw in the fireplace (without reading)*. The poem begins:

Bukowski looks out of his window
He looks out of his Hollywood window
His Hollywood Park window
Bukowski looks down from his three story window
He can see little children playing below
And he cries because someday they will die
When the fallout crosses the street they will die . . .

The poem of Bukowski's that I remember most clearly from those years is *Old Man, Dead in a Room*. In 1963 the poem appeared as the final piece in *It Catches My Heart in Its Hand*, a hand-printed book from Loujon Press, New Orleans. I remember thinking how the tone differed radically from what I had heard from the lips of my English teacher:

this thing upon me is not death
but it's as real,
and as landlords full of maggots
pound for rent
I eat walnuts in the sheath
of my privacy

and listen for more important
drummers . . .

I embraced those lines and looked on Bukowski as a soul mate,
as one who knew that the classroom was a lie and the president
a puppet. Right down the line, he understood. His rhythms
soothed me. He took ordinary words and magically combined
them to produce stark, profound images at once both hard as
rock, yet vulnerable, as Bukowski in person can be. I learned in
later years something about "the sheath of privacy" he wore
around himself like a coat of armor, to keep the world away. In
1960, however, "this . . . is not death, but it's as real," sufficed,
as talk of fallout shelters emanated from the highest levels. Even
at sixteen I knew that represented a hopeless path. The "landlords full of maggots" also struck me, especially since I had visited
his earlier apartment, a third floor walk-up on Mariposa Street
in Hollywood.

His was a natural voice for the dispossessed. Not a crusader,
still he led the charge by the single-mindedness of his vision. In
much of the poetry of his contemporaries, the jargon of the leftist
movement entered the poems, especially in protesting social and
economic injustices. Bukowski's protest had the feel of the outsider who lived beyond all limits and ideologies. Society had
failed, both from the right and left. As he said to me once: "The
difference between voting for Nixon or Johnson is like trying to
differentiate between warm shit and cold shit." He called to mind
Jackie Gleason's show, "The Honeymooners," the 1950s TV epic
of the hapless Ralph Cramden, bus driver, pitted against forces
too large for him to overcome, yet living an existence with room
for love, humor, and dreaming. Bukowski once told me, "I always
liked Gleason's comedy, the truthful, long, slow murder of humanity, filled with a Brooklynese madness of poor people pitted
against the bosses, always about to be fired. Jesus, how could I
help but identify?"

Shying away from popular culture has never been a part of Bukowski's armor. He is usually the central character in his poetry
and prose—a man who made a deliberate choice to take on
working-class jobs and live in cheap, furnished rooms. He only
asked to be left alone, feeling no responsibility for anyone but
himself. "You have to watch those who have the answers," he

used to say. "Beware of those who know why war is good or why it is bad, and what is good literature or bad literature. Those who talk peace will often be the first to stick the knife in your ribs. In other words, I distrust everyone."

I remember his excitement when Pablo Neruda won the Nobel prize in Literature. "Outside of myself, I don't know anyone with such a clean line. When he says 'blue' he means blue. The problem is when he becomes political. That is his weakness."

Bukowski's writing matured under the shadow of the big names of his youth. He could rhapsodize endlessly on William Saroyan, "Papa" Hemingway, and William Faulkner, making them come alive in his drab bungalow on De Longpre. He had come of age under the myth of the invincible writer, and, in his mind, he pictured himself protected against society by the sheer power of his poetry and prose. "You have to be so damn good they cannot deny you," he told me.

In poetry or prose, the story line remained his main anchor. The motifs he developed, whether of the indomitable landlord or the sad sack next door coming home to drink and heave up his guts surrounded by desolation, came alive in his clear narrative style, simple and unadorned. The avant-garde in art and literature meant nothing to him or his development. Nor did he see much in the Beats. He stayed with the larger-than-life writers who had influenced his youth. He was unimpressed by Ezra Pound's axiom, "make it new," and expressed his theory of composition as "just plain hard work." As he became better known, he said, "Now the professors come by with their little six-packs of beer, and they want to know the secret. There isn't any fucking secret. It's just work, day by day, banging on the typer." He denounced universities so vehemently that I fled the English department when I was attending college and entered the American History program. He would say, "Don't let them touch your writing. Stay with what you have naturally."

Since he began as a short-story writer, his poetry has retained a narrative style. He gradually developed a strong personal tone, the one I had sensed in those first chapbooks. The voice in the poem stood larger than the language: the presence of the man from outside, the tough guy who can see through everything, who can, in Bukowski's words, "spot a phony from forty thousand yards."

From his earliest poems, Bukowski has affirmed the call Walt Whitman made for a clear, articulate voice wholly indigenous to the American earth. Beyond that, Bukowski's own insistence that a poem be devoid of tricks, that it not be in line with a standardized literary tradition, is precisely the same note that Whitman struck in the preface to *Leaves of Grass*. Bukowski often spoke of "those preconceptions people have of what a poem should be . . . that's what needs to be forgotten. You must listen to your own voice." Rather than ranging far and wide over the continent, he chose to write about a particular urban environment, Los Angeles. His "I" centered work is filled with images that Whitman's common man can readily relate to, and his language is precisely the democratic tongue that the author of *Leaves of Grass* aspired to and called on others to help formulate. Bukowski is Whitman's "average man," living and creating outside of institutional settings. Whitman's commonality attracted Bukowski. He often spoke of Whitman as the one who opened the door to a freer style and to an unabashed sense of selfness in the poem.

Bukowski's presence in his writings is much like that encountered in Louis-Ferdinand Céline's prose, the uncompromising outsider. The writing is an excuse for stripping the world of pretense. Céline's *Death on the Installment Plan*, especially in the opening chapters, reads as a prelude to Bukowski. Both writers utilize humor. With Céline it is often employed with bitterness, producing an hallucinatory effect. In Bukowski's writing, humor softens the harder edges. His first novel, *Post Office*, tells of a man relating his life, which began "as a mistake."

His attitudes on life and art were forged while growing up in Los Angeles. Much of this is documented in *Ham on Rye*. Most of what is in that book I had heard in conversation during our two- and three-day drinking and talking sessions that we often taped. I later realized how those were actually work sessions for Bukowski. Yes, he was socializing and enjoying himself, but he was also working. "I didn't like my parents," he would tell me. "Come on, Hank. That can't be entirely true." He would counter, "Believe it, kid." Then I would say, "What about when they died?" He'd say, "Uh uh, nothing. Zero. They just died."

From the beginning, his father had been a stern disciplinarian. When he turned to his mother for help, she succumbed to the dominance of her husband. "My father was always right, and I was always wrong. It was a simple way of looking at things for the old man. So how the hell do you expect me to feel? It was like the final breakdown of things. In other words, my old man going insane and beating the shit out of me because after I mowed the lawn he inspected it and found one blade of grass uncut, was like America itself coming and beating me down because I wouldn't turn a lathe somewhere for forty-five years until my head turned into hamburger like my father's."

Thrift, hard work, and the hiding of one's emotions were big concepts in the house of Henry Charles Bukowski, Sr.—a man who had no particular leanings toward art or literature. "When I told my parents that I was going to be a writer, they knew for sure that their suspicions about me would more than likely come true. I certainly didn't want to disappoint them."

Perhaps his father understood that his son didn't fit into any norm. Yet Bukowski could accomplish most tasks laid down before him if he applied himself, like the time he won the ROTC drill contest in high school. "Hell, I didn't even try to win. I just went through the motions, marching to the right and to the left and I won a medal, which I threw away walking home."

His teachers sickened him, and he began looking on them as enemies. He had friends but didn't share their values, and he bore eternal enmity toward rich kids, those who would go on to universities. "I distrusted the ones getting top grades, who dressed and behaved properly at all times, as if nothing ever bothered or even entered their heads. They had dead expressions on their faces, and I can imagine how they look now with those same dead expressions."

He wandered out of the city of Los Angeles in his twenties, first to New Orleans, then to Philadelphia. He found himself in Texas once, sitting on a park bench in El Paso. We were well into a fourth six-pack when Bukowski told me this story back in 1969. "There were three or four of us, maybe five. We pooled our money to buy some wine. I think it came to a total of twenty-seven cents after I added my six pennies. I said to myself, 'This is going nowhere,' and so I walked away. Down there in El Paso there was a little brick library. When you have nothing else to do, you go to a library. I went up to the shelves and began looking at titles. On

the spine of one of those books I saw *Notes From Underground*
by a man named Fyodor Dostoyevski. When you're down for the
count on a goddamn park bench you kind of feel like the underground. I took that book from the shelf, found a chair, and began
reading. The words marched into me like lightning. I kept saying,
'This guy has got it . . . this guy has got it.' And I was right."
Bukowski saw himself in the hero of that book, a man who felt
sickened by the lies, silent and loud, apparent and hidden, all-
pervasive in the world. He knew that most people sold their souls,
including those who wrote or painted, and he vowed he wouldn't
let that happen.

Adamant that a writer is made, not born, he pointed to his first
story, written about Baron Manfred von Richtofen, the World
War I German flying ace. "It was in 1935. I wrote about a man
with an iron hand. He had lost his hand in battle, a man who shot
people out of the sky. The other kids were making love. I had these
boils on my face. You know the story. I would go to L.A. General
Hospital and the doctors would drill into my face. You want to
know something? Fear made me a writer, fear and lack of
confidence."

Enamored of the thought of being a major literary figure, like
some half-insane Theodore Dreiser erupting out of the pavement
of Los Angeles, throwing aside palm trees and hamburger stands,
he spent most of his time writing, even going without food, living
for the next story. He would send out his efforts to publishers and
they would all come back rejected. At age twenty-four he had a
piece called *Notes on a Rejection Slip* in *Story*, Whit Burnett's
prominent magazine.

In 1969 I received a late-night call from Bukowski. "Listen, kid.
We're going to be rich and powerful. I met an old school friend
who wants to invest some money in a literary magazine. You'll
edit it with me. I've even got a name, *The Contemporary Review:
A Non-Snob Compilation of Active Creativity Now.*"

"It doesn't fit. We need a tougher, wilder title, something different than the others," I said.

Less than forty-eight hours later the phone rang.

"This is Bukowski. I got the title."

"Go ahead," I replied.

"*Laugh Literary And Man The Humping Guns*, publishers, Hatchetman Press."

"You got it," I said.

The promised investment, however, was not forthcoming. We had to find the money ourselves, producing a photo-offset magazine of forty typewritten pages. We took poems from writers we knew in the L.A. area. After the first issue, hundreds of submissions began pouring in. Most were attracted by the idea of having something published in Bukowski's magazine.

"This is frightening," he said. "All this shit arrives in the mail, to my address. It's depressing."

Often we'd only read the first poem in a five- or six-page manuscript and then send the entire thing back without going further. One drunken night Bukowski wrote, "These won't do," on a rejection slip and returned it to a prominent professor of creative writing. Then I wrote, "We wouldn't publish these if our lives depended on it." After that Bukowski went into the kitchen, got an egg, and cracked it into a dish. He crumpled a manuscript and dipped it into the dish. I added beer. Then we went to work on another manuscript, burning tiny holes in it. Next we wrote obscenities on various rejection notes. By the end of the evening we had disposed of forty-five manuscripts.

The following morning we both felt a tinge of guilt, which grew over the ensuing weeks. Always, Bukowski hoped for a new discovery. He wanted "that tough e.e. cummings in bronze" to break on through. One hot summer night in 1969 he thought he had made such a discovery. He called, saying, "I have a great writer here. You must come over, immediately."

"Hank," I said, turning on a light and glancing at the clock, "do you realize it's 3:00 A.M.?"

"Doesn't matter. I have been reading these poems for hours. They have power. This is what I have been waiting for."

"Can't it wait a little longer?"

"No, it cannot," he said with finality.

I drove to De Longpre Avenue and soon found myself standing before my co-editor and a poet named Tracy Gross. He sat across from Bukowski, his eyes glazed over with impotence. And yet, I thought to myself, what do I know? Perhaps I had been mistaken when I heard him read at the Bridge in the Saturday poetry series.

Bukowski sat in an overstuffed chair next to the radio stand. Empty beer cans littered the dirty rug. He handed me Gross' stack of poems. First, I wanted to relax. We drank and talked about women, poetry, and ourselves for a few hours. Finally Bukowski asked me to do my job as an editor of *Laugh Literary*. I took a poem from the stack and began reading. The first poem was called *Twilight L.A.* It began:

The ravens call
from streets of light
where darkness darts
and women rape the wind
I stand aside
to dream wonderful dreams
of where the raven pecks
at life.

It did have something in the first four lines. Then I read another poem, worse than the first.

When I finished, I looked up at Gross and then over to Bukowski. They were smiling at one another, hardly aware of my presence. I handed the poems back to Bukowski. "Why don't you do a second reading?" He began to read. And, as the first rays of dawn entered through the curtains, forming a perfect halo around his head, Bukowski said, "Jesus! This stuff is horrible! They don't make it. Not one of them. There is hardly a line with backbone enough to stand up until noon."

Suddenly Gross shot out of his chair, grabbed his manuscript from Bukowski's hands, and turned to me as he left: "You ruined it. Things were going fine until you showed up. He loved my poems."

Bukowski leaned over in his chair and said, "I'd like to thank you for saving me from those poems," after which we drove to Mort's, an all-night restaurant on Sunset that served a $1.49 breakfast special. We would go there often, laughing at ourselves, one another, and the customers. This morning it was Bukowski's treat.

but this thing upon me
as I tear the window shades
and walk caged rugs,

this thing upon me
like a flower and a feast,
believe me
is not death and is not
glory
. . . . .
this thing upon me
crawling like a snake,
terrifying my love of commonness,
some call Art
some call poetry;
it's not death
but dying will solve its power . . .

Bukowski's "love of commonness" is what held him together
and forced him to stay with his stories, and eventually led him to
poetry. He wanted to communicate what he perceived as an intensely personal, wholly original vision. Yet he could never rid
himself of the Romantic myth of the artist.

and as my gray hands
drop a last desperate pen
in some cheap room
they will find me there
and never know
my name
my meaning
nor the treasure
of my escape.

He sees himself as the tough guy from the streets, but it masks a
vulnerable, sensitive writer unable to shake off feelings of being
somehow different. Yet being different, and his embarrassment
about it, is a theme to be dealt with: "I apologized for the beer
cans, my beard, and everything on the floor," he writes in *I Am
Visited by an Editor and a Poet.*

There are few writers as unaffected by the idea of demonstrat-
ing their proficiency, how many tricks are in their respective bags,
as Bukowski. Los Angeles, which he celebrated for the common
sights, sounds, and banalities others made light of or used as reasons for sociological essays about the profanity of modern civi-

lization, had sunk indelibly into his consciousness. His novels, *Post Office, South Of No North, Ham on Rye*, and parts of *Women*, offer keen insight into the life of Los Angeles. Bukowski's deadpan style and humor come through as a saving grace, making Los Angeles the perfect atmosphere for his characters, most of whom struggle at the low end of the social scale, just getting by.

Humor, which he once told me had been part of a dialogue he held with himself as an adolescent, was his secret weapon against the dullness he sensed around him. "Humor kept me alive. Being able to laugh at others, but also myself, helped make me a writer. This, with commonality of tone, is my strength," Bukowski said.

One of his recurrent themes in conversation centers around the image of men being turned into hamburger, working in factories or in deadening office jobs. Through writing, he became a voice for those who lived oppressed lives. People who didn't normally read, let alone read poetry, suddenly found themselves picking up his books and reading them. The humor in his work served to make him even more popular and accessible. There was no program for social action on his part. He took life and hammered it down onto the page, almost always with himself in the foreground, so that his writings became a kind of on-going journal. A reader can pick up Bukowski anywhere, at any point in his life. "When people read me," he said, "I want to think of them as not reading literature, but actually participating in life."

His narrative poems place him outside of the mainstream of post-World War II non-academic poetry. This was not a problem for him. He had built his reputation in the hundreds of small poetry journals that had published him from the late 1950s on into the early 1970s. The weekly column, "Notes of a Dirty Old Man," in *Open City*, a Los Angeles weekly newspaper, made his a well-known name throughout the city. The columns were collected in a book with the same title, becoming an instant underground classic.

By then the man who had been named "Outsider of the Year" in 1963 had clearly defined himself as a non-political, working-class man who just happened to write poetry and prose. His motifs—centering around the battle of the sexes, the impossibility of maintaining a sane and rational relationship, the crises with landlord and boss—had been poured in concrete.

Ezra Pound, T. S. Eliot, William Carlos Williams, W. H. Auden were all internationally known literary figures. The first two had fled what they saw as the vulgarities of America for European values, embracing the literary past while, paradoxically, inventing their own radically new forms of expression. Williams stayed home and spent his life insisting on "American Speech," yet he steered clear of street lingo. Eventually in *Paterson*, he began utilizing his own specialized literary techniques, formulating a virtual "policy" for the direction of contemporary American poetry. Auden fled Europe for America, but rarely stepped far beyond his rational sensibility. Even the Beat poets, from Allen Ginsberg to Gregory Corso, often weighted their work with traditional literary devices and language. Ginsberg leads us back to Whitman, Christopher Smart, William Blake, and, eventually, the Hebrew Prophets. Corso continually evokes the spirits of Keats, Shelley, and Poe. Bukowski rarely goes much further than the Los Angeles city limits. The poem *the tragedy of the leaves* captures the life Bukowski celebrates:

and I walked into the dark hall
where the landlady stood
execrating and final,
sending me to hell,
waving her fat sweaty arms
and screaming
screaming for rent
because the world had failed us
both.

Bukowski chooses Los Angeles, swimming in it. When I edited an anthology of L.A. poets with him and Paul Vangelisti, he wrote in the Foreword: "You know, I can't think of another city that takes more mockery than Los Angeles. It is the unloved city, it is the target. We contain Hollywood—and in a sense, Disneyland . . . we are corn. We are mistakes . . . I think it is important to know a writer can live and die anywhere." And, indicative of his deep personal feelings about life and literature: "The true Angelo also has a certain sophistication—he minds his own damned business."

Bukowski celebrates the aroma of hamburgers frying in the pan, the generalized daily life of the American. In his short stories he pries apart the eternal struggle between male and female, exposing the whole agonizing process while turning it into a mad, nonstop comedy. For him, the comedy of life is ever present. He grew up reading James Thurber, and echoes of Thurber's "battle of the sexes" can be seen throughout his opus. With Bukowski, people aren't so much destroyed as pulled along their varied paths of the tragic and comic, always managing to blend in with the urban landscape without succumbing to it. Even as they drown in back rent, cheap booze, lousy sex, and cars that stall as they are backed out of the driveways, they are bathed in a certain glory. The Bukowski of *Ham on Rye* is last seen playing a game in a penny arcade with a young boy. There are two boxers; one is missing an arm. The boy chooses the one-armed boxer. He wins both games. It is a bit sentimental, yet taken as a whole, a sweetly humorous snapshot of Bukowski's charm.

Poetry brought Bukowski closer to his feelings quicker than prose did. He had tried climbing to the summit of literary success with short stories and had not succeeded. In the poem, he wrote with ease, never laboring over lines. After a full day's work at one menial task or another, he would come home and begin typing. His solace was beer and classical music. The many years spent gathering a story line for his prose gave him plenty of material for his poetry. As he began corresponding with editors and other poets, and then meeting them, he wrote about the literary life, most of it humorous. What he excelled at back in the 1950s and over the next decade was a poetic style devoid of pretension. It was tough, hard, with a Hemingway-like ease of expression:

the girls shift buttocks,
and the Hollywood Hills stand there, stand there
full of drunks and insane people and
much kissing in automobiles,
but it's no good: *Che sera, sera*

There were also poems dealing with whores and life at the racetrack (Santa Anita, Hollywood Park, and Del Mar). *Longshot Pomes for Broke Players* was dedicated to the jockey Willy Shoemaker. When Bukowski worked at the post office, he would often take a day off feigning sickness, only to be called and told that he was being docked two days' pay. "Can't you make it a week?" he'd ask the supervisor.

There we were, sixteen of us, all L.A. poets, on the steps of the church on De Longpre Avenue down the block from Bukowski's place. John Thomas and I were the only ones standing. Off to one side was Bukowski with his girlfriend, Linda King, sitting on the steps. Big John Thomas was wearing a Western hat, and his arms were folded. I thought of him as the best poet in Los Angeles after Bukowski, though he kept reading and publishing the same poems over and over again. Paul Vangelisti was there, in the center, translator from the Polish and Italian, book publisher, and poet. Sitting close to Bukowski was Gerald Locklin, a heavyset bearded poet who taught at California State University at Long Beach. Steve Richmond, author of *Hitler Painted Roses*, sat on the far side of the steps, dark hair spilling over his shoulders.

Bukowski reigned. When the other poets came together, the conversation usually turned to him. This day, as we assembled for our photograph to go with *An Anthology of L.A. Poets*, it was the same. He always had a new book coming out. Some of them, like *All the Assholes in the World and Mine* and *Confessions of a Man Insane Enough to Live with Beasts*, were mimeos badly stapled together, but considered gold to collectors of contemporary poetry. Bukowski's publisher, Black Sparrow Press, had come out with several Bukowski books by the time of our group photo for the anthology. The press' founder, John Martin, understood Bukowski's importance in American literature from the first time he read his poems. He became friend, editor, and agent, literally shaping the poet's career and book projects while promising him a secure future. Martin delivered on that promise in a big way, helping to make the poet a fixture in the American poetry scene and a best-selling writer throughout Europe. Bukowski wrote a warm description of their dealings in an informative introduction to *Burning in Water Drowning in Flame, Selected Poems, 1955–1973*. He used to tell me, "Martin's my man. Anything he wants."

Another photo, of Bukowski and me with an eighty-five-year-old window washer in front of his place on De Longpre, appeared on the cover of our little magazine. My father was taking a photograph of us when Bukowski called the old man over with his washing tools. He wore baggy pants held up by suspenders and was happy to stand between the two literary lights of *Laugh Literary*.

One night in 1972 he invited me to a party for a book he and his girlfriend, Linda King, had written together, *Me and You Sometime Love Poems*. The party went well at first. Linda King's ramshackle rented house in Silverlake was a perfect place for a get-together. The house was surrounded by thick foliage and had a country feel to it. We were crowded into the small living room with plenty of beer, dancing, and lots of loud conversation. That's when the trouble began. Linda, a pretty woman, shapely and vivacious, seemed to be everywhere at once and always with a different man. Was every male in the room dancing with Linda? Bukowski drank with increased frequency as the evening wore on and shot forth a few warning signs. Finally, when the party had boiled down to me, Big John Thomas, Paul Vangelisti, a poet named Tony Quagliano, and Linda, Bukowski said, "Okay, I've had enough. Linda has been asking for trouble all evening. She can't seem to keep her hands off anyone, including you guys."

Linda yelled, "Can't I have any goddamned fun without you getting jealous?" Her cheeks turned crimson and she fell back against a table stacked with copies of their joint publishing effort.

Bukowski picked up an empty beer bottle and held it by the neck in a threatening manner. "Okay, which one of you guys is first?" he asked, backing against a far wall and looking each of us directly in the eyes.

Tony stepped forward, a massive man with a thick neck and gigantic hands.

"You want her, right?" Bukowski asked.

"No. I don't," Quagliano said, holding his ground as Bukowski took one step in his direction.

"Bullshit," Bukowski roared.

"You calling me a liar?" Quagliano asked, shifting his weight from right to left and readying himself for an attack.

Just then Big John moved in on Bukowski from one side and Vangelisti from another. Bukowski suddenly threw the bottle to the opposite wall, where it shattered. He turned and stormed out of the house. Moments later we heard his engine rev up and he was backing out of Linda's driveway.

Linda ran after him, managing to get close enough to his car to bang on the hood and scream, "I HATE YOU. OH I DO. I HATE YOU, YOU SON OF A BITCH."

When she returned, we settled down for more beer as Quagliano said goodnight, leaving with a copy of *Me and You Sometime Love Poems* under his arm.

Half an hour later, the phone rang. I sat near it so Linda asked me to answer. "Hello?" I said.

"This is Bukowski. Put Linda on."

"Linda, it's Hank."

"I don't want to talk with him!" she said loudly enough for him to hear.

"Tell me, who's with you there?" Bukowski asked.

"John and Paul. Tony just left."

"Which one of you is going to end up with Linda tonight?" he replied.

"None of us," I said.

Then he hung up.

We finished drinking and Paul went on his way, leaving me, Big John, and Linda.

Bukowski called again.

"Yeh?" I asked.

"Who's left?"

"Me and Big John. Why don't you come back? We're only talking."

"I want you guys out of there," he said, hanging up before I could say anything in response. I glanced at the clock and noticed it was one A.M.

Five minutes later, the phone rang. "YOU SONS OF BITCHES BETTER CLEAR OUT. I'M REAL MAD," Bukowski growled.

"Hank, I . . . ." But he had already slammed the receiver down.

Linda laughed and handed me another beer.

It wasn't long before he pulled up in the driveway. When he entered the room, Linda bolted from her chair, ran to him, and began scratching his face. "You ruined my party," she bellowed.

"Yeh? Well, I can ruin more than that if you want," he shot back.

Big John had slipped out unnoticed. I managed to get their attention long enough to say goodnight. As I drove down the San

Bernardino Freeway I realized that I'd left my copy of their love poems back in Silverlake.

September 20, 1963, Bukowski to Neeli Cherry:
   "I remember your bedroom and you asleep in there like a sick frog, and pictures of Hem on your wall, pictures of Hem and maybe Faulk and so forth, well, this is better for a kid than Henry Ford and almost as good as ice hockey . . . but look, someday the pictures have to come down . . . and paeans to a minor poet, c.b., must stop. It is pretty hard as you might guess, not to die before the last supper of your thirtieth birthday in our American society, and then you are never safe, you can go at any time like any Mailer, although I do not know their ages nor am I interested. The novel nowadays has become the guillotine. You can last longer in and around the poem although it isn't any news you won't make any money . . . this is stale advice from an old man to a young man . . ."
   And a few months later:
   "Writing is painting and the sooner people realize this the less dull crap will dull the market. . . . Picasso does with paint what I would like to do with words . . . a good style comes primarily from lack of pretentiousness, and what is pretentious changes from year to year and from day to day, from minute to minute. We must be ever more careful. A man doesn't get old because he nears death; a man gets old because he can no longer see the false from the good. Enough of speech making."

In the summer of 1968 Bukowski and I were going to a party up at Crazy Jack's, a small house perched on a hillside in Silverlake. For the previous two days we had been on a continuous drunk, buying six-packs and making runs for greasy chicken-to-go on Hollywood Boulevard. Mary, Crazy Jack's girlfriend, had called to invite us. "It's a celebration for Jack's new drawings," she said. "Everyone will be there." For Mary, everyone meant an assortment of hippies, addicts, and small-time hustlers. But I loved her and I loved Jack's drawings. They were done in pen and ink and often dealt with Biblical themes.
   Bukowski kept drinking on the way over, but somehow seemed perfectly sober. "Jesus, kid, I hope these people don't bore me," he said.

"You like Mary."

"I know, and Crazy Jack is wild enough. It's the others that worry me. I'm not much with crowds."

"Unless you're the center of attention," I said.

"Well, you have a point, Neeli."

We started up the steps on the narrow sidewalk leading to the house. As we walked, we were called over by a man working in his garden, separated from us by a white picket fence. He turned the earth with a tiny spade and had done a good job for an entire flotilla of petunias.

"I'm all alone," the gardener suddenly blurted out. "That's right. There is nobody left."

He was balding, with a large indentation running across his forehead. His eyes were pale brown and his lips thin. Something about his face made him suspect.

"What the hell," Bukowski said. "Why are you alone?"

"My parents died. Now there's just me. All alone in this house. All alone in the world. Where are you guys going?"

"A friend is having a party up the street," I said.

"Can I come, too?"

Immediately, Bukowski said yes.

"Hold on a minute," the man said, dropping the spade and running in the front door of his house. A moment later he reappeared with a tattered coat on and his hair haphazardly slicked back.

"Thanks for letting me come with you guys. I don't get to talk to many people. I get so lonely," he said.

A few minutes later we were at Jack and Mary's door. Mary greeted me with a hug, then turned to Bukowski. "Mary, baby," he said, handing her the six-pack we had brought along.

Our lonesome guest shook her hand and walked inside. He sat on a sofa between two beaded hippies. Bukowski and Crazy Jack were huddled in a corner with Marv Conners, a poet, and Mary. I went into the kitchen to forage through the refrigerator.

Somehow, the conversation got around to the Vietnam War. Mary said it was all madness and nobody should take sides. Crazy Jack, high on pot, began chanting, "Ho, Ho, Ho Chi Minh, the Vietcong are gonna win. . . ." As the talk went on, the tempo began to shift. Mary said that the United States had no business there. Others agreed. Bukowski cut in with "who gives a sacred fuck," and I said we were earning the enmity of the Vietnamese people. It was about then that the lonely man from down the street sprang up from the sofa, where he had been quietly sitting. He announced that he had killed ten men in Korea.

"So what?" Bukowski said.

"So I could kill ten more if I had to," the man said.

"That's sick," somebody shouted.

"Yeh!" Crazy Jack said as he threw some of his drawings onto the coffee table.

The lonely man suddenly ran toward the door, turned, and pulled a gun that he waved back and forth. "Okay, now listen up," he said. "I am a killer. It really doesn't much matter to me who I kill or where."

I tried moving slowly toward the kitchen, hoping to escape out the back door and go for help. But he saw me and motioned me back to where I had been standing. "Don't nobody try any shit," he said.

"Yeh? Who the hell do you think you are?" Bukowski retorted.

He ignored Bukowski and said to all of us, "You people never been on a battlefield. You don't know what killing is all about."

Bukowski said, "I don't think you're man enough to pull the trigger."

"Oh yeh?"

"Yeh," said Bukowski as he walked up to the madman, stuck his belly into the gun barrel and challenged him to shoot.

"Go on, baby. I'm ready to die. Shoot," Bukowski said, taunting him.

The man began to cry as Bukowski reached out and took the gun away. After emptying the bullets, he handed it back and told him to leave. The man did not want to go and began pleading to be allowed to stay at the party. "I was just kidding. I promise to be good. I didn't mean nothing bad."

"You could have killed someone," Mary shouted. "Get out of my house."

I opened the door and watched as he walked down the street to his place. Bukowski rejoined the party. The man with nothing to lose.

In 1985 *War All the Time* appeared. It included selections of poetry written between 1981 and 1984. Reading like one long poem, the tone of the book is focused into tight, prose-like lines, sustaining the image of a hard-edged observer victimized by mundane situations but never trapped into sentimentality. The speaker in the poems is somehow triumphant in his knowledge of the traps laid before him. Looking through the book, I found a poem about Linda King in which Bukowski accurately brings her into focus:

she had long hair and
wild, wild eyes, and
she danced and pranced up
there with her poems,
overdramatizing,
but she had a great
body
and she
twisted
it
and read and waved her
poems. . . .

These loose sections, sparser than the earlier work, are a further affirmation of Bukowski's original impulse to write freed from preconceptions about how a poem should be shaped. The newer work is skillful, yet often lacks the lyric depth and emotional desperation of the earlier poems. With that said, it is still easy to flip through the pages and find brilliant poems and passages:

I watch the falcon glide
gracefully
above the telephone wires,
it is a beautiful
thing
that falcon
from this distance,
and, of course,
it makes me think
of death
and death is perfectly
proper
yet I throw my cigarette

down
stamp it out,
look up at the bird:
"you son-of-a-bitch . . ."

Bukowski and I were involved in one of our wild, drunken escapades. Hours earlier we had come to Shakey's Pizza Parlor up on
Sunset, a few blocks from his place. We started at the table nearest
the door with a pitcher of beer and a basket of peanuts. After finishing the pitcher and the entire bowl of peanuts, our table was a
mess. We ordered another pitcher, thereby earning the right to yet
another bowl of peanuts. Rather than return to our table, we
went to the next one. Three hours later, eight tables had been
messed up by the two of us. Having run out of clean tables, we
left the parlor to make a beer run. Returning to De Longpre, we
began again, only this time throwing our empties on Bukowski's
rug. We talked about literature. "Steinbeck, *The Grapes of Wrath*,
think of it, man. Old John S.—*Cannery Row*, a touch of the sentimental, granted, flawing the work, but still. . . ." Bukowski
mused as we sat in his living room amid the clutter of a twenty-
hour drunk. The tape recorder had been turned off hours ago. We
now had no imaginary audience to play to. It was one on one,
"the old man," as he called himself, and me, "the kid."
    "It gives you the chills just to say his name," I said.
    "You're sure as hell not kidding, man. Those guys could lay it
down . . . blood on the line. Think of them. Think of Hemingway
running on home for the touchdown. . . ."
    "How about Saroyan?"
    "A tough daddy. You should read *The Daring Young Man on
the Flying Trapeze*. It was revolutionary in its day."
    "Wolfe . . ." I said.
    "A giant. Jesus, they were the ones I read as a kid. They stood
eighty feet tall, immortal. That's how it seemed back then. If I
read them now, I wonder?"
    He dismissed most of his contemporaries, especially the poets.
"They all fall into the literary trap, even the ones who are supposed to be rebels. It's the same old literary con game."
    "Where do you fit in?" I asked.
    That was an easy one for "the old man." He took a long swig
of beer, leaned back in his chair, belly protruding, and said, "My

contribution is obvious. I opened things up to a clear line, so that an auto mechanic without an education in literature or a dock worker in Seattle can read me."

I didn't like it when we drifted apart. I began working a political job in San Bernardino in 1972, imprisoned in a coffin-like building downtown on a federal grant as an assistant to the mayor. From time to time I would read about Bukowski. Once, he sent me an invitation to a documentary on his life. I drove to L.A. and saw John Thomas, Linda King, all the old gang. There we were, gathered in the lobby of a municipal building off Hollywood Boulevard, waiting to be called into the civic theater for the film. Amid the larger crowd, Bukowski seemed unaffected. He and I joked with each other about looking older and things like that. "They're going ape-shit over me in Germany," he said. "You got to remember, I'm the hometown boy." A bell rang and we filed in to see the film. I was going off to find a seat when Bukowski motioned me over to sit with him and Linda. When the film began, he took out a bottle of vodka hidden in his jacket. We shared a drink as the film credits flashed on the screen. Larger than life the poet stood, as he bought beer and cigars at the liquor store on Normandie where he and I used to go on our beer runs.

"How are they running at the track?" he asked the man behind the counter.

"When I first met Neeli, he was 15 and I was Bukowski," he once wrote in a preface for a book of my poems.

Twenty-two years later, in 1983, I went to see him at the house he now owned in San Pedro. He had made the move from Hollywood and rented rooms. Royalties from his book sales in America and abroad had made him a wealthy man, taking him far from the rooming houses on Temple Street, downtown, where he once wrote the stories nobody wanted.

I hadn't seen him in six years. Driving down the Harbor Freeway to San Pedro, I wondered what to say to my old friend. Maybe I'd park, walk up to the door, knock, and, when he opened it, say "Hank, I miss you." Oh no! How corny. Yet the truth was, I did miss him. How frustrating to be self-conscious with someone I knew so well. He had become famous. I feared he would be inexplicably changed, that a wide chasm would now exist between us.

Once inside the spacious living room, with its big picture window looking out on a front lawn of dying grass and flowers, I knew this man had not changed. But we were both uneasy. I glanced at the bookcase filled with his titles in at least a dozen languages. I picked up a book in German called *Fuck Machine*. "They can't get enough of me over there. I can do no wrong. So the deutschmarks keep flowing in, not to mention the francs and the lira." He handed me a copy of the magazine *Der Spiegel* that contained a story on his European tour. The Germans claimed him as their own. Just as popular in France and Italy, he was compared to Henry Miller and Jack Kerouac.

After I put the magazine down, there were several minutes of awkward silence. Then he said, "I feel like I'm meeting a ghost. It's been so long since I've seen you. You actually look the same, although I see that you have one false tooth in the front." For his part he had grayed, but his eyes were as animated as ever. Power glowed from within.

"Linda Lee will be over soon," he said of his wife-to-be, Linda Lee Beighle. "She's a good woman. Be kind to her."

We talked of old times, loosening up considerably. I told him about the literary life in San Francisco. He got a kick out of my Corso and Ferlinghetti impersonations and of all the San Francisco gossip. We dredged up names from the sixties that were best forgotten.

He asked about my writing, about what I was doing in Los Angeles. I told him briefly of my novel, *Angels Flight*, as yet unfinished.

"I have a good rule," he said. "If you enjoy writing while you're putting it down and you can barely tear yourself away from the typewriter, then you probably have something going. When it becomes a struggle, watch out." He mentioned a new book, *Hot Water Music*, and gave me a small publication from Black Sparrow Press, *Bring Me Your Love*. On the title page, he wrote, "For Neeli. Don't bring me your love."

When Linda Lee arrived, regal, good looking, obviously in love with my old buddy, we talked a while longer, then decided to go out for dinner in Bukowski's brand-new BMW. "I don't want you to feel jealous, but I bought it with cash up in Hollywood," he said. As he put the key in the ignition, he told me he was buying dinner.

We had a good time. Halfway through our meal, he began haranguing a tableful of college students sitting near us. In the parking lot, totally revved up on wine, he yelled at a man who pulled up in a BMW, "You have no right! Only I should have a BMW . . . I paid cash. It's top of the line." Back at his place, Linda Lee showed me a photograph album with Bukowski on every page: at the track, at the liquor counter, relaxing at home, behind the wheel of his car, working in his upstairs writing room.

On my way home, driving north on the freeway, I felt good about his success. Enough with those small apartments and broken-down cars. Even his old typewriter had been replaced by an IBM Selectric. It was two in the morning and I thought about Bukowski, that there were no grand visions of America in his work, no overriding desire to strike out on Whitman's road into the broad, sweeping land, no ultimate dialogue of the soul struggling for self-possession. I realized how much I admired the way he captured Los Angeles and her people, especially those who sorted mail as he had done and worked other ordinary jobs and who wouldn't know Faust from hamburger. I remembered how he had put it some years before:

this land punched-in, cuffed-out, divided,
held like a crucifix in a deathhand,
this land bought, resold, bought again and
sold again, the wars long over,
the Spaniards all the way back in Spain . . .
. . . and you take your shopping bag
outside and walk along the street
and the green beer hangs there
just above your stomach like
a short and shameful shawl, and
you look around and no longer
see any
old men.

These lines from the poem *Crucifix in a Deathhand* captured Los Angeles like no one had before. Bukowski interiorized the city, bemoaning what it had become, and, as usual, offering no escape route from the problems he identified. For Bukowski, there was no escape. The job was simply to capture the idea of the place, ravaged in some final way, just as the characters in his books are. His outlook is akin to that of Henry Miller in *Murder the Murderer*, an essay on the madness of war. To Miller, the mere idea of the conflict was insanity. Better to step aside, come home to America, take the "air-conditioned nightmare" trip, and retreat to Big Sur. Bukowski never consciously wrote an anti-war poem. His war is the war within, the war to remain an individual in the face of the mutilating effects of our society. *War All the Time* reflects this feeling of a continuing battle to free oneself of the brutal system stifling the Whitmanic song of the self.

Early September 1987. I dialed Bukowski's number and heard a message from Linda Lee, asking me to leave my name and the time I'd called. I followed her instructions. Two days later the phone rang.

"This is Bukowski. Is Neeli there?"

I knew the deep-toned, sardonic voice was his.

"Hank. I'm glad you called back. We both have answering machines."

"You have to screen out the world, kid."

"Listen. I've just sold a book. It's called *Whitman's Wild Children*. Corso's in it, Ferlinghetti, Norse, Ginsberg, and some others. You, too."

"Oh, Jesus . . ." he muttered. "What the hell."

"Don't worry. There's nothing vicious in the book."

"Yeh, I'll bet."

"No, it's true. It's a combination of humor and criticism."

"Yeh, keep the humor in there, baby. That's what can make it for you."

His statement brought back memories of the dinners we shared nearly twenty years ago. Inevitably our humor came out in full force. We would break into uncontrollable laughter midway through the meal. We usually went to Mort's, that mecca for every outsider, retired assassin, and aspiring mass murderer in the L.A. basin. We would be carving our steaks. Bukowski might say, "See that guy over there. One of his legs is too short" or "That old lady looks like a whore I used to know up on Alvarado."

We invented stories generally based on a person's face. Bukowski would say, "The guy at the counter, third from the left, see his face, kid? A zero. A great circular glob of nothing. A man's responsible for how his face looks after the age of forty. Looking at him I can see he was probably a set designer at Warner Brothers. They busted him for drinking on company time. Gave him his papers and he was out on the streets."

Then we would start on each other. "You know the trouble with you, Bukowski?"

"What? What is the trouble with me. Tell me so I'll know. Go ahead, fat man, tell me with your little fishhook mouth."

"Your monkey face."

"Yeh? Well me and my monkey face just deposited two thousand dollars in that bank across the street for a couple of short stories I wrote and some good luck at the harness races."

We were famous at Mort's. One day I went in alone. The waitress, Faye, asked me where my father was. "I saw his picture in the newspaper. He wrote a dirty story."

I began to think of a defense for the piece when she said, "You know what I like about his writing? It ain't got no big words. Your old man tells it straight."

Telling it straight: that is Bukowski. I called him on Veteran's Day 1987 to tell him that I was going to see the movie *Barfly*.

"Will you do another script?" I asked.

"No. I don't care much for those Hollywood types."

"No kidding? What about going on the morning shows?"

"They tried to get me on Johnny Carson. I said no. They wanted me on those other shows, too: '20–20,' '60 Minutes.' I turned them all down. But pick up a copy of *People* magazine. I'm in it. I let them do a story because they're just corny enough. Besides, you can buy it in any supermarket."

Back in the late 1960s, I asked my father to take some photographs of Bukowski for a projected book of his poems, *The Days Run Away Like Wild Horses Over the Hills*. This would be his second full-length book from John Martin's Black Sparrow Press.

When the day came to take the pictures, we drove to Skid Row. He told us: "When I was younger, half out of my mind, I'd come here thinking I'd find some great man of genius wandering around. But there weren't any. Then I'd go back to my room. I was going to be the new Papa Hemingway, gloves laced, taking on all comers. That was the way I thought." He kept talking like that, as my father took shots of him propped up against a religious poster on a corner about a block from the old Greyhound bus depot.

Then my father and Bukowski pretended to fight. I held the camera as they threw punches.

"Jesus, Sam, you could knock me out if you didn't pull the punches. Let's be friends. I don't like murder," Bukowski said with a grin on his face.

My father suggested we get some shots down at the old freight yard near Chinatown, not too many blocks from the area around Temple Street.

"Good idea," Bukowski responded. "You're not the only one who rode the rails. Martin might like an action shot."

We parked near four derelict freight cars. Bukowski and I walked up to one and he said: "Jesus. This thing is big when you finally get near it."

My father came bounding behind us. "Okay, Buk, jump up there and I'll get a shot."

Bukowski tried hopping into the freight car. "This is embarrassing; I can't do it," he said, turning to me for help.

I tried lifting him up, but it took my father and me both to hoist him onto the platform. Once he was up there, he struck a tough-guy pose and my father began snapping.

Getting down, however, proved more difficult than getting up. The three of us nearly toppled over one another, and Bukowski said, "Jesus, don't you guys realize whose life you have in your hands?"

After the photo session we walked into a nearby restaurant where coffee still cost a nickel and sawdust lay on the floor.

"It's been a long time since I rode the freights, Neeli," Bukowski said.

Thinking of those days when we first met, I remember him saying: "Someday, I'll make it. It's just a matter of time."

But back then, being only fifteen, I had no fix on time or the future. Nor did I have any idea of the long history Bukowski already had behind him: those years in rooming houses, the dead-end jobs, and the loneliness. When he was my age, his face had already been covered with boils. Other kids were going on dates. He would tell me: "I was on the outside by your age. The ugly kid. Maybe that's why I'd hide from people later on." He could always deliver a clear image of his aloneness and how a poet could grow through and beyond it:

I got somewhat larger
and took my first boxcar
out, I sat there in
the lime
the burning lime
of having nothing
moving into the desert
for the first time
I sang.

The Memory of Love

A poem for movie goers

I sit in the late evening
    in a quiet restaurant on
    the International Settlement of San Francisco.
My friends, the poets are gone.

Talk of opium and 4 days on horse
    riding across country. Talk of cancer
        sickness sweeping the world
As we, the poets sit. We who should be out
    on battlefields in silver suits
        drink our energies away. David
        talks of hanging wires with no connections.
    And I say we are the conductors.
No wonder Walt Whitman loved them

2.

    The records change.
    Green vines hang
down one white column on the balustrade.
There is a marble terrace at my right
and my lover walks miles away.

    On the other side of town
    where the cable car goes down
    and the neon lights stay on all night.

Orange lamps along the wall
and oak leaves sprout too small
My lover's thoughts are not
                of me at all.

John Wieners
From *Selected Poems*

"The poem does not lie to us. We lie under its law," John Wieners wrote. Now his poetry lies bound in a volume that ranges over his entire poetic life, *Selected Poems* from Black Sparrow Press. *Selected Poems* opens with the complete version of *The Hotel Wentley Poems*, originally published in 1958 by Auerhahn Press; Wieners was twenty-four at the time and Wentley was his first published volume.

I received a copy of *Selected Poems* for review. Before that, I had been asked to write an appreciation of Wieners for *Mirage*, a literary journal published in San Francisco. Both tasks seemed easy. *Wentley* is an implosion, a spiritual journey into the body and mind, the opposite of the explosive, outward-flowing work of Wieners' contemporaries. There is intimacy to his early poems, a young man looking inward, naming the aloneness he feels and cannot rid himself of while his signs are universal and his music exquisite. He cries, and the tears turn to revelation. The grim aesthetic beauty he shapes is reminiscent of Edgar Allan Poe, who was also born in Boston. Wieners is restless, even feverish in his onslaught of human feelings and passion, a great architect of the poem while the sureness of his language sustains him and gives range to the desolate memories and visions of the poet's sorrowful life. The lines are lean. There is no excess. Every word counts. He worries about self-indulgence even as his work bespeaks an enormous generosity of feeling. He searches for sustaining relationships. As his desperation grows, remaining with him through the years, so does his talent.

In reading through Wieners' poetry, I found myself going back to Whitman's *Calamus* poems where the yearning for love is so deep, where we find those "frailest leaves of me," and gain insight into the deep and sustaining sexual yearnings that Whitman felt so passionately. It is in *Calamus* that the desire for comrades is intensely celebrated. Reverberating from that poem is Whitman's private self, which is often hidden behind an onslaught of imagery ranging over the entire world. The leaves he turns over here are from a personal notebook of passion. It is that journey into the self, ribbed always with images of the land as in *I Saw in Louisiana a Live-Oak Growing*, that Wieners continues in his work.

My attempts at writing the review failed. After ten tries at an appreciation for the magazine, I was defeated. Nothing seemed right. I called the patient editor and said, "Listen, I know you've waited for my piece. I just can't get it right. Whenever I read the poems I go into a deep depression. The words flood in. I look at some of those poems and see my face staring back. I'd be unfair to the work if I sent in anything now." I couldn't get beyond a sense of grief, of personal doom, in his work. I kept reading one line over and over again, "I burn in the memory of love." Everything I wrote appeared awkward and wrong in the face of that admission. And, as I read through the later poems, which are sometimes convoluted, I felt dragged down by a sense of loss. I let the book sit on my shelf. Once in awhile, I'd take it down and read. Finally I found myself reading every night, and then in the morning and at night. I began to see things I hadn't noticed before. John stood at the center of an entire universe of tone and texture. Vistas existed I had failed to see. Entire stanzas and poems came alive. I tried to imagine him in San Francisco during the Poetry Renaissance, 1957 to 1959, far from his Boston home, busted up with his lover, Dana, of whom he writes in *Wentley*. He loved many places in San Francisco, but lived in solitude, mostly, and with the memory of love, as in *a poem for the old man*:

Remove this desire
from the man I love.
Who has opened
the savagery
of the sea to me.

See to it that
his wants are filled
on California street
Bestow on him lar-
gesse that allows him
peace in his loins.

Shadows of the land and its solitary splendor crowd in on Wieners' writings. Like Hart Crane, the immense American earth becomes internalized in his own sufferings (as with Ginsberg in
Wichita Vortex Sutra). Wieners gradually comes to a sharply defined understanding of his native land. This is seen mainly in
poems from the mid-1960s, long after he left San Francisco. He
even looks farther from American soil, toward other lands. In
With Meaning he writes:

in the canyons of L.A.
plus the journeys over oceans
and islands, to metropolis
spreadeagled the earth.
Yes rise shining martyrs

out of your graves, tell us
what to do, read your poems
under springtime moonlight.
Rise and salvage our century.

Set deep within the texture of his writing are straightforward
insights, wrapping images into tight, fiery orbs, flinging them
outward to cover consciousness, forever mocking the scalpels of
literary critics absorbed in the intellectual life of poetry, and trag-
ically blind to the whole unbefuddling, totally trustworthy and,
at root, intuitive process. The poem *Supplication* illustrates the
care Wieners takes with language:

O poetry, visit this house often,
imbue my life with success,
leave me not alone,
give me a wife and home.

Take this curse off
of early death and drugs,

make me a friend among peers,
lend me love, and timeliness.

Return me to the men who teach
and above all, cure the
hurts of wanting the impossible
through this suspended vacuum.

This caravan is laden with jewels of every shape and color and travels toward Byzantium with quiet visionary prowess. Wieners is gently oracular. He has Charles Olson's authority without the bombast, tempered not merely by his gentleness, but also because he refuses to wear the mantle of the poet as priest. "My new work which I presume / already lies scattered, lost and / in error prompts memories of / a dark address in Hell's Kitchen . . . ," he writes. John Wieners is committed to feeling through the development of his craft, as in the *Wentley* poems of his youth.

For Wieners, rules of prosody thrust themselves against his skull, and he works them into an intensely personal search, with an implicit understanding of how the process of composition reshapes our use of language. Olson, one of John's teachers at Black Mountain College, is seen throughout Wieners' work, not as an ocean or a mountain range but as himself, a man, a person, human flesh with its joys and sorrows. A person. A dead man. And what he did with language. How he held the lance and sat firmly in the saddle. Which is not to say that Wieners is on his way to Gloucester, but simply that what may seem incomprehensible in his work is, for me, very clear. His poetry is a public journal of private emotion. He wants to bring language home again. In his journey back to the body, Wieners creates a language sculpted entirely out of his own experience and sets it in a light that makes his meaning unmistakable. It is not a happy vision.

Born in 1934, Wieners was raised in a middle-class Catholic family living in a Boston suburb. He attended school there and graduated from Boston College with an A.B. in English in 1954. Following graduation he worked at the Lamont Library at Harvard University and was active in the Poet's Theater, where he acted in plays by Frank O'Hara and John Ashbery. O'Hara was immensely impressed by the young poet, then eighteen years old, who regularly wore eye makeup and attended meetings of the Beacon Hill chapter of the Poetry Society of America, which consisted of five elegant, elderly ladies plus Wieners. He had already begun to write, but it took a chance event to make poetry his life's vocation. On Sept. 11, 1954, he reports in Donald Allen's *New American Poetry* anthology, he was walking past the Charles Street Meeting House and heard Charles Olson reciting poetry. Intrigued, he walked into the reading room where he was handed a copy of *The Black Mountain Review*.

In the spring of 1955 he enrolled at Black Mountain College in the rural hill country of North Carolina. Poet Robert Duncan recalls that he and Olson were impressed by the twenty-one-year-old's talent. They soon thought of him as an equal. Olson frequently referred to Wieners as "elemental—literally like an element." Recalling Olson, Wieners has said, "Charles' manner of address causes respect, respect even for the spoof that he releases both through his pen and through his oracular power . . . we are different sides of a coin, reversed in spirit."

After a semester at Black Mountain, Wieners returned to Boston where he edited *Measure*, a literary magazine that published many of his friends from college. As Foye tells it, "When *Measure* hit the stands, John was fired from his job at the Lamont Library and drove across the country to San Francisco with his lover, Dana. There he would soon find himself at the center of an important literary scene."

In San Francisco, Wieners contacted Robert Duncan and was soon introduced to Allen Ginsberg, Kirby Doyle, Michael McClure, Philip Lamantia, David Meltzer, Bob Kaufman, and others. He sought out the company of painters, most notably Wallace Berman and Robert LaVigne and soon wrote *A Poem for Painters*.

The Hotel Wentley Poems came out just after Wieners broke up with Dana. The eight poems in the book were written in six days while he lived in the boardinghouse of that name in San Francisco's red-light district. Kirby Doyle once told me, "John's book had an immediate impact. We all felt compelled to read and study his work." Ginsberg wrote, "The whole book is the work of a naked flower, a tragic clown, doomed sensibility, absolutely REAL, no more self pity." Thinking of Ginsberg's perception, I came across these lines from *A Poem for Painters*:

At last the game is over
                    and the line lengthens.
Let us stay with what we know.

That love is my strength, that
I am overpowered by it:
                    desire
                         that too
is on the face: gone stale.
When green was the bed my love
and I laid down upon.
Such it is, heart's complaint,
You hear upon a day in June.
And I see no end in view
when summer goes, as it will,
upon the roads, like singing
companions across the land.

Go with it man, if you must,
but leave us markers on your way.

I look at John and think of him at Black Mountain, focal point/
oasis amid air-conditioning and presidential primaries. There
they were: Charles Olson, Ed Dorn, Robert Duncan, Robert
Creeley, and young, curly-haired John Wieners. Then, in San
Francisco, far from his Boston home, Wieners explodes, but not
in a volcanic way, more like a bright red rose standing taller and
brighter than others, lifting petals upward toward the sun.

"John's reputation has in fact suffered from the great success
of the Wentley poems," Raymond Foye told me. "It's one reason
why he has always written of childhood stars. At a certain point
he despaired of ever getting out from under that book. But in another sense, he hid behind the Wentley poems. They established
him as a poet, and freed him to pursue a more experimental, un-
conforming path." The Wentley poems are more approachable to
readers than much of the later work. There is the poem for painters, for fathers, for the wheat of Kansas, and for our generations
of dissent and bewilderment. There is, in *Wentley*, so much given
over to love and the need for it, and the outer boundaries of it,
that I keep returning, renewing my sense of being. If I become

unnerved, I go to those melancholic lines John Wieners created in his early poems.

We meet Wieners in New York, hoping he will join us at a reading in which Allen Ginsberg will dedicate several poems to the Boston poet, but that is not enough to entice him down into the subway. He wants to stay at the Ninth Street townhouse where we are both guests. I shake his hand. I think of the photograph of him, standing under a poster with Philip Lamantia, Michael McClure, and David Meltzer—how many centuries ago in San Francisco? Now, before me, stands a person who has been through intense pain. I see it. I feel it. He smiles and says how nice it is to meet me. I can't even understand my own words. I see a poem in his face. Knowing something of what he had gone through in the past two decades, I am not surprised. There are ruins and wounds there. His eyes speak more forcibly than he does. I think of a few lines from *A Poem for Early Risers*:

It is not doors. It is
the ground of my soul
where dinosaurs left
their marks. Their tracks
are upon me. They
walk flatfooted.

The words seemed to hang in the air of Ninth Street in Greenwich Village as we turned right at Balducci's market and walked toward the subway.

Ace of Pentacles was published in 1964 by James A. Carr and Robert Wilson in New York, when they discovered that Wieners had not had a book out for six years. The title refers to the card in the tarot deck signifying the triumph of the human spirit over despair, an enduring symbol for the poet. Among the poems of this collection, Wieners placed traditional verse: sonnet, ballad, and couplet. The most ambitious poem here is *The Acts of Youth*. The poem invokes "the middle of the night," much in the tradition of Edward Young's *Night Thoughts* and Francis Thompson's *City of Dreadful Night*. In *A Series*, Wieners takes a long journey into himself, dealing with the themes of pain and suffering in his early poetry. Through all the self-wrenching, one finds:

Dread night is gone,
you see suspended in a bar against the blackness
the mighty lord, who makes his way
Love in his eyes as a bride might say
To put away all fear.

Pressed Wafer, published in 1967, brought together poems written in Buffalo between 1965 and 1967, where Wieners had enrolled in graduate studies at the suggestion of Charles Olson, who was teaching there. Olson made him his personal teaching assistant but treated him more as a colleague.

The title of the book refers to the Eucharist, the symbol of the body of Christ. Putting Catholic imagery into his poetry was not new for the poet, but here his relationship to his own Catholic childhood becomes intensified as he continues his search for solace through sensual love:

There are holy orders in life.
I was born to be a priest
defrocked as Spender says,
an Epiphany to make manifest
                    mysteries.

There is a sense of authority in these lines and an awareness of the serious and fully aware poet that he aspired to be. He sees the burden of his muse clearly and accepts it. Yet there would be no refuge, despite the full flowering of talent evidenced in the poet's development and despite his enduring friendship with Olson and Robert Creeley. Nothing, not his past, Catholicism, or the community of poets could rescue Wieners from his emotional turmoil.

In 1969 Wieners spent a few months in a mental hospital. While confined he wrote *Asylum Poems*, published that same year, and when he came home to Boston he plunged into a lively poetry scene centered around Steve Jonas, Charles Shively, and others. Poetry readings and gay activism kept him busy as he worked on the poems for a new book.

Unlike the long, flowing lines in *Ace of Pentacles*, the *Asylum Poems* are compressed, the vision tautly drawn, almost constricted, yet filled with lyrical notes probing the natural world in poignant detail. *Private Estate* begins:

Dancing dandelions
and buttercups in the grass
remind me of other summer
flowers, simple blossoms

roses and tiger lilies by the wall
        milk pod, sumac branches

Within Wieners, contained between inner landscape and the
outer, unlimited vision thrust up from poem to reader, live these
floral gatherings, together with demons, angels, and the lost and/
or elusive beloved. Does he choose happiness? It appears that he
would like to, but in his own frantic search to be held he encounters a familiar aloneness and insensitivity. *How to Cope with
This?* portrays the poet's sense of alienation:

A mean, dark man
was my lover
in a mean dark room
for an evening

till dawn came
we hugged and kissed
ever since, first and last
I have missed

him, his mean, dark ways.

As my friends and I sat and listened to Allen Ginsberg in a high
school auditorium, I thought of Wieners and about how the two
poets differ. Allen gives of himself in the manner of a Whitmanic
bard, even in his introspective poems and the meditations on the
death of his father. Wieners is like Rainer Maria Rilke, the poet
I link to him. Both wrote poems of introspection, profoundly interiorized canvases that compel us to leave the world of sight and
sound; we enter mind and spirit. How much of himself can John
Wieners expunge? He tries to obliterate the lyric line, but fails.
He wants to leave language behind, but cannot.

Despite brief periods spent in mental hospitals, the poet continued his association with Boston-area poets. He was important
to them, not only for his poetry and his powerful presence, but
also as a gay person who had been publicly out of the closet since
age sixteen. He moved into a small walk-up apartment that he

continues to occupy on Boston's historic Beacon Hill, a neighborhood of narrow cobblestone streets. The walls of his rooms are covered with a collage of movie stars, religious figures, and pornography that is constantly being added to or altered in some other way, depending on his mood.

Ginsberg encounters himself; John Wieners finds demon or angel, fire and void. As Allen read to us at the reading John wouldn't attend, alluding from time to time to the missing poet, I returned to *A Poem for Painters*. In the first lines, Wieners spells out his yearning:

Our age bereft of nobility
How can our faces show it?
I look for love.
My lips stand out
dry and cracked with want. . . .

The timing of those lines, the placement of "I look for love" after longer, more graceful and less commonplace lines lead into the inferno that is John Wieners. His sensibility remains squarely on the dime of his own being: "I look for love" means "I look for myself."

The precocious insights of the *Wentley* poems, akin to what is encountered in Robert Creeley's early poetry, remain foremost in my mind. Personal in the extreme, there are pictures that stand out with striking clarity: *a poem for vipers* is steeped in dark, metropolitan imagery:

I sit in Lee's. At 11:40 PM with
Jimmy the pusher. He teaches me
Ju Ju. Hot on the table before us
shrimp foo yong, rice and mushroom
chow yuke. Up the street under the wheels
of a strange car is his stash—The ritual.
We make it. And have made it.

Despair, loss, desire, and an overwhelming sense of futility bind the *Wentley* cycle into a cohesiveness that is one sustained music.

Before leaving Ninth Street, I had asked John if he felt excited about the publication of *The Selected Poems*. He shrugged his shoulders and nodded toward Raymond Foye, who feigned lack of interest. The editor simply smiled and said: "Come on, or we'll be late for Allen's reading." I wanted to stay and talk, but John seemed to be saying he had said it all in *Wentley* and in his later books, like *Nerves*, *Ace of Pentacles*, and *Behind the State Capitol and the Cincinnati Pike*. The latter, published in 1975 by Charles Shively and The Good Gay Poets in Boston, received many negative reactions from John's admirers, some claiming he had even burned out as a poet. They expected a repeat performance of the earlier, more accessible poetry, not appreciating that the poet had moved on with the poem into a house of *Understood Disbelief in Paganism, Lies and Heresy*:

Prick any literary dichotomy
sung unrent gibberish from maxim skulls
West Manchester cemetery

recidivist testimony damned
promulgated post-mortem Harry Ghouls
wills pleasant chicanery hulled

in opposition to queer honesty,
flying hapless good humours
Morphe erroneous untedious mystery . . .

Reaching into himself to the sounding of words, to the langauge buried away with the pain of unfulfillment, Wieners begins to probe a complex set of meanings beyond the linear.

"I look for love," John Wieners writes in a world that he reminds us is bereft of nobility. Well, good luck, John. Keep on looking. I guess I can wrap his whole poetic outlook around those four words. John has not come to throw America back in Whitman's tender face. He has only to look in the mirror and see himself, his own sad eyes, his own face growing older, lonelier. Like Rainer Maria Rilke, he confronts the deep, evolving vision on the border of the real and gives meaning to what otherwise might remain terrifying. Thinking of Rilke's reality, however, I am reminded that the real, for John, may not exist, shaped as it is by such demanding internal struggles. It wasn't a toy chest Wieners opened up when he wrote *Wentley*. The world for the German poet was still largely ordered by a romantic vision, but John is forever surpassing the momentary visions of chaotic American reality.

Ginsberg showed me the Hotel Wentley one day as I chauffered him through San Francisco. I saw the bay-windowed, wooden building and thought of John awakening:

For me now the new.
The unturned tricks
of the trade: the Place
of the heart where man
is afraid to go.

These lines from *A Poem for Early Risers* are, again, made awesome by timing. Deftly, Wieners begins with a clipped statement, then one a little longer, and finally, a lengthy sweep that lays down the law.

In *The Duino Elegies* Rilke goes to that place Wieners writes of, for the sake of his hand and his heart—to bind them together. The *Elegies* are a new poetic order that Rilke contrasts to the old world hierarchies binding men to culture and civilization. Wieners is also obsessed with new definitions, hoping to create a map of consciousness in a universe that always remains tentative.

A terrible angel arcs over Rilke's language, wings overshadowing the intellect and imperiling the spiritual center of man, what some call the soul. Rilke has language with which to fight his way to an intimate relationship with the ineffable. This relationship ultimately must be a movement toward the unobtainable, never a goal actually reached. The poet probes. His search takes on a sacred, mythic quality, obliterating time and space. Fascinated by myth, the poet creates his own, weaving many fabrics into one, taking disparate images tossing them into the furnace, sometimes bringing them out with a soft, hot glow surrounding them, and they become, miraculously, a unified, vibrating whole.

Wieners' dissatisfaction increases as the unobtainable covers his world. Acutely aware of the decaying of the social order, Wieners retreats into himself, mirroring that decay. The poetic craft brings a sense of beauty and, paradoxically, a feeling of dread: "cheap insult's glare," as he sees in the face of a desired young man his own predicament. John rises to affirm his craft in *II Alone*, procuring some personal salvation:

Sustained by poetry, fed anew
by its fire to return from madness,
the void does not beckon as it used to.

Littered with syllables, the road does not loom
as a chasm . . .

The poet realizes just what the act and art of writing can bring
him to, where it may land him. "You poets dream on / and find
out where the path leads you . . . ," Wieners writes knowingly.
He finds renewal amid chaos, even as "the lover, Oh lover" evap-
orates. Then, "to sleep alone" becomes an obsession again, and
"to make alone / desire alone" the reality.

Wieners implores men toward Whitmanic camaraderie. He
tells all of us to strip away the desolation. Ginsberg aims *Howl*
right at the soul of the machine—controlled by Moloch—and the
madhouse becomes the doorway to the continent. Ginsberg takes
old Walt by the hand and they cross the Brooklyn Bridge together,
weeping. There is humor in their eyes, and sadness as they rip
away the delusions that blind the nation. Whitman had warned
of what could happen if this compassionate camaraderie didn't
replace repulsive class-bred arrogance. He wanted to take the
walls down. And not just in the literary and cultural world. Unlike the expansive Ginsberg, who remains sane despite the madness, Wieners would not be spared: In a *Howl* of his own, he
begins:

You took two years of my life away from me, locking me behind
bars,
for no reason other than common dishonest perpetrated malice,
running me from one cheap, enclosed kitchen bidet unto another,
in drug-induced
collaboration with Apollo and the Nine Muses;
experimenting on me involuntarily
out of statehood apprehension. . . .

Not a pretty picture, as the dark angels of the state swoop
down on this victim of the state and lock poet and poem away in
an asylum. Instead of Whitman's hoped-for society of enlightened citizens, apprehension and mental instability await us.

I wanted to see John the morning after Allen's reading, but he
had gone home to Boston. So there it was—one brief encounter

and the memory of having called him once to come read in San Francisco for a reunion with the poets of his Hotel Wentley days, which, as yet, has never happened. In my Boston call, I asked: "Will you come and read, maybe with Lamantia and McClure?" "Oh yes, of course," he answered, "and we will fly to Coit Tower and kiss the old stones and melt into the ocean, all together."

In his introduction to Wieners' *Selected Poems*, Ginsberg writes: "As that youthful idealism of *The Hotel Wentley Poems* dissolves in *Ace of Pentacles*, we see his intelligence delve deeper and deeper into the hole, or void, created by his imagination of an impossible love." There it is! That is what happens—John comes to see what a nightmare exists out there, beyond himself. There is the poet to love, the creative process to embrace, the interior world to outline, to form, to shape and reshape, to meditate on . . . but what about another person, another heart, the arms of another? It is at this point where Wieners embodies the desperation of everyman while refusing to remain quiet.

In *The Ages of Youth*, a cycle of poems from *Ace of Pentacles*, Wieners begins in the night: "And with great fear I inhabit the middle of the night / What wrecks of the mind await me, what drugs / to dull the senses, what little I have left, / what more can be taken away?" Unlike Rilke, anxiety lies right on the surface, nailed there, permanent. Rilke could soar above it and eulogize the act of rising over pain and suffering and the misery of the flesh. John transcends in another way, more hurtful perhaps by remaining grounded and dealing face to face with himself and a society hell-bent on cheapening poetic impulse. He moves between reality and the void. The cycle continues with a concentrated history of a man's horror and hope, a brief poem, *Two Years Later*, which tells us:

The hollow eyes of shock remain
Electric sockets burnt out in the
        skull.

The beauty of men never disappears
But drives a blue car through the
        stars.

In his later work, Wieners often perceives things the way we do in daily thinking, randomly and unconsciously splicing our thoughts into elements entirely apart from the preceding perception. Taken as a whole, *Behind the State Capitol* is a precise montage of this process. Because he is "radicalized beyond belief," his language has moved on from the *Wentley* poems.

"In the 1970s, Wieners began a gradual, but radical process of non-attachment," according to Raymond Foye. "Possessions, ambitions, fame, money, friends, it all went out the window. Only poetry remained." Between 1976 and 1983, Wieners, for the most part, wrote only one poem per year, for himself, on his birthday. When he reemerged in 1984 with a new manuscript, he had alienated whatever audience he had left by writing in a cryptic, private voice of obtuse, seemingly unrelated images. The reader is often left hanging, peering in at these hermetically sealed verses so radically different from those of his youth. Yet he could recapture the clarity of the earlier work:

My pillow a rock of stone
My bed a bench of board
These the treasure trove I hoard
Against the rolling morn

My symphony a choir of birds
Family the passing cars
And for friends the stars
And for company words.

In highly condensed language, Wieners sums up many of the themes common to his poetry and rediscovers a directness that reaches out to the reader. I often feel that he deliberately pauses from his later experiments with words to give the reader a bittersweet, linear note, which has immediate and universal appeal. Here is a mixture of profound suffering with a calm vision of nature made poignant in contemporary terms. Wieners has said of his career, "I am living out the logical conclusions of my books," but that does not dissuade him from continuing to write his poetry.

John Wieners, sustained by poetry, looks longingly over my shoulder. I think he is restless to go back to Boston. Soon he'll receive a $20,000 grant from the National Endowment for the Arts and Humanities and $25,000 as a Guggenheim Fellow. Not bad for a lifetime of work in a rigged society. "The right of freedom means improving what you're doing," he wrote. No wonder they gave him an award. What a sweet man. What a sad-faced man in shabby clothing standing on the beautiful floor of the Ninth Street townhouse.

One day in San Francisco, Gregory Corso and I read Auden's poem on the death of William Butler Yeats. "You got it?" Corso asked. "Do you dig that each line is important. Look," he says, "something in every line, real meaning. That's a biggie for a poet to do." That's it. That is how I feel about Wieners.

The *Selected Poems* is an adventure, from the focused lyrics of the *Wentley* poems, to a wider line, and then to a series of poems with a decisive political edge. *Behind the State Capitol* means just that. Wieners shows us that the work of the poet may reveal unseen injustice, the life behind the facade of our political structure. There is none of the rhetoric here that one associates with political poetry. Wieners is intimate and the injustices he speaks of come from his own experiences. He is even able to look at society from within the context of a mental hospital. Much of what he has to say is not far from the spirit of Whitman's prefaces to *Leaves of Grass* or the vision of America found in *Democratic Vistas*, and yet in *Children of the Working Class*, Wieners writes: "I am witness / not to Whitman's vision, but instead the / poorhouses, the mad city asylums and re- / lief worklines. Yes, I am witness not to / God's goodness, but his better or less scorn." That was written on the first of May, 1972.

"That love is my strength, that / I am overpowered by it . . ." This ironic note remains the root of Wieners' unfolding poetic commitment. The idea of love, its fulfillment or lack of it, is a primary quest for the lyric poet. Often he merges with the land in this quest. For example, *A Poem for Painters* contains the following lines:

This nation is so large, like
our hands, our love it lives
with no lover, looking only
for the beloved, back home
into the heart, New York,
New England, Vermont green

mountains, and Massachusetts
my city, Boston and the sea.
Again to smell what this calm
ocean cannot tell us.

The poem becomes a paean for the enormity of America and
shows a strong devotion to home, Boston. In a later poem Wieners wrote:

In DEvotion these orders
about poverty and deprivation
climb past New York's skyscrapers
hearkening against oceanic tides
Of humanity . . .
see you everywhere hiding
under the rubber of state VEHicles . . .

Imagine. He winds up in the streets, enlivening every sidewalk
with his song. From *Sequel to a Poem for Painters*:

Cavernous echoes obeyed lines on
       heartache, only hangover upper

       GRANT's Ave. horizon shriners
       C
       E
       ntral Park dawn moonshiners lent,

       strech small Hoosiers baker scratched
       N
       i
       ckel trays when Mary had a little
       arnd. the corner Corp.

A real projective priest for language, protecting his native language by not limiting the power of words, even single letters.
What a patriot for the Mother Tongue.

   I think the proper words for describing John Wieners' power
within language, his feeling for the poem, are "passion" and
"composure." What I have written here concerns his passion, expressed in longing, and his texture, a grasp of craft that is a matter
of composure. It is what Williams, Pound, and Olson sought for
and sublimely mastered, and what is evident in Wieners. For all

the weaknesses Wieners seems heir to, regarding love/the lack of love, he wears strong armor, or, as Ginsberg observed, "his stubborn resilient strain of New England genius." In his youth he is close to William Carlos Williams, lyrically, but later Pound and Olson loom large. Wieners is the most familiar of the three—his escapades are more familiar. Instead of tromping through a semimythic China or Italy, as Pound does in the *Cantos*, Wieners is at home in America:

I can't put my head on the pillow
but all kinds of fear ensue,
doubts plague the morning
what will I do

watch for the mail man
I feel like a jaded movie star
who missed the big-time
and ended up mopping floors

on South Street.

The lover is forever there: "The song of life, soft syllables from God" is a love song. Wieners becomes worn out by it. He would look for solace in the poem and find himself delving deeper into intellectual things, asking that a meaning be applied to the lack of love. His unfulfillment is what we have to face and to feel. We feel it because his art is deep, and his heart is never hidden. History becomes the story of his "being-in-need," his act of naming human vulnerability. Forest, river, city, and "love . . . to put away all fear" are wrapped within the language of his poetry. "Yes I am alone now" is one way he communicates his feelings, saying the same thing in a myriad of ways, captive of his fascination with love and loss.

Wieners uses strict stanzaic forms to "order" himself, to provide space between units of thought, threading those thoughts on a rhythmic line:

I am the poet of benzedrine, bus stations,
jazz, and negro lovers. I am the poet—

so many ambulances ride by, in this city
the old are dying in the cold,
can't get their welfare checks, surplus food.

I am the poet of overpasses,
railroad yards and all night cafeterias . . .

This poem, *First Poem After Silence Since Thanksgiving*, offers a
harmony of line break and rhythm enhanced by the dramatic
placing and repetition of "I am the poet." Dark, metropolitan imagery stands over all, yet Wieners remains the great affirmer,
echoing Walt Whitman in the lines: "I am the poet that stands
between / the lover and his wife." Wieners binds himself to us,
ending the poem with: "I am the poet of your life."

His editor once approached the poet, asking, "Is there a poem
you've left to write?"

Wieners answered: "I want to write a poem about an old person dying of loneliness. I want to write a poem about an old person, alone in a room, dying of hunger and loneliness. No one has
ever written a poem about an old person dying in the cold, of hunger and loneliness. Except, of course, Ava Gardner, who is always
our master."

Eros and Tamalpais

Arsonist of My Body

Arsonist of my body   He
  all that is beautiful in man
Furnace of my kingdom   He
  all that is beautiful in God
Merlin of my genitals   He
  all that is bold of touch
Firearm of my spirit   He
  all that flows into flame
Solace of my solitude   He
  O his lift and embrace
Very lion of lions   He
  O the roar
    the roar of his dance

James Broughton
From *Ecstasies*

In an earlier California than the one I know, James Broughton was awakened by an angel, "a glittering stranger," who told the three-year-old boy that he was a poet and should never fear being alone or laughed at by others. This angel would appear to him throughout his childhood, especially during times of crisis, offering protection from a mother who taught Broughton that men were dirty because they always wanted sex. James was his mother's "little darling" until he grew older and she began to take a less favorable view of his questionable masculinity. "To my mother I was developing into a sissy who preferred ballet and poetry to business or sports. My mother had a strict idea of what a man should be and I didn't fit it."

Broughton thinks of artist Joel Singer, with whom he has lived for more then ten years and collaborated with on several films, as the embodiment of that angel who came to him as a three year old. "Joel was my student. He took a film class I gave. I never thought this young man would want to sleep with me and to live with me. But when we came together, it seemed that it was always meant to be."

His mother would have been horrified, I imagine, to have seen Jean Cocteau kiss Broughton after the latter's film, *The Pleasure Garden*, won a special prize for poetic fantasy at the Cannes Film Festival in 1954. "Both Luis Bunuel and Cocteau were on the committee. Of course I was thrilled," Broughton told me. "And when Cocteau kissed me, well . . . you know he was always a great inspiration for me. I took his embrace to mean approval of my being a poet working in film."

In 1947 a collection of Broughton's poems, *Songs for Certain Children*, was privately printed by Adrian Wilson. His first films, *The Potted Psalm* and *Mother's Day*, helped initiate the underground film movement in San Francisco. Broughton remembers the late 1940s as an idyllic time: "There was a real sense of community amongst poets and other creative people. Poetry readings were intimate events, and when books came out people actually bought them." He speaks of the lack of divisions at that time, stressing that poets hadn't split into diverse camps, each claiming to be the only possessor of the muse.

It was an era in which Kenneth Rexroth, William Everson, Robert Duncan, and Jack Spicer helped to keep alive a flame that would burn nationwide in the mid-1950s when North Beach became the center of a new explosion in contemporary poetry. Broughton was one of the pioneers who helped set the tone for the era that would become known as the San Francisco Poetry Renaissance. Following his first collection of poems, other books were published locally including *The Playground*, *The Ballad of Mad Jenny*, *Musical Chairs*, and *Almanac for Amorists*. His first book from a major publisher, *True and False Unicorn*, came out under the Grove Press imprint in 1957.

Broughton earned a B.A. degree from Stanford University, joined the merchant marine, and worked as a reporter on the *New York Herald-Tribune*. As his reputation as a poet and pioneering underground filmmaker grew, he began to teach, mesmerizing students with courses of his own invention at San Francisco State College and the San Francisco Art Institute. Broughton married during the sixties and had a daughter and a son. When his son was three years old, he played the starring role in one of his father's films.

Like William Everson, Broughton came from the San Joaquin Valley. He was born in the farming town of Modesto in 1913, a third-generation Californian whose family held traditional values sacred. The poet would not look back nostalgically on his childhood and youth; as an adult he would create a series of poems called *Nursery Problems*, full of haunting echoes and reverberations from his childhood. In *Papa Has a Pig*, he writes:

Papa has a pig.
And a big pig too.
Papa plays a piggy-toe that I can't do.
O Papa has the biggest pig you ever did see.
He gave only ten little piggies to me.

Papa has the star of all the swine,
Papa shines stern in the sty.

I sat comfortably in the back seat of the spacious old-model Volvo as Joel Singer pulled out into the middle lane of the Golden Gate Bridge, trying to imagine the world into which James Broughton was born seventy-four years ago. Sitting next to Joel, white-bearded and wearing one of the flamboyant shirts he is known for, Broughton turned toward me to say that it looked like we might not have a clear day, pointing out that the weather on the Marin Headlands could be tricky. Passing Sausalito, we magically shed the fog that hovered at the Golden Gate, encountering it again as we started up the road to Mount Tamalpais. At any moment I expected to see Looney Tom the Happy Lover, a film character of Broughton's, jump onto the roadway, complete with a cast of characters projecting innuendoes of sensual pleasure and pure poetic joy back at their creator.

I had brought with me his most extensive collection, *A Long Undressing*, published by poet Jonathan Williams' Jargon Society. A collection of poems written between the years 1949 and 1969, it is mostly a joyous package of ballads, songs, sea chants, sensual incantations, Zen-American koans, and even what Broughton calls "a tapestry for voices." When I first read through the book, I recalled thinking how disarming Broughton can be. His insights are often hidden in the word-plays and the nursery-rhyme mood many of his poems exude. Some of the poems, however, merely ask the reader to surrender all erudite thoughts or lofty expectations. In *Call for a Desperate Measure* Broughton writes:

A little arson, please, a little aerification
to dare some miracle of small surprises!
At least a bauble, at least!
Or so are we stalled, in our labyrinths.

As we entered Mount Tamalpais State Park, I asked Broughton about his relationship to Walt Whitman. He smiled and said, "You know, we had the same angel. The angel that came to me when I was young was the same one that visited Whitman. When I first read *Leaves of Grass*, it was a revelation. A forbidden fruit. I've felt close to him all my life."

He reached back and grabbed my hands. "Lots of people today are afraid of something. They run from it in fear. If my films and poetry are about anything, it is the willingness to touch another man or woman. That is what Whitman was concerned with, too. He reached out for others. It isn't really a matter of eroticism, but more of understanding how capable we are of loving one another, of communicating on more than a mere verbal level."

I knew that Broughton's life was filled with a yearning to reach people. In his poems and films he sought to bridge the gulf between himself and others. He agreed with the social philosopher Herbert Marcuse that a battle was constantly being waged between eros and civilization. He once told me that he had grown up in a household of women who were, in his words, very proper, and sex was never a topic for discussion.

Driving through the fog on Mount Tamalpais, Broughton reminisced about the circle of friends in which he had come of age. They included Alan Watts, with whom he had taken LSD; the painter and sculptor Jean Varda, whom Henry Miller wrote of in *Remember to Remember*; and William Everson, like Broughton a California-born poet.

"We all thought of Tamalpais as a magic place. A divine place," he said.

I mentioned to him the reverence Lew Welch, Gary Snyder, and Kirby Doyle, poets of a younger generation, had for Tamalpais. Each had written beautiful poems centered on the mountain.

"Well, just look at it," he responded.

But the fog still lay in close. When it finally broke we were high enough on the mountainside to have a broad view of the Pacific below us. Our ultimate destination, Stinson Beach, lay within a ten-minute drive. Broughton and Singer began to discuss the weather. Both were experts on the region, and between them they believed we would find clear skies below us.

"We should have stopped at Muir Woods," I said. "Remember Whitman's promise for California and his songs for the redwoods?"

"I do," Broughton said. He had taken my hand in his and pressed it. "But mostly I think of his call for adhesive comradeship." Singer laughed and then pointed to a long finger of land jutting into the sea, at the south end of which lay Stinson Beach.

"We're almost at my village," Broughton said. "This was another of our favorite playgrounds in the old days. I love the sea. It's hard living away from it in the city. Yet it's near enough at hand."

"Your poetry is filled with the image of the ocean," I said.

"Sure," he responded, "and most of it comes from my long walks, often solitary ones, on Stinson Beach. Everson lived here, too, for a time. The land has great extremes of weather."

"Like today," I said.

"I think we'll have some sunshine," Singer said.

"Yes, and our picnic on the beach," Broughton added.

We had already gone through a bottle of Cabernet Sauvignon, but there were two bottles of wine remaining.

Years before meeting Broughton I had seen his film *The Pleasure Garden* and read his poems in literary magazines. I knew of his reputation as a teacher at the San Francisco Art Institute. The students thought of him as a guide and friend. One of them told me, "It was great having a poet teach us. It isn't so much the technical side as the poetry behind the whole process. So if you're interested in which camera to use and things like that, you have to ask elsewhere. With James, it's kind of like being the camera yourself, really feeling what you're trying to do." When I mentioned this to Broughton, he said, "Well, that's true. I've done a lot of teaching, but always in my own unique way. I could never follow a departmental directive as to curriculum or educational objectives. Learning should be fun and poetic. Instead, it's often a big bore."

His reputation for throwing wild parties also filtered down to me. One of the most beautiful was the 1978 ceremony held on a one-hundred-year-old ferryboat, the *Vallejo*, belonging to the Alan Watts Society for Comparative Philosophy. The event celebrated the relationship between Broughton and Singer, whom he had met a year earlier. The poem for voices Broughton wrote to mark the occasion includes a list of commandments.

Thou shalt surrender the miseries of thy mind
Thou shalt retrieve the innocence of thy heart
Thou shalt relish the amazements of thy body
Thou shalt revel in thy dishevelment . . .

It is just like Broughton to turn the Biblical message on its head. The key to his thinking on sexuality lies in the phrase "the miseries of thy mind." He believes that most of the misery we suffer is due to an inability to truly experience ourselves as sexual beings. For that reason, his films are usually centered on our relationship to our bodies and to those of the people around us. I have always thought of Broughton as a bodhisattva of the California dream. He personifies the best West Coast aspirations of independence and progressive thinking and remains true to the essentially wild nature of the land, much of it now covered in concrete and asphalt. His poetry offers a fully rounded, often humorous mindscape that breaks free of notions of craft, both traditional and contemporary, and connects the reader with the primal elements of delight.

Much of what he writes is considered "light" even by those who agree with him philosophically. Many critics refuse to take him seriously, unable to recognize depth in his work. I see him as an innovator, one whose breakthroughs lie in what the language suggests rather than in technique. In his films and poems we are taken on a journey through a land of erotic possibilities, unfettered by prejudice, willing to probe the deep wisdom of touch. He takes enormous risks in this regard, not caring to appear profound.

He has taken off the mask of the heavily burdened poet, the tortured literary figure weighted down with important matters, lost in elaborately built prosodic theories. What emerges is a man who deliberately strikes a whimsical pose. Broughton's Stinson Beach poem *I Asked the Sea* is a playful reverie:

Why are you so restless
said I to the Sea.

I'm calmer than you, said She.
The wind and the moon
like to toss me about
but myself I do nothing at all.
I accept whatever comes
and everything comes to me.

Often, he mixes a nightmarish vision with a lighter touch. On the back cover of *A Long Undressing*, Kenneth Rexroth wrote, "There is an old science fiction story about a couple who tumble through a hole in the Fourth Dimension and fall into the terrifying world of which nursery rhymes are a reverberating memory; they scarcely escape with their lives. This is the realm of Broughton's poems." When I came across these lines from *Summer Is a Bride*, I thought they served to illustrate Rexroth's assessment:

Merry fine lads grow fewer each day
and the sturdier ones make haste to wed,
so it's far between and it's way roundabout
when it comes to that specially well-met fellow
who will row you away in a strong houseboat,
who will row past the land of the dead.

Reading the poet, I am taken by his directness. With a purity and almost minimal simplicity he comes right out of Whitman in a way radically different from his contemporaries or the younger Beat poets who followed him.

Everything is stuck together
everything sticks in the muck together
    and we're thick in it
    we're mucked up in it
we're stuck with Original Glue.

For all the "lightness" of this passage, it is Whitman to the core and expressive of Broughton's later amorous/erotic poetry.

Graffiti for the Johns of Heaven (1982) is dedicated to John the Baptist, John the Divine, John XXIII, John Lennon, Jean Cocteau, and other holy Johns. Following this is a poem summing up his philosophy: "I believe that the greatest virtue is to leave virtue alone." The tone of *Graffiti* is close to that of Harold Norse in *Love Poems*. I see the two poets as picking up directly on the eroticism in Whitman's *Children of Adam* and *Calamus*.

Broughton and I walked north along Stinson Beach. He had just shown me the cottage he once owned on a small sandy road right off the beach. "Stinson is my village," he said. "Lying so close to Mount Tamalpais and next to the sea, it is a dramatic coming together of elements."

"So much of your work is joyful and funny," I said. "Even your movie *The Pleasure Garden*. The name alone denotes a sense of joy. Here at Stinson Beach there is something more somber."

"I've found a lot of joy in Stinson Beach and across the hill in

Mill Valley. But I know what you mean. I like the fog when it rolls in and hovers. And the storms here," Broughton responded.

Joel Singer left us to prepare the picnic we would have in the garden of a house they were thinking of renting. Walking beside Broughton, I asked him about his experiences in a military school as a youngster. "Being in that school, a kid with so much creative energy and drive, what was it like?"

"My father had died a few years earlier in an influenza epidemic. Almost immediately my mother set herself the task of finding a new husband. My brother and I were dressed in sailor suits, and we would go to these fancy resorts. She told us to be polite and generally to behave. Finally she found a nice respectable Republican bigot. Imagine how he felt when he heard of my ambition to become a dancer. One of the conditions he set for marrying my mother was that I be sent away to military school, a most un-Whitman-like thing to have happen. Naturally, he believed that would turn me into the kind of man he would expect a stepson to be."

"I remember you told me once that it really wasn't such a bad place."

"Surprisingly, it was okay," he said. "Within no time I had formed some passionate friendships with other boys, ranging from hero worship to love affairs. By age eleven I already knew the meaning of erotic love. Finding the enchantment of the male body became a great discovery. In the end, I had a lot to thank my stepfather for."

Walking back toward town, Broughton talked about a boy whom he calls Littlejohn in *The Androgyne Journals*. "Our relationship lasted for some time. He was captain of the baseball team, blond and well built and had one of the most beautiful cocks I've ever known. Also, he was exceptionally tender."

"How long did your relationship last?"

"Oh, for some time. He taught me lovemaking. All the delightful pleasures of the body. I really think he helped awaken my creative impulses."

"But you had been writing poetry for some time already?"

"Yes, that's true. I believe there was a real strong connection between my poetry and my lovemaking with other boys."

We broke off our conversation as a gust of wind came in from

the ocean. Broughton took my arm in his and we walked to where
Singer awaited us with wine and food.

After lunch I went back to the beach, now cold and empty except for two lone figures walking along the shore in the opposite
direction. I read aloud from *The Bride from the Sea*:

Abruptly the wind died away
    and I
stood blinking at the surf
only to see rolling toward me
a towering wave too high to outwit
that crashed over my head
and toppled me with it up to the beach
    where I found
myself clutching myself only
soaked to the skin.

Reading from Broughton's Stinson Beach poems, I saw his lines
as falling between Rexroth's "terrifying world" of nursery rhymes
and Whitman's centering of the self amidst the land. Broughton's
sea poems have a dark side, but the Whitmanic sense of joyous
appreciation remains a strong, constant theme. *The Bride from
the Sea* possesses a tone close to the innocence we encounter in
many of Whitman's nature poems:

Then I heard
what the song was singing:
        the shock of my joy
    that on a deserted beach
    between the waves of the sea
    and the waves of the land
I had wed my own grief for all time.

Earlier in the poem I discovered a litany of sea images, reminiscent of Whitman:

I rise on your tides,
I shower you in mist,
I salten your eyes,
I glisten your whiskers,
I sponge your thighs,

I graze your groin,
I loll in your armpits,
I glow round your temples,
I bead your misgivings,
I wean your sighing,
I lean near, I listen,
I encircle, I am . . .

When I finished I realized that Broughton had been calling to me. I walked through the sand to where he stood before a beach house built like a miniature castle, complete with turrets, and before which a German shepherd stood guard. We decided to head back to the city. With Singer at the wheel, we drove up the coast highway, carved into a precipitous cliffside, winding in and out of the deep canyons that are the loins of Mount Tamalpais.

Back in San Francisco, Singer and Broughton dropped me where my car was parked near the Fort Mason wharfs. Turning to *A Long Undressing*, I read:

Tail of the mountain
rising at my back
I face the West and become the East.

This margin of sand
is now all I have
to stand on, fall upon, or be.

Broughton, the sublime Californian, reaches to the East, feels the mountain at his backside, delves into all the meanings washed onto shore.

When I read Broughton I feel as if I have entered the grounds of a never-ending carnival, half hidden behind the towers of anybody's faceless modern city. Here I find a refreshingly unsophisticated voice, completely free from worry over current theories. I walk into the funhouse and find:

When the fog lifted
I went out to gather driftwood.
Over my head
a seagull was carrying
a sardine can.

These lines are a perfect California song, reflecting the poet's life-long interest in Zen thought. I wanted to turn back toward the Golden Gate Bridge, cross over the Marin Headlands to Stinson Beach, and invent my own koan, but darkness began to descend and I had to prepare for a class I was teaching.

Driving to North Beach, half my attention on *The Long Undressing* and half on the road ahead, I thought back to Stinson Beach. Nothing wild had happened there; in fact, we were all rather sedate, laid back, like true Californians. Broughton had radiated such calm and had been so gentle that he momentarily seemed at odds with the Whitmanic wildness of the other poets I'd been writing about. Later I ran into George Scrivani, editor and translator, and asked him what he thought of Broughton.

"Neeli, did you ever notice what he can do to a room full of people? Why, he's all over the place, touching, kissing, disarming. In a matter of minutes he's got everyone giggling, their eyes glittering. That certainly seems wild to me," Scrivani said.

There is something wizard-like about Broughton, with his colorful clothes and hands that move like they were casting spells. Yet he can excite in the most straightforward manner:

No need to be fancy
or unorthodox
just try a plain diet of
nipples and cocks . . .

During dinner at my house one night, he said, "Oh God, save me from being profound! Save me from those who are carefully literary!" He is well aware that poetry is itself a wild venture allowing for the maddest dreams and the most uncommon preconceptions, and that theory, in the end, doesn't really matter.

I wished we had stopped on the green slopes of Tamalpais. Walking with Broughton, I had a sense that I had gone back in time. At any moment Alan Watts would appear, carrying the manuscript of *The Joyous Cosmology* or maybe *The Way of Zen*. Broughton would ask us to listen a moment while he read from *Buddha Land*, subtitled "A Zen Spiritual":

There's a big bodhisattva
dishing out enlightenment

serving up enlightenment
feeding you enlightenment—
A big Bodhisattva
dishing out enlightenment
when you get to Buddha Land.
    Koan Baby, don't you cry, don't you cry!
    Koan Baby, don't you cry!

Back at home I read his *Shaman Song*, printed in a San Francisco poetry anthology, thinking how relentlessly he pursues an open and direct language. I wanted to rush back to his apartment, on a hillside that overlooks much of San Francisco, and sit with him in the comfortable living room where so many books are stacked on the coffee table and where the talk is of poetry, printing, gay liberation, and some new film project. The more I thought of James, the more I wanted to call. I would have to think of a good excuse. It must sound nonchalant. When I heard a recording on the other end, asking that I leave a message, I put the receiver down and read *Shaman Song* aloud, pausing at the lines I find most intriguing:

Come forth unabashed
Come forth unbuttoned
Bury belligerence
Resurrect frolic
Only thru body can
you clasp the divine . . .

On the night of Tuesday, November 10, 1987, I went to Broughton's seventy-fourth birthday celebration at Larry Blake's, a popular platform for poetry located in Berkeley. Several of his friends recited poems in honor of the poet before he gave his own reading. Victor Di Suvero, publisher of Pennywhistle Press, handed Broughton an unbound copy of *Hooplas*, subtitled *Poems for Odd Occasions*. Broughton read a few poems from it, including one to Alan Watts and several written on his own previous birthdays. *Hooplas* contains primarily poems written to honor his friends. They are witty, humorous, and warm, in keeping with the spirit of the man who created them.

As Broughton read, I sketched his face in my mind, his white beard, puckish eyes, and wide smile. I wrote in my notebook,

"James is a laughing bodhisattva. Even if he were not here at this moment, I believe I could hear him laughing." Only a few moments later, after telling the audience to listen to the sound of one hand clapping, and making it happen, he read:

Koan baby, don't you cry, don't you cry,
Koan baby, don't you cry.

He is a character right out of one of his films: roaming through a forest, sad faced for a moment, then smiling, looking toward the sky, down to the ground, then eyeing a woman who appears for a moment, only to quickly disappear.

"James may live in the city now, but he had to bring the grace of Tamalpais with him," I told a friend. What better life for a man whose angel brings to him both the range of Walt Whitman and the reverberations of Mother Goose.

Mostly Visible

Words I Dream

A gem with a head
a life on the brink
falling like a lute
through endless space
heart strings are felt
the wonderous look of invisible fish
drunk as sober is
the street a dream
no dreams in death
the outside inside
and the tediums of insufferable labor
Captain Stalin in Generalisimo Franco
believe me 'the turn of things'
nightmare in a glass eye
smooth and simple as Milton's dictum
Sensuous spirit
the Babels of violence
I'l say it with sputniks and spuds of desire
on the loamy earth of the heart's desire
for the grandeurs of absolute equality
There's permission of persimmon
lore of my time

the gravitational pull of passionate wavelengths
a crack on the horizon
The fireworks of nostalgic festivals in Mexican villages
soothe the footsteps
up the city beneath the sea

Philip Lamantia
From *Meadowlark West*

One evening I crossed over from my apartment on Harwood Alley in North Beach to Philip Lamantia's studio. Earlier I had heard his typewriter as I passed by on my way home from the Caffe Trieste, and so I let an hour pass before calling to arrange a meeting.

"Yes, come over around 5:00," he said, " or make it 6:00 . . . or 7:00 . . . in fact, 8:30 would be perfect." That is pretty much the way he settles on an appointment, although it may take minutes longer.

Once inside his three-room apartment, cluttered with books from floor to ceiling, I took a seat in the workroom. Within moments I was handed at least five different books, one of them the first volume of the *Collected Poems* of Thomas Chatterton. "I had to order these from England," he shouted as he walked to the kitchen to make coffee. I leafed through the book, aware of Lamantia's fascination with the poet's youthful output. His own poetry was first published in *VVV*, a surrealist journal, when he was fifteen. At age nineteen *Erotic Poems* was published by Bern Porter in Berkeley.

Lamantia reappeared with two cups of coffee. Handing me one, he said: "You should like this . . . it's Graffeo." I took a sip and nodded approval, putting the book aside for a moment. After the Graffeo he asked if I'd like to try some French Roast from another jobber. "Of course," I answered. Within moments, a fresh cup appeared. We downed our coffee quickly. I even had a chance to read one of Chatterton's shorter poems. As we discussed the poet's suicide at age nineteen, Lamantia rummaged through the kitchen for yet another kind of coffee. "From Guatemala," he said, "Antigua . . . it has a very good aftertaste." We drank that and then found ourselves tackling a cup of Mocha Java.

We read the poems aloud, trading off now and then, until he suggested we go down to the Savoy for cappuccino. I readily agreed. Once there, we ordered and drank quickly. When that was gone, it was espresso, after which we each had a caffé latte and then two house coffees apiece. A few friends joined in, but they soon left, unable to keep up with either of us. The coffee gods were now in full control. I gazed at Lamantia's leonine head, framed in distinguished gray curls, and noticed a fiery blaze in his eyes. "Let's go and read more poems," he said. This sounded good, but I wondered what we would do for coffee. As if reading my mind, he said, "Don't worry . . . I have some North Beach blend from the Caffe Trieste to try."

Making our way back to Filbert Street, I realized that Grant Avenue was rotating. The buildings on either side seemed draped over one another. Panicked, I turned to Lamantia and didn't see him. I looked down at the sidewalk, and the concrete was lurching toward Chinatown in undulating waves. "Philip, where are you!" I yelled, half expecting to see him dancing on a toppling rooftop. But finally he wobbled up beside me. "We really must drink more! Much more!" he insisted, as he staggered toward the corner. I prayed that he would be able to make the necessary turn and walk the twenty-five steps up to his place on the corner of Filbert Street and Harwood Alley. If he could do it, I reasoned I could, too.

Lamantia was born in San Francisco in 1927, the son of Sicilian immigrants who had settled in the Excelsior District. When he first began writing poetry, in junior high school in the early 1940s, he had barely heard of the French surrealist movement founded by André Breton, and yet his first poems read as if he was familiar with the poetry of Breton and his circle. *There Are Many Pathways to the Garden*, written in his teens, begins:

If you are bound for the sun's empty plum
there is no need to mock the wine tongue
but if you are going to a rage of pennies
over a stevedore's wax ocean
then, remember: all long pajamas are frozen dust
unless an axe cuts my flaming grotto.

In 1943 fifteen-year-old Lamantia made contact with the surrealist group gathered in New York. The following year he was
invited there to meet Charles Henri Ford, Parker Tyler, and other
American surrealists. Astounded both by Lamantia's brilliant poetry and conversation, he was embraced as an important young
member. His work began appearing regularly in surrealist publications and other notable journals, such as *View*, which published his poem, *Touch of the Marvelous*, in 1944, and the
Berkeley-based *Circle*, which was one of the more important pre-
Beat underground publications.

In the 1950s, still only in his late twenties, he became a major
figure in the San Francisco Poetry Renaissance and was closely
associated with Michael McClure, Howard Hart, Gregory
Corso, and Allen Ginsberg. Some of his early poems were published in *Ekstasis* (1959) and *Destroyed Works* (1962), both from
Dave Haselwood's Auerhahn Press. The first poem in *Ekstasis* is
a picture poem in the shape of a cross. Several are atypical of Lamantia, touching on his Catholic childhood and indicative of his
search throughout the 1950s for new modes of expression. In
Fragments from an Aeroplane he wrote:

I'm here alone
        Where is HE, God of the PSALMS?
Where's the way to the garden at work within the rose?
    —perfumes that made me drunk, light life—

That garden at work within the rose is the refuge Lamantia would
seek out in his later works, returning to the florid intensity of his
early poems.

These lines from *Interior Suck of the Night* reflect his many
years of taking various forms of mind-altering drugs:

        Opium
           in a butterfly's dream
    windows open on broken stem of pipe
        chimes, cuneiforms
of the marvelous and you! my innocent!

For Lamantia, drugs offered a way to enter the world of the marvelous, to continue exploring his relationship to the mysteries
that poetry provides. He wanted to forge himself in new experiences, shaking off the mundane world:

I am the master of the unpronounced word
I have come thru places where speech is fire.

During the Beat years Lamantia spent time in New York City
and the Far West. Between 1954 and 1962 he lived in Mexico.
From 1963 to 1968 he lived in Spain, Italy, and Greece. He met
the poet Nancy Peters while in Europe. They married in 1978. She
once recalled to me that when she met Philip, he was traveling
with more than twenty suitcases, one reserved for a vast array of
incense and incense burners, another containing astrological
charts and gems, and others filled with his books on Egyptian
mysteries.

While in Mexico Lamantia stayed for a time with the Cora Indians of Nayarit, a Pacific Coast state that remains largely wilderness. Having gained the confidence of the Indians, he participated in their ancient tobacco rites. Later on, he would try LSD
and other hallucinogens. In *From the Front* he writes:

Tenochtitlan!
gray seven thousand feet high
mist of dust—tin door open
to slow motion immobilized traffic
—girl at window—terrace—
terrace a heartmobile— . . .

Allen Ginsberg wrote of Lamantia: "An American original,
soothsayer even as Poe, genius in the language of Whitman, native companion and teacher of myself." Ginsberg admired Lamantia's lyric genius and his astounding word combinations. Not
a poet of the socio-political message as were many of the Beats,
Lamantia fixed more on the power of language, unrestrained by
strict linear thinking. Throughout the 1950s and 1960s he would
invoke Saint Germain, Lautréamont, and Rimbaud in his poetry
and the mythical worlds of Mu and Atlantis. In one of the poems
from this period he recalls his "surrealist youth," its original
impulse:

Oh! Go to the end of the world, Hands
of my surrealist youth! When all the trees
bent to thy rites
of savage runes and flights the sunbird made
on midnight's exploded jewel!

His *Selected Poems*, 1942 through 1966, includes a large selection from his early years. The book, published by City Lights in 1966, is divided into three sections: Revelations of a Surreal Youth, 1943–1945; Trance Ports, 1948–1961; and Secret Freedom, 1963–1966. It is a solid introduction to the poet's growth and development, tracing those first intuitive ventures into surrealism, his years as an important member of the San Francisco Poetry Renaissance, and his travels, particularly in Mexico.

Touch of the Marvelous, also published in 1966, brought together Lamantia's earliest poems, including those published in *VVV* and *View*. Four years later *The Blood of the Air* reaffirmed his belief in pure surrealist techniques. I have always thought of it as a good companion volume for *Selected Poems*. It signals a dramatic change for Lamantia from the work of the early and mid-1960s. The journey here is sensual and more purely of the mind. It begins with *I Touch You*:

I touch you with my eyes when you lie under spiders of silk
I touch you with my one hundred headed giraffes too secret to be seen
the rods & cones the morning covets awaken you
with my touch of tobacco eyes
and you rise from the snails bed of tubular hair
I touch you with the breath of jet planes
and they are gone elsewhere to touch you too . . .

The poet walks on the precipice of a new language, intuiting it with lines that astound:

I shall say these things that curl beyond reach
A fatal balloon
Resolving riddles
It's pure abyss-crackling vortex

Like the experimental jazz musicians of the 1950s, Lamantia threw himself into an abyss of self-revelation, free of the past, entering a chamber of rituals yet to be revealed. Together with Jack Kerouac and Howard Hart, he participated in jazz and poetry performances at New York City's Circle In The Square.

Looking inward, Lamantia recognized the immensity of the human imagination. With a Blakean sense that everything is intricately interconnected, he wrote:

We're off into ourselves
Every moment is light
I eat the sun I scale the moon

Nothing is impossible. Everything becomes immediate. Lamantia obliterates all sense of chronology. Time no longer restricts us:

From a jet plane window I landed into an eighteenth-century drawing
    room
Where the Marquis De Sade and I were of one mind tasting
    pineapples . . .

The poems in *The Blood of the Air* are recipes for the poetic imagination. Lamantia takes incredible risks with language, flinging himself far from institutionalized reason. He once asked me, "Reason? What does poetry have to do with reason?"

From the early 1970s on he has been living in San Francisco's North Beach. Younger poets found him to be a source of knowledge and readily accessible. He took on the role of mentor with ease and soon began teaching a summer course at the San Francisco Art Institute, meticulously tracing the history of the surrealist movement, examining both its precursors and its greatest twentieth century exponents, Breton and Péret. He has called surrealism "a vital myth through which a permanent revelation of humanity shall become a new way of life."

Lamantia's latest books, *Becoming Visible* and *Meadowlark West*, betray no lost daring. Reading the former book for the first time, I recalled him stopping me on the sidewalk one day in front of City Lights Bookstore. I was holding a copy of *Leaves of Grass* with a portrait of Whitman on the cover. I showed it to him. He glared and screamed out, "Oh you and your damn Whitmanic ways!" And then stalked on down Columbus Avenue. A few days later he called to apologize.

As I read *Becoming Visible*, especially *In Yerba Buena* and *Redwood Highway*, I began viewing him as a natural extension of Whitman's headlong charge into a new poetry. Whitman had once called *Leaves of Grass* a language experiment. I believe he would have approved of Lamantia's lines, bold and essentially American despite their surrealist stamp. In *Redwood Highway* he becomes a poet of the landscape, focusing on his own native environment:

The San Francisco Peaks blowing their tops
Runners from the Chumash sprayed
Teleported
Over sierras hot lands deserts . . .

and

Here in old Lemuria
The Oregonian stalagmites
Climb the ocean's ceiling over the Bay Area
My dream identical to Coit Tower . . .

In *Meadowlark West* strains of the wide-open poetics of *Destroyed Works* are in evidence, but a new ingredient is added. The poems are concerned primarily with environmental issues and the need for a new social and political order. He speaks of a society of anarchs, envisioning man transfigured, in tune with the ecology and living in, and at one with, the powers nascent in what he terms the "humanisphere."

The surrealist vision is intact, with its bizarre humor: "It's cozy to be a poet in a bed, on a copse, knoll, in a room / It's terrible to be a poet dragons around to bite off your wings. . . . " Lamantia is sparring with the language of surrealism. The sharp contrast between the two lines, beginning with a list of ordinary objects and ending with an imaginative image, adds to the playfulness of this passage and of many of the poems in the collection.

Some years before *Meadowlark West* was conceived, Lamantia and Nancy Peters began traveling through California and the Pacific Northwest to trace the migration of birds and to observe them in their native habitat.

"Nancy and I were at Lassen Volcanic National Park. We found a path no one had been on before. There were strange trees everywhere. Then we found birds. There were thousands. They spoke to us. I know it sounds crazy, but they did speak in a language we could understand," he said to me after a trip north.

One of the most inspired passages in *Meadowlark West* reads:

At the green bowls green the revels of time
to step into orbs of the before time
wake up where the glyphs are lit within
with purest golden light
the Dawn-Bringer Meadowlark

the inner temple the forest temple
the American destiny line carries us to the Klamath . . .

None of the nature poetry in *Meadowlark West* is program-
matic. It does not read like an editorial, nor is there a self-
righteous tone. In *There* the poet writes:

on that chain of Ohlone mountains
shafts of light on a bobcat
through the thick madrones
first seen emblems that endure cupped my nine years
the great booming voice of nature . . .

It is this voice and the booming voice of Philip Lamantia, himself
a natural phenomenon, that give *Becoming Visible* and *Meadowlark West* significance. Through poetry "the impossible is easy to
reach."

While reading *Meadowlark West* I was surprised by the lines:

. . . the seances of poets Poe Blake Whitman
Emily Dickinson Samuel Greenberg. . . .

Finally he has included Walt Whitman in his hierarchy of poets,
recognizing the influence of *Leaves of Grass*.

Meadowlark West is Lamantia's notebook of the American
West. Here he sustains a vision rooted almost entirely in California, deliberately seeking to build a new poetic myth based on Indian folklore, the varied flora and fauna of the Pacific coastal region, and the shape of the land itself. The poet seeks to galvanize
his surrealist past and his travels in Europe and Mexico with a
vision based on images uniquely Whitmanic. In doing so, he gives
credence to his years as a surrealist and his own resilience as a
writer.

Lamantia is a brilliant conversationalist and a natural teacher.
When we first met and I began to visit him frequently, either at
his apartment or in various North Beach cafés, I took notes as
inconspicuously as possible. He could become so enraptured in
conversation that a planned hour's visit would often run to five
or six hours. He might say to me, "Yes, let's meet at Malvina's
Café, but I only have one hour. We must be done by 3:00 P.M."
Ten cups of coffee and hours later, he would still be expounding

on anything from the poetic science of Charles Fort to a newly discovered theory on the location of Atlantis.

At almost every meeting, I was struck not only by Philip's erudite manner but also by his eagerness to listen. I could say anything halfway plausible regarding poetry and he would seize on it: "That's it . . . . . you have it . . . . . yes . . . . . yes . . . . . poetry is possible . . . . . impossible . . . . . invisible . . . . . comes from the other side. . . . ." His excitement couldn't help but rub off. I never left him without immediately rushing either to my typewriter or to my library, seizing the opportunity to explore new territories Philip had helped open up or simply digging in to that other side, the non-prosaic world.

Some of our interchanges were so intense that I would return home too exhausted either to write or read. One time I had left Philip's, found my way home, and climbed into bed. Five minutes later, as I was about to fall asleep, the phone rang. "This is Philip. I have it now! In Rimbaud . . . you must listen." I got out of bed, dressed, and went over to his place. He read feverishly from Rimbaud's *Illuminations* a passage he had tried to recall from memory earlier at the Caffe Roma. One of the strengths of his poetry is an element of restlessness, a gloss of language below the words themselves, an imprint of lyricism consistent in his work from the beginning to his more recent poetry in *Meadowlark West*.

Lamantia's ear is the key. He never had to develop it; it was there, in the beginning, when he discovered poetry. In both his early poetry and the work of his mature years, what remains important is not a message or set of ideas that finally build a unified edifice but the way he works with language itself. In *The Curtain of Magic Turns Over Motors of Sleep*, from *Becoming Visible*, Lamantia writes:

The purity of the dream-rivulet crosses the depth of
day
    permanent witness from the source of things
    draped: a forest of fiery signs

Lamantia leads us to the frontier of language and then plunges into a dream world beyond the linear. Chronology is set aside, and we are infused with the purely imaginative. He is obsessive in his struggle to free himself from the ordinary. Many younger poets see him as the great magician or hierophant, the one who will point the way beyond preconceptions of poetry as craft and art.

Lamantia takes it as an article of faith that a poem and its form should not be preconceived. As Rimbaud tried, through poetry, to change the nature of man, Lamantia has tried to change the nature of language, to make it a true alchemical tool for opening up realms of consciousness. Whereas Ginsberg's poems often become a mirror in which the poet reflects his own immediate triumphs or tragedies, Lamantia attempts to make the poem an arena for expressing elements of human consciousness that reach beyond the personal.

In *Meadowlark West*, the poet reshapes California. Land and language come together, and he sees in this union a key to a new area of expression. He had touched on much the same thing in poems written in Mexico that reshape the Mexican landscape. Tenochtitlán, the Aztec name for Mexico City, became a personal talisman, and he used it to mark some of his most admirable creations:

I came with banquet of lovers at ruins of Tenochtitlan
   swam the Hellespont of antique mystery
      landed on shores of Mu Atlantis Babylon
         made fast for pool of the underworld and
            ascended feet high into the sky—at rigalu of Tingis
            ate from tables of undersea gardens

When speaking of San Francisco, Lamantia can make it sound as if it were not a city at all, but still a wild, low-lying peninsula. He speaks with authority concerning the winds in the city, where they are the strongest, how occult forces converge at the Alemany Gap, close to his childhood home, or where Broadway and Columbus meet in the center of North Beach. In *Meadowlark West*, he writes: "secrets walked the winds of Market Street / and the lost paradise a black hole . . . "

He has become an expert on the Indian myths of Northern California, particularly those of the Ohlone Indians who inhabited the areas adjacent to San Francisco Bay. They symbolize for him a people close to nature and, therefore, closer to themselves than we can ever be. He would say they lived their lives poetically.

to walk a living bridge of salmon
what was once joy with the supernatural beings

Gilak in the Pomo legend
That these spirits are here now with the clunk of material letters
the yellow-billed Magpie in the dry wind

There was a time when the poet felt estranged from America. In Europe, living in Paris, living in the south of Spain, he felt at home. This was natural for a poet who had grown up responding to avant-garde European literary tradition and the Spanish influence on the culture of California and Mexico. In some of our first meetings, he would discourse on Breton's *Nadja*, Rimbaud's *Illuminations*, and other such texts with a feeling that can only be described as intense reverence. Breton, Péret, Rimbaud, Lautréamont . . . they didn't exist in history for Lamantia; they were contemporaries. He brings them alive in his small, crowded studio just as he does in his poetry. When I first read through *Meadowlark*, in fact, I came to the following:

Paris at the beginning of the Heroic Age in the Twenties making the
round of cafes with surrealist friends the young Breton
Soupault
Péret
Artaud
time of the Surrealist Research Bureau
Amber liquors . . .

All of these images are intertwined with Ohlone, Mount Shasta, and other Mexican, California, and Pacific Northwest imagery. Lamantia comes home but brings Breton along with him.

In our discussion of automatic writing, Lamantia referred to that process as writing without interference from the conscious part of oneself. I said, "Yes, I've been doing that all along. I don't think of what I'm going to write, and in the process of writing, am constantly surprised by what I discover."

Whitman's conception of poetry as a language experiment takes on supercharged meaning when applied to Lamantia's poetry. When he realized that Whitman was also searching for a language beyond the ordinary, his sympathy for the poet grew. Whitman's *Respondez!* is a poem we once read back and forth in my Harwood Alley apartment. It is written with a cynicism atypical of *Leaves of Grass*, although the same dark spirit may be found in many of Whitman's prefaces and the essay *Democratic Vistas*.

Lamantia felt particularly moved by the following lines in *Respondez!*:

Let the earth desert God, nor let there ever henceforth be mention'd
    the name of God!
Let there be no God!
Let there be money, business, imports, exports, custom, authority,
    precedents, pallor, dyspepsia, smut, ignorance, unbelief!

Lamantia once told me that he sometimes spent weeks working on a poem, emphasizing that when you revise a poem, you have to re-create the inspiration of the original writing. Above all else, I believe, Lamantia stands for imagination and would join Blake in holding up the imagination as the true key to poetic genius.

The manner in which Lamantia deals with the subject of pain, and our relationship to it, has a Blakean quality. He takes the thought "man is in pain" and creates a concise, highly animated poem. *Man Is in Pain* is probably the most widely anthologized of Lamantia's poems. The elements of music and imagination are fused. Originally published in *Ekstasis*, it is found in the *Trance Ports* section of *Selected Poems*.

Man is in pain
    ten bright balls bat the air
    falling through the window
    on which his double leans a net the air made
    to catch the ten bright balls
Man is a room
    where the malefic hand turns a knob
    on the unseen unknown double's door

Lamantia probes beyond the ordinary in a language that sometimes falls in on itself in an extremely florid cascade of surrealist images, but in *Man Is in Pain* he is lean and fluid:

Man is in pain
    with his navel hook caught on a stone quarry
    where ten bright balls chose to land
    AND where the malefic hand carves
        on gelatinous air THE WINDOW
    to slam shut on his shadow's tail

It is Lamantia's ability to "blossom" within the world of the fantastic that makes his poetic expeditions onto the land so attractive.

Moving through California and the Pacific Northwest, which Lamantia envisions as a part of what he terms "The Marco Polo Zone" (from the Chinese coast, through Korea and Siberia, down the Alaska coast and the North American coast to Tierra del Fuego at the tip of South America) he writes:

These are the gilds of free verse
Doesn't the horror of writing Am I reading?
Better not to repeat your Sovereign Powers
the astral too plain at noon black with engines slipping again . . .

Moving within this Marco Polo zone, he conceives a bio-ethics new to his poetry in its directness. In the poem *Ship of Seers* he begins: "The dust of intolerable social conditions packed like melting bombs . . . " He writes of "the earth's renewal" and speaks of an end to "the slaughter of the beautiful beasts." All of those trips to the Mount Shasta region of Northern California and to Lassen Peak, in the isolated northeast section of the state, provided the poet with fertile, new fields of nature imagery. I could imagine him, years earlier in Europe, summoning up the ghosts of Novalis and Edward Collins with the same enthusiasm he brings to this new language landscape.

In Lamantia's view there is no alternative to the poetic imagination. Through it, he believes man can reach ultimate freedom, not freedom as one of a myriad of choices for mankind, but as the only choice. Poetry becomes the great liberator because it impels man to go beyond the veil of daily logic, to unlock what Lamantia terms "the marvelous," a realm wherein language acts as alchemical agent, transmuting the ordinary into something rare and beautiful. He tells us that "Poetry knows in the unknowing" precisely because of his belief that the highest knowledge, or wisdom, comes from each individual's confrontation with the inner self, with what cannot be tested or controlled by science, with a mystery that resides in "spirit."

Flaming Teeth is one of his poems I admire most. Each line exists independent of the others, and yet they are cohesive in that they are highly charged words pressing in on one another. In the 1960s, during a time when many of Philip's contemporaries were composing anti-war poetry and polemics against the Vietnam War, he wrote some of his finest love poetry, including *I Touch You* and *The Talisman*. In *Flaming Teeth* he writes:

The earthquake slivers
The broken nails of the nazis
Mister Fly and his obsidian mask
My father on his razor
Basalt nightmares
Megalithic godplanes click the xylophones
My wracking spit spits
Words are magic beans . . .

"Poetry is magic . . . . . words are magic . . . . . yes . . . . . that is it . . . . . I've got it . . . . . don't you see?" Lamantia proclaimed that night in his North Beach apartment when we were reading Rimbaud. I saw it, opened Chatterton, and shouted a random poem.

At 3:00 A.M. one Saturday I stumbled up the steps on Filbert Street toward my apartment. A light blazed down on me from Lamantia's studio. I knocked on the door. A moment later he glared out of the window, a telephone in one hand. "I'm talking to Chicago. Wait a minute and I'll be down to let you inside." His voice was high pitched and agitated. I heard loud noises from upstairs. When he came to the door, he began a steady stream of invective against the person he had been talking to, whose name I never learned. All I found out was that it centered around André Breton and the surrealist group.

We began talking about Mexico. I told him I would be leaving for Oaxaca in two weeks. This led him to a vivid description of the Cora Indian tobacco rites.

"I was one of the first outsiders to be taken to their secret ceremonial," he told me as I sat across from him in the small, crowded studio. "It was then that I levitated. I actually found myself *floating* in the air. *Do you think me mad?*"

I didn't know what to answer. I wanted to say that I believed anything could happen, but let it pass.

"*And the moon danced in the night.* None of this is out of the ordinary. None of this is abnormal," he insisted.

The previous night I had read through Charles Fort's *The Book of the Damned*, required reading for Lamantia. Fort describes lost planets, strange lights falling on earth from heaven, black rains, chunks of ice from the sky, and a procession of the damned. His book is actually an epic poem, one any surrealist might find especially interesting.

As Lamantia talked on about Mexico, it sounded increasingly like an interzone between reality and unreality. I wondered why I had missed so much on my last trip there. I heard graphic descriptions of Breton's visit to the exiled Leon Trotsky in the Mexico City suburb of Coyoacàn, and of Diego Rivera and Frieda Kahlo's friendship with the surrealist painters and writers. I stayed until dawn, then got up to leave.

"You can disappear in Mexico," he told me as I left, "like Ambrose Bierce or B. Traven. The country is endless."

When I got home I found that sleep was useless. I picked up *The Blood of the Air* and read, "I shall say these things that curl beyond reach / A fatal balloon / Resolving riddles / it's pure abyss-cracking vortex."

My friend Jack Mueller called me. "You must have gotten in late," he said, "I've been calling all morning."

"Yeh, I got back five minutes ago. I was with the Cora Indians in Nayarit. I walked through the valley and into the hills, arriving at their sacred ritual site. They allowed me into their most secret ceremonial. I levitated. The moon howled. Blood dripped out of the sky. Frogs dropped from a triangular-shaped cloud."

Mueller answered, "Oh, you were with Philip," as across the alley the shades went down over Lamantia's studio window.

Celebrating Second April

Walking Parker Home

Sweet beats of jazz impaled on slivers of wind
Kansas Black Morning/ First Horn Eyes/
Historical sound pictures on New Bird wings
People shouts/ boy alto dreams/ Tomorrow's
Gold belled pipe of stops and future Blues Times
Lurking Hawkins/ shadows of Lester/ realization
Bronze fingers—brain extensions seeking trapped sounds
Ghetto thoughts/ bandstand courage/ solo flight
Nerve-wracked suspicions of newer songs and doubts
New York altar city/ black tears/ secret disciples
Hammer horn pounding soul marks on unswinging gates
Culture gods/ mob sounds/ visions of spikes
Panic excursions to tribal Jazz wombs and transfusions
Heroin nights of birth/ and soaring/ over boppy new ground.
Smothered rage covering pyramids of notes spontaneously
        exploding
Cool revelations/ shrill hopes/ beauty speared into greedy ears
Birdland nights on bop mountains, windy saxophone
        revolutions
Dayrooms of junk/ and melting walls and circling vultures/
Money cancer/ remembered pain/ terror flights/
Death and indestructible existence

In that Jazz corner of life
Wrapped in a mist of sound
His legacy, our Jazz-tinted dawn
Wailing his triumphs of oddly begotten dreams
Inviting the nerveless to feel once more
That fierce dying of humans consumed
In raging fires of Love.

Bob Kaufman
From *Solitudes Crowded with Loneliness*

In September 1979 Raymond Foye and I planned a benefit poetry reading for *Beatitude*, the poetry magazine founded by Bob Kaufman and William J. Margolis. For months we edited a selection of poems from various poets, together with a selection of Kaufman poems never before published and an essay on his work by Foye. When we finished editing, we put the work into photoready condition and were told we needed $2,400 for a printing of 1,000 copies. Allen Ginsberg agreed to participate in the reading, along with Lawrence Ferlinghetti, Joanne Kyger, Harold Norse, Peter Orlovsky—and Bob Kaufman. It was Kaufman's first major reading in over fifteen years. Foye designed a poster using a photograph of Kaufman in a striped jacket and a straw hat, standing in front of the old City Lights publishing offices. The event was not only a means of raising money but a long overdue tribute to Kaufman as well.

When I told Kaufman that Ginsberg would read, he said, "Allen Ginsberg is the President of Poetry. He's our Pope. We're going to install him in Rome. First, we'll have to buy him a cappuccino at the Trieste and then fly to Rome on a chartered biplane. In Rome, we will all learn Sanskrit and write a new version of the Mass."

Foye and I were surprised to find a front-page headline in the *San Francisco Chronicle* on the morning of the reading: "Beat Reunion In North Beach . . . see page two." Turning the page we found a story on our reading and background information on the starring poets. "This will help bring a crowd," I said, as we were worried about meeting expenses.

I'd run into Kaufman earlier in the day and he took me by the collar. "You'll have to run things when I'm gone," he said. "Bob Kaufman will disappear someday. Nobody will even notice. You can look for him in the bayou or in the swamp, but you won't find him."

"Don't forget, Bobby. Tonight. Seven-thirty. We need you there a half-hour before the reading begins."

Two hours before the reading the street in front of the Savoy Café and Theater looked like the entrance to a major rock concert. We quickly sold out all the seats and then talked to Ginsberg and the other poets about doing a second performance. Everyone agreed and we sold out a second show. An hour before the first performance, at 8:00 P.M., a few hundred disgruntled fans were told that no more tickets were available.

"This is an important event," I told a radio reporter who way-laid me with a microphone on the terrace of the Savoy Tivoli. "Tonight, Bob Kaufman will read *The Abomunist Manifesto*, a major poem of the San Francisco Poetry Renaissance. He has not read together with Ginsberg and Ferlinghetti for twenty years." I went on to say that Kaufman's work had been translated into French and published in two popular editions, but that his work was somehow not appreciated at home.

"Is it true that Governor Jerry Brown will be here tonight?" the reporter asked.

I shrugged my shoulders and went into the theater. Foye and Ginsberg were doing checks on the sound system, and they called me over to coordinate some of the remaining problems.

"Luckily, everyone is here," I said, glancing at my watch. It was twenty minutes before reading time and the Savoy was packed. Then we noticed that Kaufman was missing. Normally this would not be a big worry, but in dealing with the self-proclaimed "abomunist," it could mean he was on a plane to New York or across town at an all-night jazz party.

"I'll run down and see if I can find him," I said. I left the café and looked in on the Coffee Gallery, one of his old hangouts, and then down at the Caffe Trieste. "I saw him a few minutes ago," I was told by one of the poets hanging around. "I think he went up to the reading."

Running back to the café, I was pulled into the theater by Foye. Kaufman was still nowhere in sight. Behind me, Ginsberg, Orlovsky, Ferlinghetti, and the younger poets on the bill sat in anticipation. Foye began the introductions. The glare of the video lights bored in on us. We could barely make out the audience. I had a picture of myself apologizing for Kaufman's absence and reading a selection of his poems. Ginsberg called me over and said I should send somebody out to look for him again. Meanwhile, the reading had begun.

I conjured up images of Kaufman wandering alone by the waterfront docks. Just as I suggested we find a replacement, he came bounding up on stage. Ginsberg launched into *Plutonium Ode*, almost blowing the sound system apart.

"You want me to read *Second April*?" Kaufman leaned over to ask.

"What about the *Abomunist Manifesto*?" I asked.

"Where is it? What have they done to it?" he responded, looking genuinely agitated.

I leafed through *Solitudes Crowded with Loneliness*, his first book, and marked the page where the poem began. Kaufman had brought along a copy of *Golden Sardine*, a collection published by City Lights in 1967. "This is old Beatnik stuff, but I'll read it," he whispered.

It came his time to read. He lifted his thin, dark body from the chair and went toward the dais. Ginsberg smiled at him. The audience seemed to lean forward. There stood diminutive Kaufman with a serape over his flowing white shirt, brown skin radiant as the stage lights hit it. He began to read in a muffled tone that grew clearer as the poem raced toward its conclusion:

ABOMUNISTS JOIN NOTHING BUT THEIR HANDS OR LEGS,
    OR OTHER SAME.

ABOMUNISTS SPIT ANTI-POETRY FOR POETIC REASONS
    AND FRINK.

ABOMUNISTS DO NOT LOOK AT PICTURES PAINTED
    BY PRESIDENTS AND UNEMPLOYED PRIME MINISTERS.

The Abomunist Manifesto is more of a document than a poem. It has elements of the jazz humorist Lord Buckley, a touch of Edward Lear, and some of the popular philosophy of the time. In a section entitled *Further Notes*, Kaufman writes:

Krishnamurti can relax the muscles of your soul,
Free your aching jawbone from the chewinggum habit.
Ouspensky can churn your illusions into butter and

Give you circles to carry them in, around your head.
Subud can lock you in strange rooms with vocal balms
and make your ignorant clothing understand you.

There is an explicit political meaning to the work, but it is clothed
in a language that frees the perceptions from mere journalism.
Thinking of the poem, I am reminded of what the poet once said
when asked how he felt about being a third-world poet. "There
is no third world. There are thousands of worlds. They all exist
at the same time, in the same precise moment. I live in all those
worlds. That's where a poet lives."

Bob Kaufman strived toward an understanding of the univer-
sality necessary for great poetry. He felt that narrow ideological
concerns could shut down the "fountain," as he described it to
me. He once told me, "I'm Black, Jewish, white, green, and yellow
with a blue man inside me struggling to come out." Often, he begins a poem with his eyes or his head or some other part of his
anatomy, and moves outward into the world. He is not visceral
but gracefully attuned to his body as a key to opening "the mysteries" he refers to in his poetry. In *Blues for Hal Waters* he refers
to his head as "my secret cranial guitar"; another poem asks,
"would you wear my eyes?" Even in the saddest poems he
emerges joyous out of an ecstatic love for language and its possibilities, reaching out to others:

My body once covered with beauty
Is now a museum of betrayal.
This part remembered because of that one's touch
This part remembered for that one's kiss—
Today I bring it back
And let it live forever.

Believing strongly in the reality his poems created for him, he
lived comfortably with them, and that is why he became like a
poem, why those who knew him were always treated to gems of
language invented spontaneously or brought out of his memory
bank of images.

When we first met, at a book party in 1975, he said, "I knew
your uncle, Herman Cherry, in Woodstock. . . . Herman Cherry,
painted *Fruit Compote* and gave it to me. . . . Herman Cherry
flew to the top of the Washington Monument and painted *Fruit*

Compote, and then he wrapped it up and gave it to me at the Lincoln Monument. Herman Cherry is an airplane flying over America with *Fruit Compote*, a small painting in a gilded frame that he gave me in Woodstock thirty years ago. . . . I was a labor organizer. . . .Rimbaud is an orange blossom. . . .Cherry is *Fruit Compote* painted for Bob Kaufman, Poet." He then began reciting T. S. Eliot's *The Love Song of J. Alfred Prufrock*, gesturing elegantly, moving his wiry body back and forth, his fingers playing an elegant invisible instrument. Three-quarters through *Prufrock* he spliced in lines from Yeats' *Sailing to Byzantium* and *Ode to Walt Whitman*, by Federico García Lorca, as well as his own poetry. Through the years I would see a repeat of such performances in cafés, barrooms, and my own apartment, especially in those months Kaufman lived with me after the Dante Hotel burned down.

A week after that first meeting, I was wandering down Adler Alley, a narrow passageway between North Beach and Chinatown, filled with garbage from the nearby Chinese fish markets and flanked on the North Beach end by City Lights Bookstore and Vesuvio's, a bar where Dylan Thomas and Jack Kerouac used to hang out when they were in town. I felt alone and unwanted. Suddenly Kaufman appeared.

"Neeli Cherkovski," he said, looking perfectly serious, "let's find our way to Saturn."

"Bobby, I don't feel good. I'm all alone. I don't have anyone to love me." I looked directly at him, hoping he would provide some words of comfort.

"You're a poet. You can't ever be alone. You have poetry," he insisted, gripping my arm with surprising strength.

He touched me deeply with that exchange, but I never quite figured out how a man who wrote *Solitudes Crowded with Loneliness* could have said what he did.

Bob Kaufman: the son of a Creole mother from Martinique and an Orthodox Jewish father; born in New Orleans in 1926; devotee of jazz, finding his way through that improvisational world to his own song. Kaufman was committed to oral poetry. Much of his work survives because his wife, Eileen, wrote it down as he spontaneously recited it. *Golden Sardine* is filled with poems written on scraps of paper, rescued by Kaufman's friends Mary

Beach and Claude Pelieu. His last book, *The Ancient Rain*, came to fruition due to the care given by Raymond Foye to gathering all of the poet's unpublished writings from paper scraps, napkins, old tape recordings, and singed manuscripts retrieved from the poet's burned-out hotel room. Kaufman himself would have nothing to do with the shaping of the book.

Before he came to San Francisco, Kaufman had organized black mine workers in the South and had been a merchant seaman who traveled around the world several times. His ideology was a generalized protest against senators conducting anti-communist witch hunts from the halls of Congress, states conducting the ritualized, official murder of capital criminals, and generals sending soldiers into battle. In the community of poets gathered around North Beach, he found himself concerned more and more with poetry and began writing in earnest.

Kaufman lived in San Francisco until 1961, a habitué of the Co-Existence Bagel Shop, The Place, the Hot Dog Palace, The Coffee Gallery, Mike's Place, and other Beat hangouts. From 1961 to 1963 he lived in New York. His reputation had grown steadily in Europe, particularly in France where he became known as the "Black American Rimbaud." He married Eileen and had a son, Parker, named after the jazz musician Charlie "Bird" Parker.

Second April, ultimate statement of an outsider, a man looking coldly, clinically at a society fringed in nightmare, is a dream-trance of the surreal, serving up childhood memories, young-adult reveries, condemnations of a society in danger of becoming empty at the core. Kaufman affirms the power of poetry and jazz to transform, to radiate from deep within the mind, outward toward others.

Kaufman's protest, wrapped up in jazz images and the summoning of the absurd, includes a recognition of human frailty. Each section of *Second April* is a "session" as in jazz: "Session quarter zero . . . is tubercular leaves, chipped nose saints, alabaster sphinx cats . . . burning warehouses, nonchalant cops, pop-bopping black leather angels, feathered fathers. . . . " Every time I heard him read the poem I imagined myself in a vast jazz club, being led from room to room, following his sadness, his aloneness, his alienation, and his humor, and ducking underneath divine revelations and his juggling of language. "We are attacking our hair, it waves to neighbors in skies, kinky relatives," and "we cook old chaplinesque shoestrings, they watch, we have never, have we, never ever, never."

Second April impressed Ferlinghetti, who published it as a City Lights broadside back in 1959, calling it "an autobiographical journey springing out of the blind conjunction of such events as Christ's crucifixion, death, and resurrection, the A-bomb, and the author's own birth." The poem hit like a bombshell when first read in North Beach and quickly became a major weapon in the Beat arsenal:

O man in inner basement core of me, maroon obliteration smelling
    futures
of green anticipated comings, pasts denied, now time to thwart time,
time to frieze illusionary motion on far imagined walls,
stopped bleeding
moondial clocks. . . .

He sets the stage for a world in which normal chronology must be suspended, so that his interior self might jump out and reform consciousness. If in *Howl* ("I saw the best minds of my generation destroyed by madness . . . ") Ginsberg looks outward from the "I" and proceeds to range over America, condemning what made the "best minds" of his generation go mad, Kaufman takes us deep inside of himself and then slowly comes back into the "air," talking of time, telling us to be free from the enslavement of clocks. He motioned people inward and then forward: "on to Second April, ash-smeared crowns, perfect, conically balanced, pyramid-peaked heads, shuddering . . . "

I took my turn scattering Kaufman's ashes onto San Francisco Bay from a little boat filled with poets Howard Hart, Jack Hirschman, Lawrence Ferlinghetti, Jack Micheline, Bob's son, Parker, and Bob's brother George from Berkeley. Whenever I miss him, I find myself going to his poetry.

His love for the poet Federico García Lorca was obvious to those who knew him, and references to the Spanish modernist abound throughout the body of his work. In a poem entitled *Lorca*, Kaufman writes:

Spit olive pits at my Lorca,
Give Harlem's king one spoon,
At four in the never noon.
Scoop out the croaker eyes
        of rose flavored Gypsies
Singing García,
In lost Spain's
Darkened noon.

Identifying strongly with Lorca, and looking on him as the primary singer of sensuality and solitude and the territories lying between those two poles, Kaufman strove for the clarity of expression and the intensity found in Lorca's poems *Somnambular Ballad* and the *Poet in New York* cycle.

In understanding Kaufman, it is vital to appreciate his search for an anchorage amid the lonesomeness he felt so keenly.

Sitting here alone, in peace
With my private sadness
Bared of the acquirements
Of the mind's eye
Vision reversed, upended,
Seeing only the holdings
Inside the walls of me . . .

For many, Kaufman was the ultimate rebel, the man who lived outside of society. His poems, however, no matter how keen their social criticism, are those of a man who yearned to be involved. Some of his last poems are deeply concerned with "that which is out there" in America. He lived in poverty all his life, yet felt himself to be a voice for the people, a new Whitman who, despite "private sadness," developed an expansive vision of the land:

THE AMERICAN SUN HAS RISEN,
THE OTHER SUNS HAVE LEFT
THE SKY, THE POEM HAS ENTERED
THE REALM OF BLOOD. BLOOD IS
NOW FLOWING IN ALL SKIES AND
ALL THE STARS CALL FOR MORE
BLOOD . . .

Kaufman's interior vision goes back to his earliest poems:

I wish that whoever it is inside of me,
would stop all that moving around,
& go to sleep, another sleepless year
like the last one will drive me sane . . .

To be driven sane . . . for Kaufman that may mean to lose what
he saw as the unlimited joy of poetry. It isn't for nothing that he
signed his name "Bob Kaufman, Poet." Yet, with this joy—the vocation of poet—also came the preoccupation with the themes of
death, loneliness, solitude. *Solitudes Crowded with Loneliness*,
far from being a sad book, has a playfulness throughout the text.
It isn't always overt, but it is there amid the alienation he saw so
clearly:

What of the answers
I must find questions for?
All these strange streets
I must find cities for,
Thank God for beatniks.

He could sweep the reader into his deepest sorrows, into his intense feeling of being on the outside cut off from others or from
himself, yet he always marches back with keen wit.

In clear language he invoked surreal moods, tossing out one-
liners that became, piled against one another in a poem, visionary: "The radio is teaching my goldfish Jujitsu . . . / My old lady
has taken up skin diving & sleeps underwater / I am hanging out
with a drunken linguist who can speak butterfly / And represents
the caterpillar industry in Washington D.C."

By the time Bob and I first met in 1975 he had written most of
his poetry, and the Kaufman legend had been fixed in concrete.
People would say, "Bobby didn't speak all through the Vietnam
War" or "Bob stopped talking after President Kennedy's assassination." In his preface to *The Ancient Rain*, Raymond Foye
wrote, "Kaufman took a ten-year Buddhist vow of silence,
prompted by the assassination of President Kennedy." Later I
would hear his old friends say things like, "He spoke all the time,
man," or "Hey, Bob would speak now and then." I can believe the
silence, especially in light of some of his more memorable lines.
Sometimes I would read his poems and feel guilty, as if I were
responsible for the deep, profound vision so often threaded with

sorrow: "THERE ARE TOO MANY UNFUNNY THINGS HAPPENING TO THE/COMEDIANS," he wrote in *The Travelling Circus*, typical Kaufman wordplay from *The Ancient Rain*. In the same poem he writes of "publishing two volumes of my suicide notes." Plagued, fearing nothing when he holds the banner of the poem aloft:

THE POET NAILED ON
THE HARD BONE OF THE WORLD,
HIS SOUL DEDICATED TO SILENCE
IS A FISH WITH FROG EYES,
THE BLOOD OF THE POET FLOWS
OUT WITH HIS POEMS, BACK
TO THE PYRAMID OF BONES
FROM WHICH HE IS THRUST
HIS DEATH IS A SAVING GRACE

CREATION IS PERFECT . . .

Death and creation are juxtaposed dramatically in the heated vortex at the center of Kaufman's vision. The poem becomes a death sentence, isolating him, opening up the terror of ultimate truths; and yet it also served as a great light, a way to express the fury of being unable to triumph over the vast emptiness permeating existence. Every line counts. Each poem is a final statement, not really part of a process but a hard thing nailed to a hard thing. Something meant to be permanent: "The blood of the poet flows out with his poems." Bob Kaufman, Poet.

I remember: Kaufman sits in my kitchen across the table from where I hold a black binder filled with soiled pages on which I have typed poems. His eyes cover me, invade my own private sadness as I read aloud. I find myself slowing down when I am on sure ground and speeding up when I am not . . . hoping he'll pass over the rough spots. I cannot fool him. He is with every word, all of the line breaks. And this is the man I had consigned to a vague, anonymous fog when we lived together in Harwood Alley.

I try to pull myself back, thinking of Kaufman's *Hollywood* poem or the long, wild poem that opens *Golden Sardine*. He describes the execution of Caryl Chessman by the State of California as it takes place on the backs of a visionary bison herd, images of PTA women and Kiwanis Club men attempting to chop down the tree from which the poem grows . . . I am pulled into Bobby's darkness . . . I am alone . . . I am unutterable and yet words begin to form. Bob Kaufman, obsessed with that "inner basement core" of himself, declared:

I refuse to have any more retired burglars
picking the locks on my skull, crawling in
through my open windows, i'll stay out forever,
or at least until spring, when all the wintered
minds turn green again . . .

That's about as playful a mask as I've ever seen a poet wear. Kaufman climbs out of himself, ranges above his own fragility and vulnerability, but will come back again when the human mind (and heart) "turn green again," when men are warm, when love rules.

We would sit in Harwood Alley during the winter we lived together—both of us probably thinking of springtime and green things—as we shivered in the kitchen. "Bob, what are you thinking?" I'd often ask. Usually, I'd get a cold stare or he would simply look off into space, but occasionally he'd say, "Nothing . . . nothing." The sure-fire way of eliciting a response was to start reading Hart Crane, Federico Garcia Lorca, T. S. Eliot, or Wallace Stevens. He felt close to Crane's blazing meteor of a life, reciting pieces of *The Bridge* from memory or fragments of *White Buildings*. Frequently, in the North Beach cafés, Bob would quote Stevens' *Music then is feeling, not sound* or launch into a fanciful version of Lorca's *The King of Harlem*.

One evening I read the first few pages of Whitman's *Song of Myself* to Kaufman as he sat at the kitchen table. As I read, he tapped his fingers on the table with his right hand, following the big Whitmanic tone I tried to approximate with my voice. When I stopped for breath, he cried: "More. More Whitman."

Bob once wrote that the first man was unable to survive the first truth and so he invented suicide. Throughout his poetry, he throws the proverbial naked truth in our faces, hot with music and cool with steady wit. He could retreat, not only into himself but to the memory of his youthful days as a sailor or into childhood reveries as well. In *Night Sung Sailor's Prayer*, Kaufman sails off the page:

Voyager now, on a ship of night
Off to a million midnights, black, black
Into forever tomorrows, black
Voyager off to the time worlds,
Of life times ending, bending, night.

The lines bring me to " . . . Sappho, rolling drunks in coffee gal-
leries, cock robin is / posthumously guilty, chicken little was right
all along, Vachel's basic savages drive Buicks now, God is a parking meter. . . ." In these lines he captures so much . . . summoning forth Sappho and Vachel Lindsay. The image of Lindsay's
middle Americans, the people he "sang" his poems to through the
raucous 1920s, in big Buicks rambling down the highways, their
spiritual values wrapped in the idea of parking meters, in the idea
of time and money.

I read again Bob's poem on Caryl Chessman, the long and
thunderous beginning to *Golden Sardine*. The poem could easily
be tacked on to *Leaves of Grass*.

CARYL CHESSMAN INTERVIEWS THE P.T.A. IN HIS SWANK GAS
CHAMBER BEFORE LEAVING ON HIS ANNUAL INSPECTION OF
CAPITAL, TOUR OF NORTHERN CALIFORNIA DEATH UNIVERSI-
TIES, HAPPY.

Chessman, a convicted kidnapper, became a symbol for people
around the world who opposed the death penalty. Kaufman, in
joining the protest, brought his ironic sensibility into full force:

CARYL CHESSMAN KNOWS, THE GOVERNOR OF CALIFORNIA
KNOWS, GOOD JOHNNY THE POPE KNOWS, SALVATORE AGRON
KNOWS & ALL THE LEAKY EYED POETS KNOW, IN THEIR
PORES. NO ONE IS GUILTY OF ANY THING AT ANY TIME ANY-
WHERE IN ANYPLACE . . .

The most stirring and memorable lines of the poem come when
Kaufman's protest takes flight, soaring over the American landscape, irony still intact, a wide and all-embracing vision of America at its historical center (rendered hysterical in Kaufman's word
juggling). The poet in San Fransciso, a child of New Orleans,
roams the continent, leaping back in time to the torment and turmoil of a nation undergoing violent birth pains. At the end of this

passage, Kaufman makes reference to his son, Parker, whom he calls to witness Chessman's truth—the taking of a life by the state is murder. Here is a vision worthy of Whitman:

... CARYL CHESSMAN WAS AN AMERICAN BUFFALO, THUN-
DERING ACROSS CALIFORNIA'S LYING PRAIRIES, RACKED WITH
THE POISON THE ARROWS OF AUTHORITY, GUARDING THE
BRILLIANT ... VISIONS OF MILLIONS OF GENOCIDED RED CRA-
ZYHORSE PEOPLE, DEAD IN THE MAKESHIFT GAS CHAMBERS
OF SUPPRESSED HISTORY ...

"Lorca ... Federico García Lorca!" Kaufman yelled from my living room where he had been sleeping on the floor. I walked in to find him sitting on a chair with a small lamp beside him, chain smoking and sipping from a Coke.

"What about Lorca?" I asked.

"The night that Lorca comes will be when the Negroes leave the south ... when Lorca comes, Harwood Alley will move to New Orleans ... we'll live on the clotheslines. ..."

He was half-quoting from one of his latest poems—a poem that would be included in *The Ancient Rain*. It begins:

THE NIGHT THAT LORCA COMES
SHALL BE A STRANGE NIGHT IN THE
SOUTH, IT SHALL BE THE TIME WHEN NEGROES LEAVE THE
    SOUTH FOREVER ...

"North Beach is home to me," Kaufman once told me. "When I'm in bed at night, and Billie Holliday is singing the blues outside my window, and Paul Robeson is singing the Soviet National An-them in my head, and I can't sleep, I go outside and walk the streets of North Beach. And I know I'm home." Once describing himself as "the poet of the Bagel Shop," he sat in that long-gone coffeehouse on Grant Avenue with other habitués, drinking cof-fee, smoking endless packs of cigarettes, and dreaming up new poems. When I first came to North Beach, the storefront had be-come a dress shop. Today it's North Beach Video.

After the Bagel Shop closed (Bob wrote a poem about that North Beach event) there were still other places: the Coffee Gal-lery, 12 Adler Place, and Vesuvio's. In the latter, he once leaned over and whispered in my ear: "T. S. Eliot is my father." That seemed funny to me at the time. I thought how different Kaufman dressed and lived from the St. Louis native who had fled to England in fear of his barbarous homeland. Eliot had an ear for those compelling mysteries that make a poem real. According to Raymond Foye, Kaufman broke his long years of silence by reciting Thomas à Becket's speech from Eliot's *Murder in the Cathedral* at a North Beach gathering.

Kaufman and I once drove out to the state beach at Land's End. He said nothing on the way there, preferring to chain-smoke. I parked on a high cliff so we could see the Golden Gate Bridge, the Marin Headlands, and hear the seals below on the rocks. I suggested that we walk down toward the rocks. Kaufman remained silent, but followed.

"Everything living that passes through death walks with head lowered," he said.

"Is that your line?" I asked.

"Lorca," he said. "I wrote it for Garcia Lorca a long time ago, when he was a gypsy in Seville . . . when I was washed ashore. Endless moon. Dreamless Spain."

Now he quoted himself. I began reciting random lines from Lorca's poem for Whitman. "*Y tú bello*, Walt Whitman, *con su barba* . . . "

I forgot the rest of the poem and wanted Kaufman to finish the lines. But he wasn't beside me. I ran down the path and couldn't find him. A wave of panic swept over me. Jesus, people fall from these cliffs, I thought, and looked down the narrow path to the jagged-edged rocks and threatening sea swells below.

"Bobby . . . where are you?"

Silence weighed heavily on me as two men passed with a poodle following obediently behind them. I took a path that forked into a clump of thick bushes and then sloped toward an embankment of sand. In the bushes, it was cool. The moment I reached the sandy clearing, I might as well have been in the Sahara.

"Come on, Bob . . . "

Then I saw him, far below, sitting on a boulder. I ran down to him.

"How did you get here so fast?"

"I'm from New Orleans," he said, "and when I sailed away, I sailed away forever. . . . "

He pointed to a massive tanker whose prow was pointed toward the bay. We watched together as it sailed under the bridge.

"Visual beatitudes," he said.

Soon we were back in the car, racing to North Beach. I glanced at him as he lit another cigarette. Hoping to catch him off guard and glean a little biographical information, I asked, "What was it like when you were sailing? Did you read a lot of books? When did you first go to sea?"

"Negroes . . . Negroes . . . Negroes" he shouted. "The world is full of Negroes . . . and the king of Harlem lifts a spoon over Whitman's beard full of butterflies."

Whitman and Bob Kaufman were meeting yet again.

In 1983 Kaufman and Lynn Wildey, fellow poet and girlfriend, rented a small house in the Russian River town of Guerneville, ninety miles north of San Francisco. I drove there with a younger poet to visit and to do a poetry reading at a nearby café.

"Neeli Cherkovski! Eric Walker! How are you? Did you bring Grant Avenue in the car trunk?" Kaufman said as he greeted us at the front door.

The first thing he wanted to do was have a drink. Lynn, however, had already made a meal, so we ate, then visited a neighbor. Kaufman, as usual, remained silent. Later we drove to a riverfront beer bar where Lynn and I tried to coax him into talking about his early youth. We hoped to get enough biographical information so I could begin a long projected profile.

"Listen, Bobby, just tell me a few things, like your father, what did he really do?"

"We were Jewish and Catholic. My mother took us to church. Sometimes we went to the synagogue. I played in Bayou Saint John. Now, buy me a beer, Neeli." Kaufman pressed his hand into my wrist. "Just one beer and I'll tell you everything."

I bought the beer, but noticed that his expression denoted a complete lack of interest in the interview. I switched to small talk about the river, the weather, and if he liked living so far from North Beach.

Then I asked a question regarding writing. "Bob, why do you like Whitman so much?"

"Another beer," he said with a demon-like glint in his eyes.

I bought another round of draft beers.

"Whitman invades America," he said.

That was his final commentary on Whitman. I used a new tactic. "What would you say to young writers?"

His eyes came alive. He stood up from the wobbly chair he was sitting on, almost tipping our equally wobbly table, and said, "Write! I'd tell a young writer to write! Write it all down! Don't hold it back!" With that said, he sat back down, stared into his remaining beer, drank it, and asked for another. I found his reticence annoying, though it was nothing new. There must be some other way to get him to talk. While I ordered more beers, Lynn began to demand that he open up. I saw his face framed in the greenery outside the window at the end of the cavernous barroom, and I knew him well enough to realize he was definitely finished with the interview.

In his early years Kaufman had tried to make changes in society. He threw himself into the political arena as a labor organizer. Those who knew him then speak vividly of his passion while addressing a crowd or explaining whatever oppression he wanted to end.

Later he retreated into his poetry, finding in it all the necessary ingredients for battling oppression. Poetry, in and of itself, became a means of defining life and of dealing with all the social, political, and personal issues that had concerned him. Lorca saw great poetry, and all great art, as possessed of *duende*, a mysterious essence that radiates from within, having little to do with a preconceived idea of craft and more with an embodied spirit that somehow captures the purest essence of what it means to be human, to live, and to die. It is a spirit that must be sought but can never be confined or completely analyzed. Kaufman longed to embrace this spirit of *duende*, to confront the demons that inhabit a poem.

Bob talked frequently of death in his last few years. Late one evening in Specs', a bar across the street from City Lights, he entered and addressed the crowd. "I don't live here anymore. I live on Mount Olympus now. I only use this body for dirty bookstore purposes." Later, as the bartender gave the last call, the poet proclaimed, "I have seen my own death. One day I shall be walking down Grant Avenue. And a pay telephone will ring. I will pick it up. It will be Jean Cocteau on the other end. And he will say, 'The Blood of the Poet.'"

When Lynn Wildey called on a Sunday morning in 1986 to tell me, "The poet Bob Kaufman is dead," I went to his poem *Awe*:

At confident moments, thinking on Death
I tell my soul I am ready and wait
While my mind knows I quake and tremble
At the beautiful Mystery of it.

After my fellow poets and I had each taken a turn scattering Bob's ashes into San Francisco Bay from the small boat that had taken us out, Ferlinghetti turned to me and said, "When I retire, I think I'll live on a little boat out by Mission Rock." I almost responded, But the shoreline there will all be filled with condos and office towers by then. . . . Instead I smiled. I leafed through a copy of *The Ancient Rain* and read to myself.

Turning back to Ferlinghetti, I said, "What do poets retire from?"

Charles Bukowski in 1970, at the Terminal Annex Post Office,
downtown Los Angeles. (Photo: Sam Cherry)

Above: A major force in the underground poetry scene since the late 1950s, Charles Bukowski has published more than twenty-five books of poetry and prose. He is one of the best-selling authors in Europe. (Photo: Michael Montfort)

Above, right: A gathering of L.A. poets in 1972, with Charles Bukowski (left), Neeli Cherkovski (standing), John Thomas (standing), Paul Vangelisti (center), and (bottom right) Steve Richmond. (Photo: Sam Cherry)

Below, right: John Wieners visiting New York City in 1986, the year that his *Selected Poems* was published by Black Sparrow Press. (Photo: Raymond Foye)

Above: Philip Lamantia's books include *The Blood of the Air*, *Selected Poems*, *Becoming Visible*, and *Meadowlark West*. A native of San Francisco, Lamantia has lived in Spain, North Africa, and Mexico. (Photo: Rob Lee)

Right: A "Bodhisattva of the California Dream," James Broughton, seen here with his lover, the artist Joel Singer, is known equally as a poet and filmmaker. (Photo: Nina Glaser)

Bob Kaufman in the Caffe Trieste, one of San Francisco's
oldest coffee houses. Kaufman wrote three books of poetry,
Solitudes Crowded with Loneliness, *Golden Sardine*, and *The
Ancient Rain*. (Photo: Ira Nowinski)

Allen Ginsberg takes time out to work on a manuscript while
visiting at a friend's apartment in San Francisco. The poet's
Collected Poems was published by Harper & Row in 1986.
(Photo: Ira Nowinski)

Above: Caffe Trieste, early 1970s (left to right): Lawrence
Ferlinghetti, Manette LaBlanc, Peter LaBlanc, Howard
Schrager, Allen Ginsberg, Harold Norse, Jack Hirschman,
Bob Kaufman. (Photo: Diana Church)

Right: Young Bob Kaufman in the Co-Existence Bagel Shop in
North Beach, a popular poets' and artists' hangout in the
1950s. (Photo: Sam Cherry)

Above: Four poets (left to right): Bob Kaufman, Gregory
Corso, Harold Norse, and Neeli Cherkovski at a publication
party in North Beach, 1978. (Photo: Mark Green)

Right: Allen Ginsberg and Lawrence Ferlinghetti on the
terrace of the Savoy Tivoli in San Francisco. Back to camera is
Gregory Corso. (Photo: Ira Nowinski)

Above: A native of California's great Central Valley, William Everson is a true visionary in the lineage of William Blake and Walt Whitman. Among his books are *The Residual Years, The Hazards of Holiness*, and *Man-Fate*. (Photo: Chris Felver)

Right: Gregory Corso and his son Max in San Francisco's Washington Square Park, 1979. Corso's poems *Marriage, Bomb*, and *Power* are classics of contemporary American poetry. (Photo: Raymond Foye)

Above: In the City Lights' office (left to right): Robert
Duncan, David Gascoyne, Mrs. Gascoyne, Lawrence
Ferlinghetti, and Harold Norse. (Photo: Ira Nowinski)

Right: Harold Norse is the author of *Hotel Nirvana*, *Beat
Hotel*, *Carnivorous Saint*, and *The Love Poems*. Norse is one
of the leading voices in the movement toward a free and open
sexual consciousness. (Photo: Rob Lee)

Lawrence Ferlinghetti achieved worldwide acclaim for *A Coney Island of the Mind*, published in 1958 by New Directions. He is a leading spokesperson for the populist voice in contemporary poetry. (Photo: Ira Nowinski)

Standing by His Word

Death News

   *Visit to W.C.W. circa 1957, poets Kerouac Corso Orlovsky on sofa in
living room inquired wise words, stricken Williams pointed thru window curtained on Main Street: "There's a lot of bastards out there!"*

Walking at night on asphalt campus
road by the German Instructor with Glasses
W. C. Williams is dead he said in accent
under the trees in Benares; I stopped and asked
Williams is Dead? Enthusiastic and wide-eyed
under the Big Dipper. Stood on the Porch
of the International House Annex bungalow
insects buzzing round the electric light
reading the Medical obituary in *Time*.
"out among the sparrows behind the shutters"
Williams is in the Big Dipper. He isn't dead
as the many pages of words arranged thrill
with his intonations the mouths of meek kids
becoming subtle even in Bengal. Thus
there's a life moving out of his pages; Blake
also "alive" thru his experienced machines.
Were his last words anything Black out there
in the carpeted bedroom of the gabled wood house
in Rutherford? Wonder what he said,
or was there anything left in realms of speech
after the stroke & brain-thrill doom entered
his thoughts? If I pray to his soul in Bardo Thodol
he may hear the unexpected vibration of foreign mercy.
Quietly unknown for three weeks; now I saw Passaic
and Ganges one, consenting his devotion,
because he walked on the steely bank & prayed
to a Goddess in the river, that he only invented,
another Ganga-Ma. Riding on the old
rusty Holland submarine on the ground floor
Paterson Museum instead of a celestial crocodile.
Mourn O Ye Angels of the Left Wing! that the poet
of the streets is a skeleton under the pavement now

and there's no other old soul so kind and meek
and feminine jawed and him-eyed can see you
What you wanted to be among the bastards out there.

Benares, March 20, 1963

Allen Ginsberg
From *Collected Poems 1947–1980*

The first thing Allen Ginsberg ever said to me was "You're fat." I answered: "And you're bald." Things were never smooth between us after that. I was not one of "Allen's boys." He told me, soon after arriving in town one day in 1977, "I have a young friend I'd like you to meet. He's straight, and he only makes it with me. Don't try to go to bed with him." When the young man came to show me his poems, he very quickly advised me, "I only make it with Allen," and then read a few of his offerings, lightweight reflections of Jack Kerouac's *Mexico City Blues* with a little Buddhism thrown in for good measure.

When the young man left, I thought of the time a leader of an Orthodox Hasidic sect called me a few days before the Jewish high holidays and began reciting *Please Master*, a Ginsberg poem graphically describing the poet's desire to be sexually dominated by a youth. Listening to him, and knowing that he would use any method to bring me into the fold of Orthodoxy, I felt a deep sense of embarrassment.

"Neeli," he said, after finishing his recitation, "I think Ginsberg would have made a good Jeremiah."

"How do you mean?" I asked.

"Well, look at his power. Listen to those words. His rhythms. The pictures he paints. His directness. Even if the lines are shocking, even when they evoke images of sodomy, they cannot be denied."

The Hasid's words came back to me one night when I leafed through Ginsberg's *Collected Poems*. I read the first five lines of the poem he had recited over the telephone:

Please master can I touch your cheek
please master can I kneel at your feet

please master can I loosen your blue pants
please master can I gaze at your golden haired belly
please master can I gently take down your shorts . . .

I understood all too well the sentiment that the poet was expressing but still found myself uncomfortable reading, "please master touch your cock head to my wrinkled self-hole." Yet, the poem has life and expresses what Jack Kerouac once called "the unspeakable visions of the individual."

In the 1960s I used to think of Ginsberg as a modern prophet, a poet with an ethical and spiritual message to deliver both to the people in power and those over whom they ruled. The image was an easy one, yet I saw justification in it. When the Hasid spoke of Jeremiah, I thought of Allen Ginsberg chanting before the Pentagon demanding an end to the war in Southeast Asia or reading *Wichita Vortex Sutra*, in which the specter of America growing dead at the center through misuse of language and apparent lack of care for its own youth is evoked.

Still, I wished that the Hasid had read from *Kaddish*, the elegy for Ginsberg's Russian-born mother, Naomi. Written not long after her death in 1956, the poem memorializes an entire way of life symbolized in the poet's mother, a world where the call for social and political justice was paramount and people did not hide their emotions from one another. The poem begins with a dream-like image: "Strange now to think of you, gone without corsets & eyes, while I walk on / the sunny pavement of Greenwich Village. / downtown Manhattan, clear winter noon, and I've been up all night, talking, / talking, reading the Kaddish aloud, listening to Ray Charles blues / shout blind on the phonograph. . . ." It was an old Hebrew place deep in his heart that caused the poet to choose *Kaddish* as the title for his poem, the name of the Jewish prayer for the dead, written in Aramaic and recited at the end of religious services.

In *Kaddish* Ginsberg wears no prophetic mask, nor does he hide his grief or memories behind a rhetorical wall. Like a newsreel of the all-too-human he writes: "You once kicked Elanor in the leg, she died of heart failure later. You of / stroke. Asleep? within a year, the two of you, sisters in death. Is / Elanor happy?" Further on there is a graphic description of his mother: "Naomi, Naomi—sweating, bulge-eyed, fat, the dress unbuttoned at / one side—hair over brow, her stocking hanging evilly on her legs—scream/ing for a blood transfusion—one righteous hand upraised. . . ." Here, the references are highly personal and charged with primal emotions. *Kaddish* becomes a hymn to Ginsberg's culture as he experienced it growing up and living through his mother's mental illness. He wrote: ". . . blessed daughter come to America, I long to hear your voice again. . . ." The poem contains home-made sodas, Uncle Max, the Graf Zeppelin, and a boy remembering: "Eugene got out of the Army, came home changed and lone . . ." Reading it, I get the feeling that I am sitting in a magical theater watching an explosion of words blossom into a way of life that is utterly gone. This leads me to read the poem as if it were a photo album filled with captivating pictures: "O glorious muse that bore me from the womb, gave suck first mystic/life . . ."

Ginsberg's prodigious achievement begins partially in the memory of his mother, "struggling in the crowds of Orchard Street" on Manhattan's Lower East Side. His parents were in their early thirties when Allen Ginsberg was born in Paterson, New Jersey, in 1926. Louis Ginsberg was a school teacher and a widely published lyric poet. In *Allen Verbatim*, Allen Ginsberg says: "I began writing poetry 'cause I was a dope and my father wrote poetry and my brother wrote poetry and I started writing rhymes, like them, until I went to Columbia and fell in love with Jack Kerouac, and then got into a sort of emotional rapport, a much deeper sense of confession."

Ginsberg recognized an immense talent in Jack Kerouac, the young, exuberant writer from Lowell, Massachusetts, and began a lifelong friendship and advocacy of his work, often referring to the author of *On the Road* as the kind of expansive individual Walt Whitman spoke of as necessary for a viable, lasting democratic society. Kerouac introduced Ginsberg to Neal Cassady, for whom Ginsberg wrote numerous love poems: "N.C., secret hero of these poems, cocksman and Adonis of Denver. . . ." One need only read "The Great Rememberer," Ginsberg's introduction to Kerouac's book *Visions of Cody*, to get a sense of how he felt about his two close friends: "Two noble men, Americans, perished younger than old whitebeard prophets' wrinkled gay eye Archetypes might've imagined like Whitman."

While at Columbia Ginsberg began to realize that Walt Whitman's visions of fervent comradeship were more than mere visions; they were practical realities that could be pressed into service as guiding principles for one's life and art. Reading Rimbaud and Whitman and learning about the genius of William Blake and Oswald Spengler from his older friend William Burroughs, whose writing he would champion in the 1950s, Ginsberg was becoming the open-hearted and open-minded individual whose revelations of self would become a major literary event.

After Columbia, still years away from public honors, Ginsberg did a stint in the merchant marine, traveled throughout the United States, worked as a copyboy, spent time in Mexico and Tangiers with Kerouac, Burroughs, and Gregory Corso, and lived in the San Francisco Bay Area. Through the painter Robert LaVigne, he met Peter Orlovsky, who became his companion and lover of many years.

In Whitman, Ginsberg recognized an astute critic of American democracy, not the cherubic optimist so often portrayed by critics. What became central to Ginsberg's way of thinking was Whitman's fundamental belief that only through a society based on "intense and loving comradeship"—real, lasting intimacy, unabashed—could the nation survive. He recognized Whitman as a kindred spirit, a rebel against both the literary establishment of his time and the government. Whitman's longing for a truly civic America, devoid of class distinctions, probably melded well with Ginsberg's own upbringing. As a young man he was exposed to left-wing thinking through his communist mother and socialist father. But at Columbia, and afterward, the young poet gradually developed a political philosophy based on American anarchism as expressed by the Industrial Workers of the World, known as the Wobblies, and poets such as Kenneth Rexroth and Kenneth Patchen. He identified with the notion of an enlightened American literary rebellion, expressed by the Midwestern populists and West Coast poet/free-thinkers like Philip Lamantia and William Everson.

Ginsberg wanted to do more than simply endure when he first began writing. He hoped to overcome. He became messianic and has remained so, perhaps inspired by his own Jewish background, filled as it is with visions of a messianic future. In his work, there would be no Kafkaesque finality, no house of horrors from which there is no escape. Always there is light, even in the poems that dwell on death.

As a young poet in Paterson, New Jersey, he was fortunate to have as a neighbor William Carlos Williams, who wrote in the introduction to *Empty Mirror*, Ginsberg's early poems: "And when the poet in his writing would scream of the crowd, like Jeremiah, that their life is beset, what can he do, in the end, but speak to them in their own language, that of the daily press?"

When Ginsberg walked down the stairwell of the Greenwich Village townhouse where we were celebrating Halloween with a small gathering of friends in 1987, I noticed that he bore himself in an atypical manner. Pensive, subdued, and reflective, he greeted me with a warm embrace. I am used to seeing him with a manuscript in hand, or a few books, busily preparing for a public reading or some other event of importance. He seemed burdened with a sweet sorrow, as if he stood between William Blake's lines from *Auguries of Innocence*: "Every Night & every Morn / Some to Misery are Born / Every Morn & every Night / Some are Born to sweet delight. . . ."

"I hear you're teaching," I said.

"Yes, at Brooklyn College. John Ashbery and Jack Gelber are there also."

"You're teaching Blake?"

"Anything I want to, but I am going through Blake's prophetic books. Teaching is something I enjoy. That's one of the reasons I began the poetics school at Naropa."

Ginsberg's experiences as co-director of the Jack Kerouac School of Disembodied Poetics at the Naropa Institute, Boulder, Colorado, have added dimension to his own studies of Blake and other authors to whom he feels a close relationship. At Naropa, he has also studied and taught the objectivist poets and has explored early Greek writing and Asian literature. Joining him at the school have been William Burroughs, Gregory Corso, Gary Snyder, W. S. Merwin, and Michael McClure.

Among the handful of guests that evening were the noted Italian translator, Nanda Pivano, and Raymond Foye. Before ordering a Chinese take-out dinner, Pivano suggested we place a call to Charles Bukowski, prompted by a discussion of the film *Barfly*, which had received favorable notice in the *New York Times*. I dialed Bukowski's number and heard his wife's recorded voice requesting that a message be left. Speaking loudly into the receiver I said: "Linda Lee! Hank! Pick up the telephone! This is your old pal Neeli calling from New York. I'm here with Nanda Pivano, Raymond Foye, and Allen Ginsberg. They all want to say hello to you."

"Hey kid, what the hell are you doing in New York?" Bukowski picked up.

"Meeting with my publisher at the Parker Meridien Hotel."

"Jesus, I'm jealous."

We talked for awhile; then I put Pivano on the line. They reminisced over her last visit to Los Angeles. Then she handed the receiver to Ginsberg. Foye had turned on the speaker so we could hear Bukowski's voice on the other end. They exchanged the usual pleasantries, and then Ginsberg began to talk about writing, mentioning that he now had a literary agent who handled all of his poetry. Bukowski protested the idea of a poet having an agent. "You end up getting all tied up with business."

Ginsberg countered: "No. They do the business for you."

"It wouldn't work for me," Bukowski said. Then he mentioned that he had begun work on a novel called *Hollywood*, based on his experiences writing the script for the movie *Barfly* and working with its cast. "After that, I'm going back to writing poetry. Allen, you gotta keep close to the poem," Bukowski warned the both of them.

During the meal, I told Ginsberg that Bukowski had once written a long essay for a mimeographed literary magazine based in Chicago, where he stated: "I believe I'm high enough now to say that Ginsberg has been the most awakening force in American poetry since Walt W. It's a goddamn shame he's a homo . . . not that it's a shame to be a homo, but we have to wait and let the homos teach us how to write. Whitman, I understand, used to chase the sailors. That manly man with those white whiskers of contemplation, with that beautiful face! . . . chasing sailors. Can you blame the schoolyard boys for saying that the poets are sissies?"

"I never saw that before," Ginsberg said, amused and obviously flattered.

"I'll send a copy," I promised. "I think it was written back in 1965. The magazine was called *Olé* and really had a wild feel to it."

Later in the evening we played the game Trivial Pursuit, which Ginsberg found boring. I kept stealing glances at him. He still looked as if he was between misery and delight, but the old power had come back to his face. His beard, part gray and part black, perfectly framed his intense eyes. Yes, I told myself, this is the same man who peers from the darkness of America to the sparkling lights of Manhattan and writes a poem that Whitman would not have failed to praise. Hebraic melodies and screeching subway gears, coupled with epic love visions all coalesced in *Howl* and *Kaddish*, midway between heaven and hell.

Two days later Raymond Foye and I took the subway out to Brooklyn College and sat in on Ginsberg's Blake class. He read passionately from *The French Revolution*, one of the prophetic books, stopping every so often to explain the lines. "This poem had a direct influence on me while I was writing *Howl*," he said, pointing to the political commentary and surreal language Blake employed.

Try as he might, this poet never completely leaves New York City, at least not in *Howl*, even though it was written on the West Coast. There must have been a secret extension of the Lexington Avenue subway line that ran to San Francisco when the inspiration came. The smell of Atlantic waves, pounding against jagged crags of language, and the odors of the East River are in the long lines that read so much like Walt Whitman's.

Whitman's "child who went forth" had come of age in an America quite different from the one envisioned in *Leaves of Grass*. Ginsberg doesn't have to take a wild raft ride down the Mississippi like Huck Finn. The wide-eyed youth in an old photograph found enough adventures in Manhattan with night-stalking and drug-ingesting friends to last a lifetime. Compressed into *Howl* is an anthem, hardly muted by the passing of time, to the poet's friendship with people who felt dispossessed by the emerging post–World War II dream of America. Ginsberg did not buy the package of goodies offered by the emerging consumerism the country was experiencing, nor could post-war optimism over a healthy economy placate yearnings for a greater sense of freedom.

Howl is a mirror of America. Ginsberg took the long, low grumble of Theodore Dreiser, the small-town sufferings and yearnings found in Sherwood Anderson, the witty, often bitter and socially conscious poetry of Kenneth Fearing, and the tonalities of such social critics as Sinclair Lewis and blazed a trail of language whose roots go straight back to Whitman. It is the poet's explosive New York energy that creates a portrait of America, touching universal elements that awaken something in each of us. Autobiographical elements merge with the poet's desire to become the public bard Whitman aspired to.

Whenever I read *Howl* or *Kaddish*, memories come back of the hours I spent as a youth reading from Jewish prayerbooks. The long litanies swept over my mind like waves on a sandy beach, and my body would begin to sway, as if it had been embraced by the language, becoming part of it. The repetition of words and phrases has a hypnotic effect, serving to heighten the immediacy of the words.

Is *Howl* a love poem? A protest poem? An urban poem? A crazy Hebrew-Buddhist-New American melody machine? Think of it as having many of the same elements found in J. D. Salinger's *Catcher in the Rye*. In both works there is the voice of a young person speaking and a sense of longing for an imagined paradise somewhere in the future. Nothing seems to work in literature like the young person seeking new experiences, setting out on the road to define the echoes cresting and pounding deep inside the mind, or the youthful rebel demanding that society turn toward idealistic concerns.

Holden Caulfield is not one of Ginsberg's heroes who "chained themselves to subways for the endless ride from Battery to holy Bronx," yet he is a young man acutely aware of the falsity of the life around him. The adolescent yearning Salinger evokes is also found in *Howl*. For me that is what makes the poem so endearing. I have always thought of it as an initiation hymn or a poetic rite of passage from innocence to experience. The poet is enraged at the lack of companionship and compassion offered in the modern, industrial world. The opening litany of *Howl* is a piling up of all this outrage inflicted on a generation. It is followed by the image of the city as a place of desolation.

Yet the poem's adolescent quality saves it from melodrama. There are cartoon elements, bordering on the slapstick, that add to its power. Far from being a work of nightmarish imagery, it is written in a style as clear and delightful to the ear as Bob Dylan's lyrics. Without this kind of graphic, semi-surreal, humorous language, the poem would suffer from rhetorical overdrive. Ginsberg utilizes such word combinations as "grandfather night," "platonic conversationalists," and "saintly motorcyclists" almost in the manner of a Jewish comedian in some visionary approximation of the Catskill resort hotels:

who bit detectives in the neck and shrieked with delight in policecars
    for committing no crime but their own wild cooking pederasty and
    intoxication . . .

When I read these lines, I thought of the word weaving done by Gregory Corso and William Burroughs. Both writers share Ginsberg's ability to make the surreal phrase both comical and pictorial.

Howl is a poem of love, not the love of popular romanticism preoccupying American culture, but one approaching Whitman's fervent adhesion of man to man, possible only through a sustained self-expression, one man, inviolable, cooperating with others in building a lasting commonwealth of feeling. Whitman saw this as a practical aspiration. The rule of law existed not to perpetuate institutions but to aid man in an ever-evolving articulation of liberty. Essential to this way of thinking is a belief in the power of feeling.

Ginsberg will not see America destroyed. There is time for rebuilding. And, despite the nightmare he shapes in *Howl*, his language does not disturb in the manner of Baudelaire or Rimbaud. He remains a poet of hope, and no matter how much evil he might see, this hope remains and is integral to his vision. Even in the most disturbing lines, *Howl* has enough proto-surrealistic slapstick that the nightmare of America is softened: "who lost their loverboys to the three old shrews of fate the one eyed shrew of the heterosexual dollar," and "who ate the lamb stew of the imagination or digested the crab at the muddy bottom of the rivers of Bowery." The poet becomes a popular columnist of the poetic imagination, bridging people into his work with language they can readily relate to, because, in its soothsaying, it is not austere and never wholly literary. William Carlos Williams was accurate when he compared Ginsberg's writing to the language of the newspaper.

Howl is my ticket to Manhattan, one of the disembarkation

points for America, the whole floating, spoiled mass of the land. It is feverish, but, at nearly every juncture, the poet's reasoning mind slows down the action. The poem portrays the vastness of America and the poet's sense of how small he is within it. Ginsberg wrote his quintessential New York poem from the vantage point of California, the very state Whitman had seen as holding profound promise for the American future. Several of the shorter works in *Howl and Other Poems* are specifically Californian: *A Supermarket in California* and *Sunflower Sutra*, the latter invoking "Frisco" imagery, then reaching home to New York for the proper amount of "condoms & pots, steel knives."

The language of *Howl*, often described as violent, is actually tender at its roots. In his introduction to *Howl and Other Poems*, William Carlos Williams emphasizes the explosive power of Ginsberg's language, but, in concluding, he writes: "He avoids nothing but experiences it to the hilt. He contains it. Claims it as his own—and, we believe, laughs at it and has the time and affrontry to love a fellow of his choice and record that love in a well-made poem."

Before *Howl* Ginsberg had written *Siesta in Xbalba*, subtitled "and Return to the States." The poet is in Mexico, but it is his own mind and body that he explores. His introspection reaches into the outer world:

my eyes were opened for an hour
            seeing in dreadful ecstasy
the motionless buildings
            of New York rotting
under the tides of Heaven.

There is a god
dying in America . . .

It is a vision that would grow inside the poet, broaden in scope, and finally come to fruition in *Howl*. Looking homeward, he offers a bitter prophecy:

The nation over the border
grinds its arms and dreams
            of war . . .

The Ginsberg collections brought out by City Lights after *Howl and Other Poems* became guideposts for the reader of the poetic journey of Allen Ginsberg: *Kaddish and Other Poems*, *Reality Sandwiches*, *Planet News*, *The Fall of America*, which won the National Book Award in 1971, *Mind Breaths*, and *Plutonium Ode*.

Walt Whitman's civic religion, with the president as the elected high priest, is unthinkable today. The one representation of a president and poet together in the twentieth century remains Robert Frost reading a poem at the inauguration of President John F. Kennedy in 1961. That is about as close as the country has come to Whitman's idea of the poet as legislator of the national spirit. I believe Whitman would have been excited seeing Frost in the Soviet Union lecturing to their top leaders as he did during President Kennedy's term of office.

Whitman's poems for President Lincoln are elegies bemoaning the loss of a great leader who had led the nation through its worst national tragedy. The Lincoln poems are intimate. It is as if a father had died. The evocation of lilacs in remembrance of the national leader is charged with profound emotion. Whitman brings the tragedy to his own home: "When lilacs last in the dooryard bloom'd."

Whitman's retelling of the Lincoln funeral procession as it moved slowly through the streets of Washington is haunting and highly pictorial. Torches in the night, silent faces of ordinary citizens lining the funeral route, and churches filled with mourners soothed by organ music and the clanging of faraway bells are all intertwined. Then the poem vaults out of Washington and into Whitman's broad and brawling land.

Few poets have explained Whitman as well as Allen Ginsberg did when he envisioned him in the supermarket eyeing a beautiful young man. The poet whom he portrays is lonely and aching for a warm body to press against his own. He has no desire to sanitize Whitman by ignoring his homosexuality. Instead, he anoints him as a saint in the pantheon of poets: "Ah, dear father, graybeard, lonely old courage-teacher."

In 1975 I went to visit Whitman's house in Camden, New Jersey, where the lilacs bloomed. The attendant showed me the upstairs bedroom and pointed out various personal items. She asked if I wrote poetry. When I told her that I did, she said, "Do you know Allen Ginsberg? I like him a lot. He's a nice man. But when he comes here, he acts like he owns the place. One time, he told me that the living room needed cleaning."

In 1983 I read with Ginsberg at the University of California at Riverside's Writer's Week. Before the reading I had fantasized that after I recited my poems he would come onto the stage and embrace me, whispering "Oh Neeli, you are wonderful. I salute you as a member of the tribe." I read and received a good round of applause. As I was leaving the stage, however, wistfully glancing back at the nine hundred people crammed into the auditorium, Ginsberg leaned over and said: "Neeli, you were too close to the microphone."

The poet, not the prophet, scholar, or socio-political commentator, that is who I was looking for and whose approbation I desired.

Back in 1967 I wandered down Haight Street with a group of friends. We were attending an anti-Vietnam War rally at Kezar Stadium in Golden Gate Park. Psychedelic banners were everywhere . . . streets jammed with smiling and spaced-out young people. A girl approached me and said, "Hi! I'm Nirvana Sunset. Wanna go home with me?" Then I saw a short, heavily bearded man walking directly toward me, near the intersection of Haight and Ashbury. As he came closer, I noticed he was flanked by members of the Hell's Angels motorcycle club, who seemed to be acting as his guards. Closer and closer he came, until I realized, finally, that it was Allen Ginsberg. My friends tried to push me close to him as he passed, encouraging me to strike up a conversation, but the famous poet seemed intent on making an important appointment, and, besides, he was well protected from intruders. I missed my opportunity to speak with him. But what would I have said? Most likely, "Allen, thanks for *Howl*, it really influenced my life.'" We went to the demonstration after that. A friend from Los Angeles was selling what he called "genuine Vietnamese peasant hats," and we heard from the old anti-war activist, A. J. Muste. I forget whether or not Ginsberg spoke, which didn't matter as he seemed to be speaking everywhere else. Hardly a day went by without my reading of a new poetic proclamation.

Ten years later I stood in Adler Alley, San Francisco. My hair was long and I wore a beard. On my jacket I wore some old anti–Vietnam War buttons and I held a manila folder stuffed with papers. Around my neck hung a set of African beads. A young man came slowly toward me, obviously awestruck. He said: "Thank you so much for all you have done through the years. Your poetry means so much to me." I was touched to think that my small poetry books had moved someone so profoundly. As I was about to respond, my admirer continued, "Yes, Allen Ginsberg, *Howl* had a tremendous impact on us all."

My time had not yet come . . . but Allen's came just about one hundred years after Walt Whitman published the first manifestation of *Leaves of Grass*. I always wanted to ask him if he had planned it that way, but never got around to that either.

Much of the rhythmic power of *Howl*, the poem's long lines and powerful, sweeping breaths, are reminiscent of that tradition in English poetry embodied by Christopher Smart and William Blake, both of whom share Ginsberg's bardic passion. Ginsberg talks of poetry as "a rhythmic articulation of feeling." Placed in the context of his *Collected Poems*, *Howl* takes on added power as a concentration of all that is good in his poetry: tenderness, deep feeling, love for comrades, sustained rhythmic power, all cradled in the vast unfolding of consciousness. In fact, reading through the *Collected Poems*, I became more patient with some of the rhetorical elements I find in his poetry, especially in *The Fall of America*. I began to think of the poet's enormous outpouring as a poetic autobiography, and much of the flatness I had seen there didn't seem so flat anymore. Still, I began leafing through the massive volume, making an imaginary "Selected Works of Allen Ginsberg," remembering what Bukowski once said: "No matter who it is, Shakespeare or whoever, you probably won't like it all, and, in truth, you may only find very little that is any good, but that one poem or ten poems might be enough to lift your soul."

Until recently, there has been little published on Ginsberg, but now the reviews and articles have become critical volumes and biographies. He is now "collected," and a book on the shaping of *Howl* has become a standard in the study of contemporary American poetry. Few poets have found themselves so public a personage. Like Robert Frost before him, he is the uncrowned poet laureate of "these states," unfortunately known more widely for his social and political pronouncements than for his poetry.

Whitman saw a direct correlation between the poet and society-at-large, believing in a poet's obligation to be involved in shaping a new world and in preserving principles of individual liberty. His call for "intense and loving comradeship" is included on the dedication page to Ginsberg's *The Fall of America*. The statement ends saying that this comradeship offers "the most substantial hope and safety of the future of these States."

On November 20, 1984, during a visit to China, he wrote *I Love Old Whitman So* and the lines: "I skim *Leaves* beginning to end, this year in the Middle Kingdom / marvel his swimmers huffing naked on the wave / and touched by his desperado farewell, "Who touches this book touches / a man" / tip the hat on my skull / to the old soldier, old sailor, old writer, old homosexual."

Hardly a more telling sign of his "intense and loving" feelings for Whitman exists than *A Supermarket in California*. Written in what he calls the Whitmanic strophe, a long line as in *Leaves*, it is a tribute to his teacher:

> Where are we going, Walt Whitman? The doors close in an hour. Which way does your beard point tonight?
>
> (I touch your book and dream of our odyssey in the supermarket and feel absurd.)
>
> Will we walk all night through solitary streets? The trees add shade to shade, lights out in the houses, we'll both be lonely.

Being lonely has been a Ginsberg preoccupation. Rarely lacking friends, literary collaborators, and loving comrades, he still experiences the essential aloneness of the individual. He had hoped that poetry might lead to a solution, but it has only provoked more questions as to why we are ultimately alone. Throughout his life he has sought out gurus who might lead him to true self-realization. Perhaps his most important teacher has been the Tibetan master Chogyam Trungpa Rinpoche, with whom he has studied Buddhist meditation and who founded the Naropa Institute. Many of his poems concern the teachers he has gone to for instruction and are suggestive of his inner search: *Gospel Noble Truths, Father Guru,* and *Guru Om* among them. In *Don't Grow Old*, he writes:

Suffering is what was born
Ignorance made me forlorn
Tearful truths I cannot scorn . . .

    Ginsberg's better poems are like magic boxes of learning and observation. *A Desolation,* remarkably terse, offers a theme touched on from time to time in his poetry, that of the choice between family and aloneness:

Now mind is clear
as a cloudless sky.
Time then to make a
home in wilderness.

What have I done but
wander with my eyes
in the trees? So I
will build: wife,
family, and seek
for neighbors.

        Or I
perish of lonesomeness . . .

    The poet chose not to have a wife and family. He has lived his adult life openly as a homosexual. In place of family, he has remained close to the friends of his formative years, identified strongly with his parents and their relations, and has enjoyed the devotion and respect of the young.

    Ginsberg once spoke to me of his admiration for Charles Reznikoff, the objectivist poet whose works only reached a large audience late in the poet's life. Ginsberg was attracted not only by the accessibility of Reznikoff's work, but also by his attention to detail and the rich New York imagery. Reznikoff stays with concrete expressions. His concerns are for the world directly before his eyes: factories, working people, shop owners going about their chores. Reznikoff is a chronicler of the life directly at hand, the ordinary, common, everyday life:

Sometimes, as I cross a street,
a pack of automobiles come speeding towards me.
But, of course, I am much better off

than the traveler in a forest—long ago—
whom a pack of wolves pursue.

Like Ginsberg, Reznikoff's ideas come from the things he witnesses yet lead us beyond the mundane to greater awareness.

Wichita Vortex Sutra (1966), written in the heartland of America, was forged in the civic turmoil caused by the protests over the Vietnam War. The groundwork for the poem came from Ginsberg's own involvement in the anti-war movement. Here the poet becomes a spokesman for an entire community of dissent, probing newspaper headlines, summoning the names of President Johnson, Robert McNamara, and General William Westmoreland—all of whom were advocates of the unpopular war—and writing of the "secret heart" that he sees as the key to ending man's divisiveness. Ginsberg appeals for an end to war. The work also contains sensual passages, evocative of the poet's love poems, here set in a context of Whitman's camaraderie surpassing the personal:

So, tender lipt adolescent girl, pale youth,
                    give me back my soft kiss
          Hold me in your innocent arms,
                    accept my tears as yours to harvest
                    equal   in nature to the Wheat
               that made your bodies' muscular bones
                    broad shouldered, boy bicept . . .

These lines establish a haunting, searching tone for a poem concerning America in crisis, eaten away by the fear and suspicion generated by our continued presence in Southeast Asia. They are a good balance for harsher images used to suggest the turmoil that the war caused:

          How big is the prick of the President?
               How big is Cardinal Vietnam?
          How little the prince of the FBI, unmarried all these years!
               How big are all the Public Figures?
          What kind of flesh hangs, hidden behind their Images?

Ginsberg seems overshadowed by the sheer size of what he is attempting. The moments where he is most firmly rooted, and in which he shines, come with self-awareness. No longer looking toward the White House or Vietnam or boys with blue eyes, the poet writes:

I'm an old man now, and a lonesome man in Kansas
    but not afraid
        to speak my lonesomeness in a car,
        because not only my lonesomeness
            it's Ours, all over America,
                o tender fellows— . . .

The personal yearnings that the poet expresses bind the poem into a cohesive unit. It is easier to understand the national pain and trauma that the poem describes through seeing how it affects the speaker in the poem itself. I am reminded here of Whitman's *When Lilacs Last in the Door-Yard Bloom'd*. On one level, we understand it as a memorial to the fallen president; yet I see the poem as a dirge for an older America, forever changed by the Civil War. In his poem Ginsberg offers us the rage of Jeremiah, the sweet longings of Whitman, and his own refusal to accept the destructive power of his own country.

   Wichita Vortex Sutra carries on the theme of alienation and aloneness developed in *Howl*. The sense of being alone is spurred by unfeeling leaders who know how to manipulate words for their own ends. Just as Whitman had seen the need for an American tongue defined and renewed by the common man and by the poet of the people, so Ginsberg's poem concerns itself with the loss of a vital connection between the people and the language they speak, a language cheapened by war. Ginsberg writes with authority, in a priestly tone:

      O but how many in their solitude weep aloud like me—
        On the bridge over Republican River
        almost in tears to know
            how to speak the right language—
               .   .   .   .   .

I lift my voice aloud,
    make Mantra of American language now,
        I here declare the end of the War!
           Ancient day's Illusion—

I ran into the poet Kaye McDonough one day shortly after Ginsberg's arrival in San Francisco, and she said, "My God! That Allen just doesn't stop. He goes on and on. I heard he was on the streets here until about four in the morning. And look at all those poems. . . . Good Lord, Neeli . . . and we complain about not having time to write."

I remember visiting Harry Smith, Ginsberg's friend who lived with him at the time. I arrived with Jessie Cabrera and Raymond Foye, and, as we conversed with Smith, Ginsberg made it clear he didn't want to be bothered. Not twenty minutes into our conversation, he appeared from another room with an armful of photographs to show me, asking if I could identify any of the San Franciscans. I found it difficult to believe that he had snapped all those shots, but the proof lay before me. After showing the photos, he talked about several trips to different parts of the world and the need to prepare an exhibition of his photographs and work on forthcoming volumes of his collected prose, letters, and interviews.

Almost any poet I have ever mentioned to Ginsberg will finally excite him. Once I mentioned a recording I had run across of Vachel Lindsay. "You should hear the Lindsay tape," I said. "He recites *The Congo*, and there's even a poem about San Francisco's Chinatown." Allen asked me to send him a copy. There followed an authoritative discussion of Lindsay's poetry and its place in American verse.

He said that Lindsay, Carl Sandburg, and their peers had gone out onto the land to recite their poetry and that is what he most admired about them. Like most of Whitman's wild children, they believed in the oral tradition. Poetry belonged with the people. Lindsay was never more at home than when he stood before an audience reciting. Sandburg read his poems, spun folk yarns, and sang ballads, accompanying himself on the guitar. They foreshadowed an interest in oral recitation that would reappear in the mid-1950s during the San Francisco Poetry Renaissance.

Ginsberg has read through the entire Blake opus a number of times, isolating himself to study the prophetic books. From his days at Columbia, he sensed a kinship between himself and the author of *Jerusalem*. Yet Ginsberg is never academic. Whatever erudition is in his poetry is not half so interesting as the anarchical gleam in his best writing. His understanding of literature is not burdened with systematic critical insights. Yet he yearns for a sense of order. Time after time, he attempts to explain his poetics. He is certainly good at talking about sources, teachers, the environment out of which his thinking and his poetic instincts grew, but the explanations might just as well be left to others.

Finally, it is with his realization of the depth of talent in Kerouac, Burroughs, and Corso that he realized a new sense of literature was about to unfold in America, a personal and visionary writing primarily of the body, a poetry closely connected to the spirit found in Whitman's work.

The first piece of writing he ever read of William Burroughs was *So Proudly We Hailed*, a prose piece describing the sinking of the Titanic. To Ginsberg it accurately described the terror of America on its way down—the fall of America—and he admired its open-ended visionary tone. The piece had no limits and sailed beyond the page, outside of time. Burroughs wrote prose, but, for Ginsberg, it had the feel of poetry. He felt the same was true for Jack Kerouac. *On the Road* became a mission for Ginsberg, who recognized it as something wholly new in American literature. All the literary conventions had been thrown aside. Long, poetic lines became the rule, not the exception. Everyday talk became the stuff, as it were, for his writing. In *Visions of Cody*, Kerouac even included long transcripts of taped conversations between himself and Neal Cassady. Concerning Corso, Ginsberg wrote, "He's probably the greatest poet in America."

> The warm bodies
>   shine together
> in the darkness,
>   the hand moves
> to the center
>   of the flesh,
> the skin trembles
>   in happiness
> and the soul comes
>   joyful to the eye— . . .

Here, in the poem *Song*, is a focus and simplicity that Ginsberg does not often achieve. *Love Poem on Theme by Whitman*, *To Aunt Rose*, and *My Sad Self* are three other poems in which he attempts to unlock the sorrows, fears, and triumphs of his own heart. *Mind Breaths* has much the same mood:

Thus crosslegged on round pillow sat in Teton Space—
I breathed upon the aluminum microphone stand a body's length away
I breathed upon the teacher's throne, the wooden chair with yellow
pillow
I breathed further, past the sake cup half emptied by the breathing
guru
Breathed upon the green sprigged thick-leaved plant in a flowerpot . . .

Whitman's wild child continues to go forth from his Lower East Side apartment, yearning to build an ever larger poem of "these states" and his own "mind breaths" breathing deep within his dreams. I still want to hear him read *Howl* in Manhattan or at least walk with him along the East River, venturing onto the rickety old pier whose pilings groan softly below, where I had stood one dark night and looked back at the trembling lights of the city.

On one of Ginsberg's visits to North Beach, we spent an evening moving from café to café. Remembering that, I think of muted neon, seemingly endless cappuccinos, loud conversation, cigarette smoke, and a steady stream of people coming up to our table to say hello. Kaye McDonough joined us at the table, and somewhere along the line Kirby Doyle, Bob Kaufman, and Howard Hart became part of our caravan of poets.

We eventually landed on the terrace of the Savoy Tivoli. The conversation ranged from Charles Olson to Central America to the future of American poetry. After several hours, people began leaving. Finally only Ginsberg and I were left. We walked down toward the bright lights of Broadway, and I hoped that he would want to talk more. But he decided to go back to Shig Murao's place and get some sleep. The old beatnik Hube the Cube was standing at the corner of Broadway and Columbus, across from Ferlinghetti's bookstore. He grabbed me by the arm and said, "Was that Ginsberg? He walked by so fast I couldn't tell."

"Yeh," I answered.

"I knew him in 1955 when he read *Howl* at the Six Gallery," he said.

"Were you there?"

"No. But I heard about it," Hube said, flashing an enigmatic smile.

November 1987: it is nearing 10 P.M. when Ginsberg hires a car to drive himself, Raymond Foye, and me back to Manhattan from Brooklyn College. As a San Franciscan used to short distances, I wanted Brooklyn to come to an end, but it just kept on flying past. As I was about to ask the driver if we were lost, the Manhattan Bridge appeared ahead. The lights of the city shone brightly, and I began to think of Henry Miller looking at those same lights from a secret vantage point in the 14th Ward, Brooklyn, his childhood neighborhood, long before. We began to cross the bridge. In the backseat, Ginsberg kept up a steady stream of talk, telling Foye of the many new enterprises he wanted to begin and enlisting the young editor's help on a possible new poetry project. They bandied names back and forth. My God, I thought to myself, these guys are shaping yet a newer new American poetry. What about me? My name? Alas, I had to content myself with a slight glimmer of recognition from the driver. Then, through the rear-view mirror, I caught sight of Ginsberg and rhapsodized in silence: Ah, what does it matter? Ego? Lights ahead of us? Ginsberg looked powerful, professorial, poetic, and sweet, his big eyes gathering in the still-distant glow of nighttime Manhattan. I wanted to vault into the backseat and say, "Allen! Look! Your town! Whitman's City! Allen! What about Crane? Remember his Bridge?" I would glance over my shoulder at the old Brooklyn Bridge. Then I would say, "Whitman crossing over on the ferryboat, and Miller dreaming of a passage to an imaginary China right here, right over the East River, and Joseph Stella with his big bridge painting." But that would have been audacious and somehow ridiculous. I turned from the mirror just in time to watch the buildings on the East River slide by. Expertly, as if reciting *Howl* or one of Blake's prophetic books, Ginsberg gave off a litany of directions to the driver: turn here, go there, take a right, a left. I could almost hear him chanting, "Carl Solomon, I'm with you in Rockland." We arrived safely at the Odessa restaurant, an inexpensive place across from Tompkins Square. "I've been coming here for thirty years," Ginsberg said, as I opened the door to let him outside.

Singing the First Song

The Summer of Fire

"California is burning!" The voice of the newscaster,
Portentous and somber, tolls off a hundred spotfires
Strung up the State, from the South San Gabriels
To the Siskiyou chain.

          Ten days back
Thunder rattled us out of the house at dawn
To scan the sky and watch dry lightning
Walk on the hills.

        Why the Santa Cruzes
Never caught fire no one could guess.

               But eastward,
Across the inland oven of the Central Valley,
The entire Sierra felt the whiplash fall,
And in the withered tinder of a two-year drought
Canyons threw smoke like the belch of chimneys
Tonguing the sky.

        North of us
Mount Diablo wrapped itself in a crimson mantle
And claimed its name: a surging inferno.

              To the south
Big Sur exploded: impacted brush,
Flattened by heavy snowfalls of the past, lay on the slopes,
Fifty tons to the acre round the Ventana Cones,
And the runaway burn tore rugged country
Like a raging bull.

William Everson
From *The Masks of Drought*

"Do not sing those old songs here tonight," William Everson wrote in one of his earlier poems. Yet it was to the old, even ancient songs of Catholicism that he went to in his mid-thirties, almost at the same age that Whitman began writing *Songs of Myself*. The old songs would have their sway over the poet, driving him to passionate self-revelation, the creation of a personal mysticism dependent on a search for God, finding harmony with the land of California, and, a striking avowal for so religious a poet, the search for sensual fulfillment. His commitment to man as a fundamentally religious being is unshakable, though his writings are pierced with struggle and doubt, much like the works of his fellow Catholic poet, Thomas Merton. Unlike Merton, however, whose poetry moved toward simplicity of expression, Everson chose to unfold a chart of linguistic richness and heartfelt song that would map out his journey toward peace and the answers to ultimate questions. Land and body find their unity and integrity in the poem, yearning and despair their place in creation; God is approachable here.

Born in Sacramento, California, in 1912, the son of an immigrant Norwegian musician and printer and a mother who grew up on a Minnesota farm, Everson graduated from high school during the depression in 1931. He enrolled in Fresno State College for a semester but soon returned home. He worked summers at the Libby McNeil cannery making syrup and entered the Civilian Conservation Corps in 1933. After one year he returned to Fresno State College where he came across the work of Robinson Jeffers. "I only began to write in earnest after I read Robinson Jeffers," he told David Meltzer in an interview. "When I encountered Jeffers everything coalesced." He quickly shaped his own voice and began to make poetry his vocation.

There is a sense of upheaval, of immense change, of a struggle toward self-identity in Everson's poems, especially in the writings including, and coming after, the long poem of World War II, *Chronicle of Division*. Few poets are as vulnerable in their work. But the first manifestations of his new songs, including *Red Sky at Morning*, *Fog*, and *The Homestead*, are more reflective of the pastoral concerns that also occupy him. Never wholly gentle, his voice is filled with an all-embracing sense of man's frailty in the midst of natural forces.

After the world convulses,
Heaving the hills and the gray-green water,
There will be men warring against the wind,
And toiling lean-limbed beneath the slow span of the years.

His early poems have a fast-paced, almost breathless quality. Laden with concrete imagery, they brush against the abstract, hinting of the meditative energies that would grip him in later years, flinging him into religious excess. From the beginning, the poet envisioned the life of poetry as an act of spiritual unfolding. Physical man and his environment become part of this spirituality: "Back of this valley like an ancient dream in a man's mind, / but it sleeps at the roots of his sight."

Never enamored of the precisionist methods of Ezra Pound or William Carlos Williams, Everson trusted his raging doubts and deep torments. Like Whitman and D. H. Lawrence, he did not seek a methodology but developed his own primal impulses. From *The Screed of the Frost*:

I cried out to the Lord
That the Lord might show me the thing I am
Who showed me frost.

Comes cold: those days in the bright
Youngness of the year, warm of sun,
With earth a glow, each new thing
Cut in a tingle of green:
Short grass here, long grass there,
All in the damp-set clods of Winter.

The plea "That the Lord might show me the thing I am" is Job-like and suggestive of the doubts that plagued the Hebrew prophets. This factor of doubt and supplication is found often in Everson's work. Here it is intertwined with the changing seasons and serves to suggest the changes of the human heart. Everson does not seek to affront his God or to simply implore. He will identify his own anguish and seek out his own solutions.

On one of my stays in Bixby Canyon, halfway between Carmel and the Big Sur post office, I began reading *Man-Fate*, subtitled *The Swan Song of Brother Antoninus*. Everson had finally decided to forsake the vows of a lay brother in the Dominican Order and live with the woman he loved. Reading the poem, I could feel the pain and turmoil he experienced in making a break with a way of life that had given much to him. I read by the light of three oil lamps placed in a semicircle, the largest propped on an edition of *Leaves of Grass* that belonged to the owner of the cabin, Lawrence Ferlinghetti. Earlier I had been on Bixby Beach, so vividly portrayed by Jack Kerouac in the novel *Big Sur*, watching the sun go down, which made the first lines of *Tendril in the Mesh* particularly powerful: "So the sea stands up to the shore, banging his chains, / Like a criminal beating his head on the slats of his cage." And on I read: "For he bears in his groin his most precious jewel, the sacred / fire of his crime, / Who pursued, like the beam of a laser its solemn command . . . "

Thinking of how well Everson drew word portraits of the Central Valley of his youth and brought California into his poetic vision, I began reading Whitman's *Song of the Redwood Tree*, a poem envisioning California as a land of fulfillment of the American destiny. "I see the genius of the modern, child of the real and ideal." I wondered if Whitman might have perceived that two of California's future poets, Jeffers and Everson, would delve deep into their own metaphysical mindscapes, finding new frontiers from within, and reflecting on the myriad moods of the physical environment surrounding them.

Few contemporary poets sing so passionately the song of self as does Everson. He is the central character in his large poetic dramas. When vast areas of the state are dry and on fire through prolonged drought, there is a fire raging inside of him. When he reflects on the vicissitudes of the weather, he will hasten to dwell on the dramatic changes in his own temperament. His spiritual growth, recorded throughout his mature life as a poet, joins the geographical. His introspective nature, coupled with the Catholicism that became so important to him as an artist and as a man struggling for equilibrium, caused him to write a devotional poetry of the self—and of the self in relationship to a creator larger than the self—that has much the same intensity as the poems of the Spanish poet Saint John of the Cross, whose lamentations and psalms of praise are rich in images of personal struggle.

Even in his most tortured and solitary musings, Everson is keenly aware of and in communication with his environment. In those opening moments of *Tendril in the Mesh*, I feel as if the poet and the sea have merged. In a single phrase, "So the sea stands up to the shore," the poet sets up a mood of discontent, of deep and troubling discourse. The language is Biblical, even grandiose, but befitting what follows as the poem moves on to describe a man adrift, seeking solid land on which to stand.

I put the book aside and thought of taking a walk on the path back to Bixby Beach with a flashlight in hand—a dangerous adventure considering that the path through the canyon is dark and irregular even during daylight hours. Yet, as a patriot of the California ode, I wanted to go outside a moment and perhaps find the inspiration to begin a new poem, inspired by Everson and the Bixby night. Instead, I returned to the book and read on, coming to these lines from the Epilogue:

Dark God of Eros, Christ of the buried brood,
Stone-channeled beast of ecstasy and fire,
The angelic wisdom in the serpentine desire,
Fang hidden in the flesh's velvet hood
Riddling with delight its visionary good.

Written while Everson was still a Dominican, the poem reflects his passionate religious fervor, even in the midst of his self-doubting and desire to break free of his vows. The "Dark God of Eros" cannot lead the poet from his confusion or out of the labyrinth of sensual desire that pushes him ever onward toward that release. Throughout the poem there is the image of a woman, not a temptress, but a fact of life, one that the poet may not turn from. Throughout the poem, the feminine archetype is summoned up and so is a rich sexual imagery, steeped in fecund language:

Crotch and thigh; she is reft. Let me break white flesh
    asunder to cock this woman.

In the glimmer of night a wedge of fern configures her croft.
Maidenhair snuggles the cleft. Its shadow conceals and defines.
When I dip my lips to drink of that spring I throat the
    torrent of life.

The "Dark God of Eros" lies at the poem's heart and, like an all-embracing spirit, impels the poet toward the woman he loves. Far from denying his faith, however, the poet remains a devout Catholic; yet he wishes to make a passage from one form of devotion to another and to affirm his faith in God through a celebration of love. The poem is a love ode, a nature epic, and a meditation in a time of personal crisis. In his preface to *Man-Fate*, Everson explains that *Tendril in the Mesh* was written with no firm intention of leaving the Dominican Order. He was in turmoil, still unaware of how profound it would become.

Everson's evocation of nature is often an expression of his need for love: "I am the grizzly that grapples his mate in his hug of sheerest survival, / The salmon that jells his milt on the clutch his woman had sown in the gravel." Such generative imagery is shot throughout his work. Much freer than Jeffers in the use of language, his images of the environment are at times Rimbaud-like in their richness and multi-colored tonalities. Jeffers, bound to a classical past of Western ideals, did not have Everson's boldness. For Everson it was Henry Miller who pointed the way toward the abandonment of aesthetic ideals and toward an intuitive trust in words as they emerge from the mind onto the page. No need to reshape old ideas or play himself off against old myths, he could write true meditations of the heart, responding to his own subjective concerns.

On the morning after I read *Tendril in the Mesh*, I walked to the beach and thought of Everson looking toward the sea as the source of life. A true prophet and believer in the shamanistic vocation in poetry, Everson trusted his own natural music, growing more and more to appreciate the broad, panoramic sense of his own instinctual feelings for the direction of a poem. As a religious poet, he meditated on the silences that interplay with the loud yearnings that come from the vast sea of the mind.

Everson published his first book, *These Are the Ravens*, not long after his encounter with the poetry of Jeffers. In the older poet he found a voice that was unique in its day, one that defied all convention. He felt attracted by this new stance and by the religiosity in Jeffers' work. Not yet a Catholic, the young poet settled in California's Central Valley, working as a farmer. With the coming of World War II he served at a camp in Waldport, Oregon, as a conscientious objector. Here he became a master printer and met other writers. The intellectual ferment of Waldport spurred him on as poet and printer. *Chronicle of Division*, Everson's most ambitious early poem, is a meditative work, foreshadowing his later religious poetry. It is shorn of the exalted flourishes that mark the major work of his later years. This long poem is a meditation of the heart, a spiritual notebook in which the presence of ". . . some vast abstraction / some dominant myth" takes shape within the woods around Waldport. What had begun as a series of glimpses of ordinary life—"That morning we rose, / Who man and woman, / Rose one from another our spacious years" and "The face puffed with sleep, / The tousled crown"—becomes a record of the spiritual complexities faced by an individual in the process of undergoing profound change. Intimacy with the land is established almost immediately and remains significant, as the poet ponders the state of his personal predicament and that of a world plunged into the chaos of war.

The prophetic tone is tempered here; yet there is a distinctly Biblical feeling predicated largely on the poet's interest in permanent values and communion with a supreme essence. The poem is a mystical "exercise" by a man in search of freedom on a physical and spiritual level. He wants to break free of his incarceration at the camp where he is forced to spend World War II and to be free from bondage to the agonies of losing the woman he loves. In characteristic fashion, he builds toward an image of self-awareness that will allow him some solace amidst his personal turmoil.

Throughout the poem, ultimate questions are asked. "Who is there to measure the length we will stay?" Irony provides a tentative resolution: "This much we known / Blood will be poured." Then follows a record of dreams in which the poet faces the realization that no one is immune to doubt, that neither saint, idealist, nor martyr holds the key to fulfillment. Only the earth itself, bearer of both abundance and drought, remains constant.

An immense obsession is revealed, the need to be humane, to

live by the commandment, "Thou shalt not kill," and to be at peace with the surrounding world. In the poem, it is as a pacifist that Everson seeks to unlock the gate leading to paradise on earth, but what appears as he leaps into deep thoughts is a vision of "Those walls at the world's end / Where all questions die." This recognition comes from a mind in crisis, one facing the deep divisions of a world at war and a separation from his wife and familiar surroundings.

The poet is being transported to the Waldport Camp as the *Chronicle of Division* begins, to serve the war effort as a conscientious objector:

The Bus begins,
And brings the traveler his known cities,
His familiar fields;
But these are outrun.
The sun draws down to inexistence,
And night closets all.

Then, in the camp, amidst his spiritual yearnings, the poet writes, with an open and realistic heart:

The man struck from the woman—
That is the crime.
As the armies grow
So gathers the guilt,
So bloom the perversions,
So flower the fears,
So breed the deep cruelties . . .

He speaks for every man through his personal experience, writing of desolation, loss, and possible defeat in the face of a world that has lapsed into the madness of war. He looks at the environment into which he has been thrust, communes with it, enduring the pain of separation from known things, and finally begins a journey into the soul. "Each evening, the mail, / Flown from the regions of our desire, " comes to the camp. His wife writes him a letter informing him that she has gone to another man. "She will not wait, / But will pack her small bag." From the collapse of his personal life and in recognition of the loss of balance in the world, with its attendant growth of divisions, a sense of hope emerges.

The man looks down his life,
And regards from his vantage that obsolete hope.
It is canceled out.
But yet remains the possible future,
Like some huge new world needing discoverers.
He touches again his crude corrections,
And masters his hand to proceed.

The poem evolves into a battle between bitterness and hope. Out of an inner chaos fed by doubt, frustration, isolation, and the reality of the war, the poet focuses on the fact that someday he will return to familiar things but will not find consolation.

He will be given again to the indifferent world,
Go south to a city,
Muse over coffee in small cafés.

And from there he will stare at the indifferent cosmos, but will "never quite know what one wanted to know." He will journey inward, unable to forget that the end of war, peace, was earned bombing Nagasaki.

In the end, a fury of language is unleashed that consumes the presence of the poet:

Sweet Jesus, boned and gutted on the phallic tree!
Open your blood-filled mouth and speak!

Sea and land converge in the meditative mood found at the beginning of the poem. The poet blends his philosophic musings with the landscape that he lives in:

The sandpiper's cry,
Flung over his back,
Stringes the sea-voice,
The round eye
Gams and glitters,
And stares him down.
In the necropolic heart,
Where crime and repentance
Merge in the attitudes of fear;
Where pity and hate
Grope together and are one . . .

The poem ends with the anguished, searching, and probing poet in the "imperative presence," binding man with the world, offering hope for renewal and new knowledge. There is a desire for self-examination that leads to fuller knowledge. The basic questions centered on life, love, loneliness, and death, however, are never fully resolved. There is no brushing aside of the need to seek further.

The religious yearnings portrayed in the *Chronicle of Division* break down the barriers that strict religious thought erects against a more expansive spiritual dialogue. Everson's religious vocation, which grew stronger after the war, allowed for doubt and self-questioning. Reminiscent of Ralph Waldo Emerson's thinking, there is a feeling that all things are touched with godliness and the infinite and the mind must be free to probe everything without constraint. The image of Christ remains a fertile field for exploration, and the poet tackles it passionately. No matter how often he muses on God and Christ, there are William Blake and Whitman to consider. In both he sensed a mystical presence akin to the Biblical prophets and his own muse. The Christian cosmology is a burden and a means of escape. He wrestles with the need to be a disciplined Catholic and to live with a sense of temporal equanimity, and yet he is ready to transform himself.

His output as poet and printer while interned at Camp Waldport was prodigious. New Directions would soon publish many of the works previously available only in small editions printed at Waldport under the title *The Residual Years, Poems 1934–1948*. In 1949 he joined the Catholic Church and quickly entered into the Dominican Order. He took the name Brother Antoninus. It was under that name that his poetry reached a wider audience.

During his Waldport years he came into contact with the works of the San Francisco poet Kenneth Rexroth, whom he considered the best poet of his generation. When Everson moved to San Francisco, his religious transformation existed simultaneously with a lively interest in the literary life centering around Rexroth and his circle. He shared with his new-found friend a commitment to poetry as a public art, wanting to put poetry back on the platform.

With the popularity of the Beat Generation in the 1950s, Everson was well aware of the impact on Catholicism his identifying with such a group could have. In 1959 the Archbishop of San

Francisco, John J. Mitty, attempted to silence Everson/Brother Antoninus after a feature article on the poet appeared in *Time* magazine. As a result, he found his public readings restricted to the San Francisco Bay Area.

During this period, Everson wrote *The Hazards of Holiness*, containing poems written with clear Biblical themes in mind. There are also meditations revealing the depths of the poet's religious experiences:

Black bridegroom,
Dear and dreadful Christ,
Deliverer,
Possess me.

Giddy I live,

Unable to die,
Drunk of the illusion,
The ruttish wine,
Lurching with deceit,
Unfit . . .

Giddy I live on.

Still, Everson reined himself in with what he described as "The splendid and terrible anguishes, / the sublime insuperable hurts." A Christ both "dear and dreadful" remained a goal, a force to be known, a spirit to become one with in the end. The Christian archetypes were a field of endless spiritual journeying as the poet's aesthetic intuition led him on to *The Beheading of John the Baptist*:

John cried out—the excoriate definition
Of the invincibly sane. Naked adultery
And the greed of caste lolled notorious
In the royal sheets. The true tongue damned it.
Herodias, that corrosive female wrath . . .

Jeffers, Rexroth, and Everson share in common a love of nature and wilderness poetry. Jeffers would often play this off against civilization, which for him was the great enemy. He saw the concerns of mankind as insignificant in the face of the natural world, in the timeless beauty of a cliffside or of the sun itself rising in the

morning or setting at night. *New Mexican Mountain* ends with
the lines, "and the rockhead of Taos mountain, remember / that
civilization is a transient sickness." It would be a mistake, however, to think of Jeffers as a nihilist. As Everson saw, there is an
essential affirmation of life at the core of his writings. The Whitmanic scope of Jeffers takes hold of the primary motivations of
human interaction and lays them out against the rugged Big Sur
coast with its isolated, wind-swept hillsides and deep gullies that
fill with darkness or shelter the shadow of a lone hawk, and man
comes out the loser. Yet the beauty of language is never lost. Jeffers graphically illustrates the failures of man to find his place
within the vast scheme of nature, but he doesn't call for the obliteration of man. He would like to see man transcend his apartness
from nature and be in harmony with it.

Rexroth's nature poems are written in common speech and
read matter-of-factly. Unlike Jeffers, he does not play off nature
against man. For Rexroth his time in the mountains, at the sea,
or in the woods is more a direct communion between himself and
his surroundings. He writes:

The skirl of the kingfisher was never
More clear than now, nor the scream of the jay,
As the deer shifts her cover at footfall;
Nor the butterfly tulip ever brighter
In the white spent wheat . . .

Rexroth often looked toward Asia from his California vantage
point for inspiration, and many of his poems, especially those of
his later years, have a grace typical of Oriental poetry.

Everson remains Whitman-like in his long line and is intensely
Biblical in his rhythms. His later poetry grows clearer in a vast
vision of the land:

They stand in the clearing of Kingfisher flat,
Twin giants, *sequoia sempervirans*, the ever-vernal,
And take in the arms of their upper branches
The last light crossing the bench-ridge west,
Sinking toward dusk.

Perhaps one of the greatest tributes any contemporary poet has
made to Walt Whitman is Everson's arrangement of the original
preface to *Leaves of Grass* into verse. Entitled *American Bard*,

the work was originally published by the Lime Kiln Press in a handset limited edition printed by Everson. Produced by Everson close to his seventieth birthday, the work is an homage to a poet who embodied the visionary tradition that Everson himself feels so much a part of and has aspired to continue. In a note placed at the end of the work, Everson tells us that he sees the preface as "essentially a poem," possessed of the same vital passion as *Leaves of Grass* itself.

Robinson Jeffers: Fragments of an Older Fury contains a series of essays and poems by Everson (then Brother Antoninus). Both a critical book and an appreciation, the title speaks for Everson as well. Like Jeffers his poetry often touches on the grandiose and does not make concessions to contemporary speech: "Finger of God! A stipple of terror shudders my skin when / you touch me." Yet his sensibility is filled with a mood not unlike that found in *Leaves of Grass*:

Now crawl to me shivering with love and dripping with rain,
Crawl into my arms and smother my mouth with kisses,
Like a little green frog slit the cleft of your thighs athwart me.

Obviously he is not trying to be current in his choice of words. To me the music of certain phrases calls to mind the poetry of another religious poet, Gerard Manley Hopkins. The vocabulary heightens the religiosity of Everson's poetry, providing an atmosphere in which one immediately expects a meditation on his relationship with God or the idea of man in communion with ultimates.

The first poem I ever read by Everson is *Annul in Me My Manhood*. It is a deeply religious document, written after he had become Brother Antoninus, and was included in the San Francisco issue of *The Evergreen Review* in 1957. A statement of submission to the rigors of monastic life, it begins:

Annul in me my manhood, Lord, and make
me woman-sexed and weak
If by that total transformation
I might know thee more.
What is the worth of my own sex

that the bold possessive instinct
Should but shoulder Thee aside.
. . . . .
And no bride, usurps the energizing role, inverts;
And in that wrenched inversion caught
Draws off the needer from his never-ending need, diverts
the seeker from the Sought.

Verbs such as "usurps," "inverts," and "diverts" are reminiscent of those found in the poetry of Jeffers. With Everson, however, they play a greater role. In his panoramic long lines, the hard verbs are often like boulders jutting from a smooth plain. Far from discordant, they add depth and color to the poetry. In the long poem, *The Screed of the Flesh*, he writes: "I had a savior in my soul / but I riddled his brow with prickles / I had a good redeemer / but I nailed him to a post." The verbs serve to give variation to the softer tones developed in the language as a whole. His meditations are given added texture by this choice of vocabulary.

As a Jew, and one who occasionally writes poetry with my Jewish upbringing in mind, I am always struck by Everson's approximations of the Hebrew prophets. In his self-journeying, I see Job probing to find an end to suffering and to know why he was chosen to suffer, or Jeremiah wanting to be relieved of knowledge, to be freed from the task God chose him to accomplish. Everson is in dialogue with God, especially in the later poetry, establishing an intimacy particularly Christian. However, I am reminded of Martin Buber's essay, *I and Thou*. The dialogue here is perhaps as much universal as Jewish in its orientation. Buber emphasized the necessity of defining one's uniqueness within the context of spiritual communion. While beseeching God, Everson remains true to Whitman's inscription for *Leaves of Grass*: "Oneself I sing."

Notes written by me after a William Everson reading at the first National Poetry Week, San Francisco, April 1987:

"I was supposed to say a few words of introduction before Everson's reading, but was too carried away by his physical presence. I had known him previously as a tall, ramrod-straight man wearing a buckskin jacket and bearclaw necklace. When I met him on the parking lot an hour ago with Jack Foley, Everson was supported by two friends holding either arm and helping him walk toward Greens for a quick lunch before the reading. He was so bent over from the ravages of Parkinson's disease that his eyes only addressed the ground. Was this man the spiritual warrior, the sensual map-maker I had found in his books? But when I introduced myself, he looked up at me and his eyes were as fiery as ever and his smooth, light skin, half hidden by a long, gray beard and cascade of hair, seemed to glow with good health. Jack and I both offered him our hands and then went off on our own.

"Jack and I went up to the auditorium on the third floor of the building across from Greens. I had read there two hours previously. When Everson entered, the festival organizer gave a short, perfunctory introduction. Everson took his seat. I sat right next to him, facing the audience. He was silent for a full three minutes, gazing over the assembled crowd, and then down to his books of poetry, then back to the audience again. Before he spoke, many of us wondered if he would even be able to read. He looked both frail and powerful; frail because of his illness, strong because his eyes radiated vigor. If ever I felt the presence of a poet it was at the moment he actually began. His voice, at first very low, grew stronger and stronger until the entire room vibrated with it. Before long the audience was riveted to his every inflection; silent spaces between words took on a weight disproportionate to their reality. I felt as if a half hour had passed between some of the pauses, when they had only lasted seconds.

"The poem he began with was about Holy Thursday, appropriate enough since it was that very day on which the reading took place. After reading, he spoke on the relationship between poetry and prophecy, emphasizing that the popular notion of the prophet as predictor of the future was not what the concept meant. Rather, the poet as prophet worked with revelation of archetypes and aesthetic intuition, probing and seeking definitions of ultimate values. He spoke of Whitman, Blake, Jeffers, and of the obligation that a poet who tackles the prophetic tradition must handle. I understood why some post-modernist poets might look on him as an antiquated voice. I thought of how his poems accurately graced the land in which they were written and that they often praised. The poet as priest invaded much of his work, but the land was there . . . and I see that as a saving grace."

One vast spiritual notebook, the poems of William Everson. In *The Masks of Drought*, actually written during a time of drought in California from 1976 to 1977, he gives us some of his most engaging earth-centered nature poems. The meditative poet in turmoil with religion suddenly finds himself immersed in the clear wind of California, his native land, observing the marks of drought on the hills, valleys, and coastal areas. Looking outward from himself, he is caught wholly in the great tragedy of the bad weather that has cast a mantle of darkness over the land:

A rainless winter; week on weed sun edging the hills,
And the frost's gray grip.

            Summer broke dry,
A tightness of heat clenched the sterile coast . . .

Yet then, from *The Summer of Fire* in the book *The Masks of Drought*:

And what of me? Has age brought peace?
Imposing a wry chastity
On the flammable mind?

            To the contrary.
The pummel of suppressed exultance
Rages through me, crying.

            "Burn! Burn!
All you dead grasses, fallen under the scythe,
Wild iris, leopard lily, sweep skyward in flame,
Meet fire in heaven with fire on earth!"

The passionate language, so evocative of Saint John of the Cross, seems less florid than earlier poems, but the spiritual traveler is as intense as ever, still seeking, still questioning, finding in the realm of the spiritual ever new territory to open and to know. The drought of the soil and the drought of the soul become one, each illuminative of the other. Whether he or the land are deluged with tragedy, Everson comes through as a celebrant of the sacred. His faith rests in the creative process. It is unyielding. Bob Kaufman once said, "I'd die for poetry," and this same commitment comes through in the life of William Everson.

I am alone on the beach. Someone tells me this is Thurso's Land-ing, described in Jeffers' poem of that name. Part of me wants to rush up to the Peckinpah's cabin farther up Bixby Canyon, bor-row the telephone, and call the library up in Monterey. But I am content leafing through *Man-Fate*. Reading Everson alone, pac-ing up and down the beach, is good enough. I begin to compose my own California songs.

The dazed highway above seems like a joke, yet it is what I will travel on when I go back to San Francisco.

If I try, maybe I'll be able to touch the Sierra from here. Or even put my hands on the great Central Valley lying closer than the mountains. Or close my eyes and dream my way to Yosemite.

Still I feel the snows of Donner Summit and the waters of the Salton Sea and the heated passions of my heart and the wild mus-ings of songs yet to be written and of Everson's songs already sung, and I close the book, walking up the canyon to the cabin where my meditation had begun. I think of the fire I must build and the new wood I'll have to chop in the morning.

I sit alone by the ocean and read aloud from my poem, *Red-wood and Responsibility*, for William Everson:

> there are places
> in the puzzle I cannot
> conceive of.
> but I know a redwood tree
> when I see one
> and a slope
> that leads to a clearing
> in the woods
> when it leans against the memory
> of waves.
>
> the ranger drives by
> in his green truck marked:
> "United States Department
> of the Interior," or maybe
> "Forest Service,"
> with a little stick-on flag
> that says: "if you've seen
> one tree you've seen them all."

government is what melts way, finally. Catullus
        and Sappho remain
long after the pomp and surliness of those who
        re-arrange the forest
and bulldoze hillsides . . .

Revolutionary of the Spirit

Hunch

Luck is of chance made
A lady, a beginner
Is Fortuna
A spin of the wheel
Either good or bad
Either win or lose
Fool's play! the game—

Blessed be the hunch
The hunch is not a gamble
A hunch is nothing to lose
To play one's hunch is to invariably win
Not to play one's hunch is opportunity missed
Hunch is *feeling*— prophetic
A hunch victorious hath engaged the future
To play another's hunch is to throw the dice
Another's hunch is another's feeling leaving you cold
The only hunch worth its worth is your own

Go rub a hunchback if you will
Look up the definition of "hinch"
                                   while you're at it

As for me
        I've a hunch it's a cinch

Gregory Corso
From *Herald of the Autochthonic Spirit*

The poet Jack Mueller and I were sitting on the terrace of the Savoy talking about an upcoming poetry reading when Gregory Corso suddenly appeared. We joined him out on the street, which was usually where one spent time with Corso. From early in the morning until late at night he could be found wandering around North Beach or hanging out on a corner somewhere. "You guys want a drink?" he said, pulling out a half-pint of cognac hidden beneath his vest. We each took a slug while Corso talked to a North Beach habitué.

We continued on to the Caffe Trieste, looking inside to see who we might invite along. Finding no one, we walked past the Church of Saint Francis, one of the more prominent North Beach landmarks, and turned onto Columbus Avenue. As it was dinner time, I suggested we eat at the U.S. Restaurant, a plainly furnished Italian café offering enormous plates of calamari, osso buco, and pasta.

"That's a good idea. You like to eat. You like to eat anything, man. You don't have the *delicato* touch with food."

Silenced by his comment on my eating habits, I crossed the street toward the restaurant with Jack and Corso trailing behind in a heated discussion concerning the relative height of ancient man. When we got there we had to wait in line a few minutes, along with some locals and families who had come into North Beach from the outlying areas of Marin County and Berkeley. Once inside the waitress said, "I'm going to have to seat you with some other people. Do you mind?"

"Yeh, sure, anything you got," Corso told her.

We were led into the main dining area, a noisy triangular-shaped room with green walls and large windows that looked out onto the busy North Beach night. We were shown to a large round table where two uniformed policemen were eating. "Will this be okay?" she asked.

Corso nodded and sat down. Mueller and I joined him, but we both had an uneasy feeling. I hoped Corso would not bring out his bottle of cognac in front of the policemen, but he did, brandishing it about and taking swigs. He offered the bottle to Mueller, who declined.

"I'm sorry, sir. We don't allow liquor," the waitress announced as she handed us each a menu. Sheepishly Corso put it away, muttering that it wasn't fair.

After ordering, Corso began telling us about his recent trip to Italy, telling us how well he was treated there. "Poets are taken care of in Italy," he said. "And the food. Oh wow, you should taste the food!" He then launched into a vivid and knowledgeable description of the drug scene in Rome, describing in intimate detail how to score heroin. His voice became increasingly shrill as diners at nearby tables turned to look at the strange man with the mop of black hair falling over his forehead. The policemen, both of whom were red-faced, beefy men, stared at him, obviously annoyed. One of them put his fork down and leaned over, asking in a gruff tone, "What the hell are you talking about?"

"Heroin. I'm talking about *heroin*," Corso yelled, rising to his feet. At this point the entire room began to shake as pieces of the ceiling fell in large chunks onto the floor. We even got a few flecks of paint on our table. Nobody in the restaurant stirred. Outside, however, people were running down the street, excited. The next morning's *Chronicle* reported a 4.5 earthquake. "Gregory always did have good timing," Mueller remarked.

Gregory Corso is not a poet of nature, yet I remember being with him on several occasions when he would suddenly stop to admire a strange cloud formation, a sunset, flowers in an outdoor pot, or a subtle change in the weather with the longing of a nature lover. In a passage from the book *Elegiac Feelings American*, evocative of Whitman's vast American vision, Corso portrays the oppression of the Indian in vivid natural imagery:

Requiem, america, sing a dirge that might stalk the white wheat black
    in praise of Indianever again to be, gone, gone, desolate, and gone;

Hear the plains, the great divide, hear the wind of this night Oklahoma
    race to weep first in the dirge of mountains and streams and trees
    and birds and day and night and the bright yet lost apparitional
    sled . . .

It is the green world that a poet listens to, utterances of wind,
horizon, tree, and grass that tug at the emotions and make even
the smallest things of nature and the mind significant. Sometimes
I felt as if Corso had long ago fled a legendary kingdom, bringing
with him the secrets of its libraries and of its wise men to our own
mundane world. He can be as audacious as Whitman, who wrote
"shut not your doors to me proud libraries," yet introspective in
the manner of Emily Dickinson, defining himself amidst colorful,
evocative language that plays fanciful tricks on our notions of
love, death, and immortality.

This may seem at odds with the origins of the poet. Born on
the corner of Bleecker and MacDougal streets in New York City's
Greenwich Village in 1930, Corso came of age in that once-Ital-
ian neighborhood. His "advanced" education took place in Danamora Prison during a three-year sentence for burglary in his
teenage years. Often dressed in corduroy pants, velvet sash, pur-
ple shirt, black vest with pinstripes, and a sparkling ring, he personifies the image of an elegant bohemian, who, like Edgar Allan
Poe, one of his heroes, might have been found in Pfaffs Tavern on
New York's lower Broadway back in the 1850s, beguiling William Dean Howells and Walt Whitman.

Most of my "Corso imprints" are centered around nighttime.
That is when I usually saw him. He would magically appear as if
from nowhere, always seeming to blend with the decor of the
North Beach neon and the well-lit cafés. There were times when
I'd run to him whining, "Gregory . . . I'm so lonely," and he might
answer, "I'm not interested in your condition." But whenever I
was really down, another side of the man would appear. While I
sat despondently in my apartment late one night, Corso rang the
bell. I let him in and he sensed something was wrong. I told him
my story of woe. He responded by turning to a poem of John
Keats. "You have to get into this poem . . . see, it's one of his last,
and it seems so modern":

This living hand, now warm and capable
of earnest grasping, would, if it were cold

and in the icy silence of the tomb
so haunt thy days . . .

I wasn't surprised that Corso had fallen in love with that poem.
It compresses so much thought into a few short lines, moving rap-
idly from life to death, sparing nothing in between. The sponta-
neous essay that ensued, once he had finished reading the poem,
took me far from my troubles. What he pointed out that night
was the economy with which Keats expressed himself. I would
later find this idea of "trimming" the poem down to its essentials
a major concern of Corso's poetics.

Corso speaks eloquently of life in Greenwich Village when he was
a kid, describing in conversation the combination of Italian immigrants and the bohemians living there. He is also quick to mention that Edna St. Vincent Millay and e.e. cummings shared the
neighborhood, along with what he calls "the sharpest heads" of
the time. But his childhood was far from idyllic. He was yanked
from his home and jostled from one set of foster parents to another, eight in all, living in many neighborhoods of New York
City, often in an orphanage. At age ten his father took custody of
his son again and brought him back to the familiar streets of the
Village.
    Corso's formal education stopped with the sixth grade. From
then on he went to the library, devouring books on rhetoric and
grammar. The New York Public Library, at Forty-second Street
and Fifth Avenue, was where Corso did most of his reading during those hard and lonely war years. It was where he wrote his
first poem, *Sea Chanty*, later to appear in *The Vestal Lady on
Brattle*, published in 1955, in Cambridge, Massachusetts, by a
group of the poet's friends. This poem is as close as the poet ever
comes to his mother:

My mother hates the sea,
my sea especially,
I warned her not to;
it was all I could do.
Two years later
the sea ate her.

    Unlike Whitman, Corso pauses to consider what will fit into
his poetry. There are few poems equivalent to the long Whitmanic

list in his corpus, although several of the longer poems from the 1960s come close to that expansiveness. Corso can be all over the place. His titles range everywhere: *Paranoia in Crete, Discord, Written in Nostalgia for Paris, Police, Poets Hitchhiking on the Highway*, all from *The Happy Birthday of Death*. Yet there is a sense of caution in his body of work. He has picked and chosen his subjects carefully. Where Whitman is outgoing, gathering the cosmos to his breast and then flinging it back onto the world, Corso takes a different tack. *I Gave Away . . .* begins:

I gave away the sky
along with all the stars planets moons
and as well the clouds and winds of weather
the formations of planes, the migration of birds . . .

Whitman is equally irreverent in *Respondez*!:

Let the reformers descend from their stands where they are forever
    bawling! let an idiot or insane person appear on each of the stands!
. .   .   . .
Let insanity still have charge of sanity!
Let books take the place of trees, animals, rivers, clouds!
Let the daub'd portraits of heroes supersede heroes!

Marriage is the first Corso poem I ever read. As with Bukowski's and Ferlinghetti's work when I came in contact with them back in the 1950s, it had the same mood of rebellion I was seeking. I remember the eagerness with which I read *Marriage* to the adults I knew. Corso's unrelenting jabs at middle-American life were a delight. It was as if he had penetrated the secret vaults of suburban life. For a kid growing up in the Kennedy era, the poem had a lot to say about the straight and narrow pathway to normality. I visualized the narrative coming alive in my mind's eye:

Should I get married? Should I be good?
Astound the girl next door with my velvet cape and faustus hood
Don't take her to movies but to cemeteries
tell all about werewolf bathtubs and forked clarinets
then desire her and kiss her and all the preliminaries
and she going just so far and I understanding why . . .

"What is Gregory's work space like?" a young poet asked during a period when Corso was staying in my apartment.

"Look around you," I said as we stood on the busy San Francisco intersection of Broadway and Columbus.

"No, I mean his desk, his office."

"He doesn't have one," I said. "He does carry notebooks. And I guess, when he has taught, there's an office, like at the State University of New York at Buffalo or the Jack Kerouac School of Poetics in Boulder, but otherwise . . ."

In true Whitmanic fashion, Corso refused to sign a loyalty oath required of all staff at Buffalo in the 1960s. This became a cause célèbre for students and faculty members and eventually contributed to the abolition of such oaths in the state of New York. Though he would differ from his fellow poets on other political issues, the themes of freedom and social and artistic integrity would play a major role in his life. Corso personifies the kind of citizen-poet Whitman wrote of in *Democratic Vistas*. His politics is indigenous to his character, never explained in an expository manner but deeply manifest in his view of man, standing alone, addressing the universe.

Unlike the writers with whom he is most closely identified, Ginsberg and Kerouac, Corso generally avoids the personal. He puts up a wall between himself and the reader that is rarely pierced. In poems about childhood, quick glimpses of a practiced observer of life come through. Little in the way of personal anguish or self-doubt is revealed. The poet is careful not to reveal himself confessionally. Only in his more mature years does a strong autobiographical element come into play, and the range of emotions broadens so that we see a more rounded personality emerge.

Between the years 1950 and 1953, Corso worked as a manual laborer, a reporter for the *Los Angeles Examiner*, and, for a short time, as a merchant seaman. By the time I met him in 1977, he had long since lived as a fulltime poet. In 1955 a play, *This Hung-Up Age*, was produced at Harvard University. His allegorical novel, *The American Express*, was published in Paris by Olympia Press (1960). He has lived off and on in New York City, Paris, and San Francisco, as well as in Italy. When he is in San Francisco he usually lives in North Beach.

Corso is fascinated by the sense of madness that can be found in ordinary things and commonplace occurrences. What the surrealists would call "the marvelous" is found throughout his writings: the ability to imbue the ordinary with a sense of fantasy and unreality. Unlike Philip Lamantia, whose usage of surrealist techniques remains orthodox, for Corso it is just one more device to use in the making of a poem. "Philip sees surrealism as an end in itself, but I take it as just another toy to play with," Corso has said. He comes close to Lewis Carroll in writing of childhood as a time in which this sense of "otherness" or the marvelous is given full play. Corso's world is inventive, profoundly personal, and imbued with the surreal. In *Birthplace Revisited*, all of Corso's fascination with surrealism comes together:

I walk up the first flight; Dirty Ears
aims a knife at me . . .
I pump him full of lost watches.

The macabre elements Corso derived from Poe blend with an admiration for Emily Dickinson, which may come from the quick, decisive way she alters reality and the economy of her impression. For Corso, poetry is at its best when it can create a totally unexpected expression. In Dickinson he has found this sense of astonishment. *I heard a fly buzz when I died* . . . and *I taste a liquor never brewed* are two Dickinson poems Corso is fond of quoting. This sensibility is found in his first books, *The Vestal Lady on Brattle* and *Gasoline* (1958). From *Cambridge, First Impressions*, a passage illustrates Corso's own unique playfulness and ability to surprise with a gentle interplay of language:

Tired of walking,
Tired of seeing nothing,
I look out from a window
      belonging to someone
      nice enough to let me look.

Yet Corso ranges far beyond nineteenth-century America. As Whitman, who took his lead from the bardic tradition of the ancient world, so Corso draws inspiration from the classic. He would often bring from his back pocket a paperback copy of Catullus, or Sappho, or from within his coat an edition of the Greek Anthology. He handled these books like sacred objects, and his knowledge of their contents was profound. With Catullus, he would find individual lines, illuminating their meanings in a manner that made them appear contemporary. Whenever I spent time with Corso, I would make a mental file of quotes from these poets of the past. Along with the classics, the English Romantic poets, particularly Byron, Keats, and Shelley, played a significant role in Corso's evolving conversations. His poetry is populated with other literary figures from the past. "Poets, worms in hair, beautiful Baudelaire, / Artaud, Rimbaud, Apollinaire" are all part of the French pantheon of writers from which Corso also finds inspiration.

Corso's early poetry is filled with concise super-realistic snapshots. Only later did he begin to write longer poems centered on particular themes: *Power, Army, Food, Hair,* and *Bomb.* These poems would find their way into *The Happy Birthday of Death* and *Long Live Man* (1962). His angel is bitter and sweet, loving and demanding, and capable of uttering the unutterable. No terminal stillness exists in his world. Nothing is spared. Conventional thoughts of morality and propriety just don't work when trying to piece together the puzzle of Gregory Corso. There were times I spent with him that now seem like a fast run through a carnival. Whether guzzling wine, smoking joints, or feeding one another lines from Edgar Allan Poe's poetry, I always expected a surprise and was rarely disappointed. At the most unsuspecting times Corso might say, "You have to hear Vivaldi's piccolo concertos" or "Can you spare a few dollars for a half-pint of whiskey?" Sudden thoughts on the paintings of Pieter Breughel or the novels of Stendhal might come at anytime. Once we were in the backseat of a car, returning to San Francisco from a trip to Santa Cruz. He kept talking about food, offering fanciful recipes and combinations of dishes. "Chicken cacciatore, man, with lots of sauce . . . the mushroom number . . . then, there's always caviar and champagne, just to get the symposium started." Then he would suddenly shift to Lord Byron. "Oh boy . . . watch out with your Byron. Not just the poems. The letters, too. They're elegant."

His reverence for the past is obvious in his choice of an archaic vocabulary, his lifelong interest in classical mythologies, and his references to historical figures, primarily literary. For Corso, this is a living tradition. He truly spends his days in conversation with Ovid, Catullus, and Sappho. I read the poem *Nevermore Baltimore* in manuscript, making my way through the crossed-out

lines and notes scribbled into the margins. The poet brings Poe
directly to the reader with stark, comic images:

And Mr. Poe
died from a drink
for every vote
the fop of Harvard
great-grandson of Calvert
tumbled the tumbler
with a twist of the wrist
and called the unnamed by name
With sand in his shoes he vomited on Maryland . . .

Once Corso and I were at a bookstore on Polk Street, across Russian Hill from North Beach. He said to the clerk, "Hi, I'm Gregory Corso." The clerk paid no attention. "You know . . . I'm the
poet," Corso repeated. "You have my books here." Now the clerk
responded, "I never heard of you." "Corso . . . the Beat Generation," he emphasized. "You know, Ginsberg, Kerouac, Burroughs." "Oh yeh," said the clerk. After that, Corso offered to
sign a few copies of his books in return for five dollars so that he
and I would have drinking money. "Sure," said the clerk, "it
sounds like a fair deal." Back on the streets, money in hand, Corso
hummed a tune, "Hi diddly dee . . . a poet's life for me." The sun
was going down as we entered a nearby bar.
    It didn't take long for the money to disappear in alcohol. Just
then a heavyset man with balding blond hair and small brown
eyes asked if he could buy us a drink.
    "My name is Jim. I'm so lonely. I don't know what to do. No-
body talks with me," he said with downcast face.
    "Spare me, but I do like to talk. I like to listen. Buy me a drink,"
Corso replied.
    Immediately, he ordered a double shot of expensive bourbon
with a beer chaser. I followed suit as our backer also ordered a
drink. After finishing our first round and listening to Jim's long,
sad story, we all went to another bar. Jim kept buying the drinks
and became especially excited on hearing that he was in the presence of a famous Beat poet. "I don't know much about poetry,"
he said, "but I did read *On the Road*."
    "That's the best," Corso said.

"I always wanted to write," Jim revealed, "but I don't know what to write about."

"Your fucking life," Corso hollered. "Write about it. You liked *On the Road*. It's about a man's life, right? Then you got it."

"I want to call my mother," Jim said.

"He wants to call his mother!" Corso mimicked, finishing off another double shot of bourbon.

Jim telephoned his mother, who lived in Palm Springs. He called us to the phone and asked that we each speak to her.

"Hi mom!" Corso said. "How are you doing? Does Jimmy write home? If I had a mother I'd write to her."

Afterward Jim realized he had no money left. It was time for us to leave. We walked over the hill from Polk Gulch to North Beach, leaving our benefactor bewildered at the bar.

When Corso searched for an appropriate title to a projected collection of poetry back in 1979, he approached friends in North Beach to test out the titles. One of them was "Heirlooms." He liked the idea of a one-word title, which he hadn't used since *Gasoline*. After some thought, he came upon the idea of "Heirlooms of the Future," a typical Corso double take. "You dig that, man? I can topple the whole contemporary scene with a title like that." I reminded him of the list of possible titles included in *The Happy Birthday of Death*, his best-known book. One was "Fried Shoes," followed by "Pipe Butter." The chosen title was toward the bottom of the list that Corso had grouped under the heading "Saleable titles."

One day I heard Corso tell George Scrivani, "I got it now. It's the best shot. 'Revolutionaries of the Autochthonic Spirit.'" Only a few days before he had proclaimed Shelley "a revolutionary of the spirit." Actually, he had been thinking of calling the book "Revolutionaries of the Spirit" in lieu of "Heirlooms." I don't remember why he added the word autochthonic to the title, but in his inscription to me he wrote, "Hi, for an autochthonic soul Neeli!! whoa boy! Love, Gregory." After leaving for New York with his completed manuscript, he settled on the title *Herald of the Autochthonic Spirit*. *Herald* was chosen for Corso's middle name, Nuncio, "the announcer." When discussing his search for a title, Corso asked Scrivani for an exact definition of autochthonic. Scrivani said that the original meaning of the word was

". . . springs of itself out of the earth." Corso replied, "Yeh, right. That's why I'm always washing my hands . . . because I come from the earth and my hands are always dirty."

After giving the manuscript to New Directions, Corso told me that his book would "kick off the eighties." He was eager to be at the crest of whatever new movement might be developing and, in fact, saw himself as one of the "daddies" of the past two decades. He used to say, "Ginsie and Kerouac and I . . . we're the daddies of the hippies and that's a big one. If we hadn't been there before them, nothing would have happened. There wouldn't have been any flower children."

Not long after this experience, I ran through the gamut of emotions I felt concerning Corso and his poetry. For one thing, I could never get over Ginsberg's words on *Gasoline*, "Open this book as you would a box of crazy toys. . . ." Something in Corso retains the spirit of a child, the spirit of selfness that lies beyond the constraints of adulthood. But this was not enough. It came down to simple questions, like What is Gregory really like? and Why do I feel compelled to read and re-read certain of his poems? I knew what made me turn away from some of the works in *Elegiac Feelings American* (1970). Sentimentality marred a few of them, like the title poem itself, dedicated to Jack Kerouac. I knew why I liked *The Mad Yak*. In my twelfth-grade English class I wrote a paper expressing how amazing it was to find a poem written in the voice of an animal, humorous and yet tinged with sadness:

I am watching them churn the last milk
    they'll get from me.
They are waiting for me to die;
They want to make buttons out of my bones.
Where are my sisters and brothers?

This led me to touch on Corso's preoccupation with death, a subject our teacher had brought up in relationship to Dylan Thomas, citing such poems as *And Death Shall Have No Dominion* and *Do Not Go Gentle Into That Good Night*. The poem of Corso's I went to and read before my English class is from *The Happy Birthday of Death*. Entitled *Death*, it begins:

Before I was born
Before I was heredity

Before I was life
Before I was—owls appeared and trains departed . . .

Typical of Gregory, as I think of the poem now, to begin by toppling our expectations. We are brought to death through a "side
door," as it were, a "before life" experience, and only then does
the word itself appear, as in *Death*:

Death is not a photograph
Nor a burning mark on the eye
Everything I see is Death
Not Grim Reaper scythed and hourglassed . . .

Those last two lines are what stuck with me back in 1962. The
English teacher thought them entirely too pessimistic, but I could
hardly sleep for a week after reading the poem.

The first poem in *Herald* is *Columbia U Poesy Reading—1975*,
which sums up Corso's public life as a poet and his intimate relationship with the muse. Written in two parts, *Prologue* and
Poem, it is a self-revelatory work probing his relationship with
his contemporaries. The poem serves as a prelude to a book that
includes a number of autobiographical poems reaching all the
way back to early childhood. In the *Columbia U* poem, Corso is
unsparing in his view of himself and others:

What a 16 years it's been
Since last sat I here
with the Trillings again seated
he older . . . sweetly sadder'
she broader . . . unmotherly still

"Since last sat I here" is a deliberate transposition, giving to the
phrase an oracular tone. Corso becomes the humorous and sometimes disdainful observer. He writes of Ginsberg:

Al volleyed amongst Hindu Gods
Then traded them all for Buddha's no-god
A Guggenheim he got; an NBA award;
an elect of the Academy of Arts & Sciences;
and the New York Times paid him 400 dollars
for a poem he wrote about being mugged for 60 dollars

O blessed fortune! for his life
there is no thief . . .

The poem recalls that Corso and his peers were once "put down for being filthy beatnik sex commie dope fiends." He describes how the Beats have since been legitimized, except for himself: "Me, I'm still considered an unwashed beatnik sex commie / dope fiend." Reading that line, I thought of the times when I could barely keep my eyes open as Corso danced around my apartment, alternately slugging on a whiskey bottle and inhaling Thai weed. He has no apologies to make. Yet he does say, "I'm as much a Communist as I am a Capitalist / i.e., I'm incapable of being either of 'em; / as for Dopey-poo, it be a poet's prerogative." He defines himself and his friends as writers of "a subterranean poesy of the streets / enhanced by the divine butcher: humor," and calls his generation "Revolutionaries of the Spirit!"

What follows, under the heading *Poem*, is a drama between Corso and the muse. I think of it as a telephone directory of historical personages in the lineage of the creative spirit, a perception right in line with the tone established at the onset. Here, Corso dons his persona with the same grandeur as the flamboyant clothing he wears and becomes the focal point for his biting satire:

Summoned by the Muse
I expect the worst
Outside her Sanctum Sanctorum
I paced up and down a pylon
of alabaster poets . . .

Cocky and self-assured, the elements of self-doubt can surface in the later work, but still the surliness dominates. "I can ride Pegasus at anytime I feel; / though my output has been of late / seldom and chance . . ." The muse, whom he calls "Miss God," appears. He is subjected to an interrogation:

"What thinkest thou the poppy?"
My silence seemed the lapse of a decade . . .

His response is, with his typical set of wry one-liners, irreverent as ever:

Dear carefree girl of Homer, Madonna of Rimbaud;
morphea is poet-old,

an herbal emetic of oraclry,
an hallucinatory ichor divined by thee . . .

Following this, Chatterton, Coleridge, and De Quincey become part of the Corso cosmology, Shelley, Emily Dickinson, and Shakespeare having been dealt with earlier. As a whole, the poet has created a mini-play, absurd in the extreme, yet compelling in what it reveals of his own self-image.

Indeed, he does not spare himself. The muse has already asked, "Do you love drugs more than you do me?"

"I'm not ashamed!" I screamed . . .
Seated on a cold park bench
I heard Her moan, "O Gregorio, Gregorio
You'll fail me, I know"

Walking away
a little old lady behind me
was singing "True! True!"
"Not so!" sang the spirit, "Not so!"

One of the more sustained conversations I had with Corso took place in my old apartment in North Beach. By the time I met him, it had become a gathering place for older beatniks and aging hippies. He had been staying with me a few weeks. We were sitting around the kitchen table one evening talking about the Romantic poets and attempting to recall the first stanzas of Shelley's *To a Skylark*. We got the first stanzas down all right, where Shelley writes of "unpremeditated art," but couldn't get beyond it. Out of frustration, I launched into a poem I knew we both had down, Poe's *To Helen*. "You got it!" Corso said, "the agate lamp . . . think of it . . . this is before electricity and Poe writes of an agate lamp . . . wow!"

Soon afterward, we came to François Villon. Corso's eyes came alive. He identified with Villon's poetry and his life as an outsider, as one beyond the law. We read from a copy of Villon's poems in a paperback edition with an introduction by William Carlos Williams. In *Dear Villon* Corso writes:

Villon, how brotherly our similarities . . .
Orphans, altar boys attending the priest's skirt;
                    purpling the coffins

Thieves: you having stolen the Devil's Fart
And I stealing what was mine
(not because like our brother Kerouac said:
everything is mine because I am poor)
Rather: Nothing is mine, a Prince of Poetry
made to roam the outskirts of society
taking, if I need a coat, what was taken
                    from the lamb . . .

For all his wildness, Corso manages his poetry well. He is a true craftsman, constantly revising. He wants no excess.

"If you got the humor in the life, you should put it in the poem, a hard number to do. Watch out when you try," Corso told me. *The Last Warmth of Arnold* is one of the more lyrically inspired poems from the poet's early years. The boy Arnold was a playmate of Corso's in his Greenwich Village days. The poem is particularly interesting in that it foreshadowed by two decades the childhood reveries Corso would include in *Herald of the Autochthonic Spirit*. Like the later poems, this one is filled with fully drawn New York pictures, snapshots from youth, similar to a secretive photo-album finally revealed:

willing to walk you home, to meet your mother,
to tell her about Hester Street Park
about the cold bums there;
about the cold old Jewish ladies who sat,
hands folded, sad, keeping their faces
away from the old Jewish Home.

Plucked from memory's garden, Corso chooses images that reveal a myriad of feelings. In a few lines he can sweep over Manhattan and home in on those confronted with old-age dependency. From cold bums to old Jewish ladies and then to thoughts of death, Corso skillfully memorializes the New York of his youth.

There is a more expansive tone to his poems that came after *Gasoline*, especially *Marriage*, *Power*, and *Man*. He would take one theme and work with it down the page, exploring all its ramifications and mixing it in his cauldron of penetrating wit. He is a Dionysian personality whose poems are often Apollonian. His interest is in communicating ideas in poetically inspired measures of thought. His measure is a matter-of-fact structure sustained by an elegant, highly ordered use of language. The poet's musical ear is what transforms his expressions into poetry. I recall *Three Loves* from *Long Live Man*:

Love.
It is a barren site in me now.
A pierced property with single ruin
—Me.
And though I'd the heart to traverse that vast acre
I'd only this inch of it, here where I sit . . .

While he has written poems of social consciousness, especially in *The Happy Birthday of Death*, he holds back a step from the more concentrated social concerns of his contemporaries. No ideologue, he finds his center in the very idea of the poem. In *Upon My Refusal to Herald Cuba*, written at a time when Ferlinghetti and Ginsberg were praising the Cuban Revolution, Corso writes: "Ever fast the world! / Best to tease all sides with awakening vibrations; / Cheerful remedies, calm or drastic solutions—"

Demeter, Isis, Osiris, and other gods and immortals from classical antiquity people the poetry of Gregory Corso. He never tires of talking about Greek and Egyptian mythology and religion. *For Homer* is one of those poems that happens when Corso's humor meets his veneration of the past:

There's rust on the old truths
—Ironclad cliches erode
New lies don't smell as nice
as new shoes
I've years of poems to type up
40 years of smoking to stop
I've no steady income
No home . . .

Corso explains himself to Homer in what he would probably call "a straight shot." He goes on to say:

I've no religion
and I'd as soon worship Hermes

And there is no tomorrow
there is only right here and now . . .

There are occasional flashbacks to the crazy language found in
Gasoline, but in the recent work Corso leads from the left-hand
margin in composing a poem and uses each line as a single frame
of thought or as discrete facets of an idea he carries down the page
to resolution.

"Revision is where you really find out how skillful you are,"
Corso has advised me. "You have to be like a magician." I remembered the many drafts he made at my kitchen table while
working on poems for *Herald of the Autochthonic Spirit*. Even
in my copy of *Elegiac Feelings American* he revised the title
poem, explaining that he wished he had trimmed it more before
publishing it. In his revision he began by striking out specific
words and then went back and took out whole stanzas. Once in
awhile he added phrases. In place of "the planet boned" he wrote
"the planet in need of repair" in the margin.

Another Corso revision, this time of the long poem *Mutation
of the Spirit*, which is included in *Wholly Communion*, an anthology of poems read at the Royal Albert Hall in London (1965,
with Ginsberg, Ferlinghetti, Ernst Jandl, Andrei Voznesensky),
was done at my place. Over the poem he wrote: "Corrections
done in Neeli's house, S.F." In place of "A life unquestioned / did
well enough unquestioned," he wrote

None know death
Not the strong
Not the dead
but the living alone.

At the end (possibly to complete the poem or merely as an after-
thought in the margins) he wrote: "Behold the born again poet
Nunzio be his name, Poor Gregory a sham for sham, all to gossip
are gone."

Dionysus and Apollo meet in Corso's world. Whatever tension
exists comes from a subtle intertwining of the two elements. In a
mood analogous to the one set up in his poem on the *Columbia
U* reading, he writes in true Apollonian style:

The days of my poems
were unlimited joys

of blue Phoenician sails
and Zeusian toys . . .

The Dionysian element, ever present in the life of the poet, sur-
faces dramatically in such poems as *Wisdom*:

I feel there is an inherent ignorance in me
deep in my being
to the very core
I know its presence
by an unforgettable smell
    first experienced in childhood:
A nose clogged with blood
    mixed with the odor of an old man's belongings

When he writes of his youth, whether of a dead friend as in *The
Warmth of Arnold* or in *Youthful Religious Experience*, his lyrical tenderness reveals itself. From the cruel observer, he can cross
over into a gentler sensibility, looking back on the years and returning from his musings with a poetry ordered and comically
touching:

When I was five
I saw God in the sky
I was crossing a bridge
on my way to buy salt
and when I looked up
I saw a huge man
with white hair and beard
sitting at a desk of cloud . . .

These lines, from *Youthful Religious Experiences*, are the beginning of a narrative poem capturing the poet at ages five, six,
and seven. The last part of the poem is about "a fat little boy / I'd
never seen before," who faints in church. The two men who carried the boy out of the church, with a little glass elephant "cupped
in his chubby hands," return to sit on either side of the young
poet-to-be. After relating this experience, he writes:

Was I next? I wondered
I who had seen the glass elephant?
I never saw that boy again

And to this very day
I cannot totally comprehend
what it all meant . . . if it meant anything at all.

There are few narrative poems like this in his published work. Rather, that idea of a topical poetry, touching on a vast array of subjects, makes up the bulk of his output. He deals with familiar things, giving them his own "take," which usually involves either a shocking turnaround of the sacred or a word-game that plays with a subject from all sides. Like William Carlos Williams, his range of subject matter is wide. He is careful not to dilute his poems with rhapsodic excess. Trimmed down to the essentials, he mixes both common speech and such "Gregorized" words as "afeared," "cerement," and "cauldronous." Also, he reaches back for archaic usage such as "thy," "poesy," and "ere."

I drove over to Andy Clausen's house in Oakland with Allen Ginsberg to see Corso, who was staying there. On the way over, Ginsberg asked, "What can be done with Gregory? Maybe he needs a few months in the country somewhere . . . away from drugs and drink." Ginsberg emphasized the Dionysian Corso. Yet only a day earlier we had talked of Corso's poetry, particularly his newer poems, and commented on their lyric grace.

We arrived at Clausen's to find Corso wild eyed and red faced. He paced up and down the living room, disappearing once in awhile, returning with renewed energy. Nothing Ginsberg said seemed right. I tried to imagine what it must have been like—their first meeting in a Manhattan bar back in 1950—Allen twenty-four and Gregory twenty, Gregory just out of prison and Allen already steeped in the wise madness of William Burroughs and Jack Kerouac.

There was no literary talk at Clausen's that night, no reminiscing on long-gone times. Ginsberg and I made sandwiches in the kitchen, devouring them just as Corso bounded back into sight. He screamed: "WHAT DID YOU TELL THIS MAN? THIS MAN THINKS HE'S A POET, BUT HE'S GOING TO DIE, SEE? AND HIS POETRY WON'T BE REMEMBERED."

"I didn't say anything, Gregory," I replied.

"Oh yeh!" he exclaimed, backing up several steps and jumping into the air. "YOU'RE BOTH JEWISH YENTAS. ALL YOU CAN DO IS PRY INTO OTHER PEOPLE'S BUSINESS." Then, he broke out laughing.

"I do so love thee," Corso said when he and his baby son, Max Orpheo, were guests at Harwood Alley. The baby had just learned how to say "Daddy," and we were all excited one afternoon when he suddenly pointed a finger at a reproduction of a Renoir street scene on the wall and said, "What's this?"

One evening, as we were all getting ready for bed, Corso came into the bedroom my friend and I shared and asked if he could watch us make love.

"Ginsberg and Peter Orlovsky never let me see. I want to know what happens. You and Ginsberg . . . all you homosexuals are so secretive."

"Go to sleep, Gregory," I said and pulled the curtain down between our room and the hallway.

In the morning, he met my former girlfriend. "Wow! What a beauty," he exclaimed on watching her come up the steps to Harwood Alley. It wouldn't be long before he and Lisa were living together. Max would have a mother and the poet an exquisite muse.

Watching them together, I was reminded of when I first met Gregory Corso. I was spending the afternoon with Kaye McDonough. We were on our way to City Lights when Corso appeared with Andy Clausen in tow. They looked like a pair of sailors who had just left a tramp steamer up from the South Seas. But somehow Corso's unkempt appearance looked noble. He had on an ill-fitting vest, pants that were too long, his hair a mess, and only three front teeth. I came up to him and said, "Hi, Gregory!"

"That's presumptuous," he barked back, swinging his right hand out in a wide, elegant gesture.

"I can imitate you disrupting an Allen Ginsberg reading."

"Yeh?" he replied with interest.

I tried to pucker up my face in a gargoyle-like manner, approximating his countenance. Then I said, "Imagine a crowded auditorium at Harvard. Ginsberg is reading and you enter the hall. He looks down from his dais and sees you. With a worried expression, he begins to recite his latest poems. You dance up the aisle, flirting with the coeds and then yell out at the top of your voice, 'HEY, ALLEN! IT'S ME, YOUR GREGORY. I'VE COME TO SEE YOU, MAN.' How's that?"

"I dig that," he said. "What's your name?"

Clausen introduced us and Corso said, "Mister Cherkovski, would you like to go with us for coffee."

"I had the best teachers," Corso told me late one evening during the summer of 1982, while sitting at my kitchen table. "There were some guys in prison. I was seventeen when I went in and nineteen when I got out. You dig it? Those are big years. I was a problem in society. So, you know what I got in Danamora?"

"What?" I asked.

"Stendhal's *The Red and the Black* and my Shelley. That's a good thing in life to find Shelley when you're a kid, when they got you locked away for being a menace."

"But wasn't it hard being in jail?"

"You make the time your own. I used it to get the literary gems. I even read the dictionary in jail and learned all the words."

"I grew up in the streets" was a phrase reminiscent of Henry Miller. As Corso spoke to me of those early years, I thought of Miller's Whitmanic anthem in *Black Spring*, where he memorializes the heroes of his youth, his playmates on the streets of Brooklyn. And of Ferlinghetti's years in Bronxville, living with foster parents, grasping for his identity in the small town, hearing echoes of a greater land sprawling out from there in all directions.

Later, on the terrace of the Savoy, Gregory and I were joined by several younger poets. After a few rounds of drinks, Corso smiled, proclaiming, "I'm the elder now. A daddy. You who do so love your Gregory got the goodie gum drops from me, Ginsberg, and Kerouac." And then, with a pied piper magic only he possesses, we all marched off through the streets of North Beach.

Becoming a Man

I'm Not a Man

I'm not a man. I can't earn a living, buy new things for my
    family.
I have acne and a small peter.

I'm not a man. I don't like football, boxing and cars.
I like to express my feelings. I even like to put an arm
around my friend's shoulder.

I'm not a man. I won't play the role assigned to me—the role
created by Madison Avenue, *Playboy*, Hollywood and Oliver
    Cromwell.
Television does not dictate my behavior. I am only 5 foot 4.

I'm not a man. Once when I shot a squirrel I swore that I
    would
never kill again. I gave up meat. The sight of blood makes me
sick. I like flowers.

I'm not a man. I went to prison resisting the draft. I do not fight
when real men beat me up and call me queer. I dislike violence.

I'm not a man. I have never raped a woman. I don't hate
    blacks.
I do not get emotional when the flag is waved. I do not think I
    should
love America or leave it. I think I should laugh at it.

I'm not a man. I have never had the clap.

I'm not a man. *Playboy* is not my favorite magazine.

I'm not a man. I cry when I'm unhappy.

I'm not a man. I do not feel superior to women.

I'm not a man. I don't wear a jockstrap.

I'm not a man. I write poetry.

I'm not a man. I meditate on peace and love.

I'm not a man. I don't want to destroy you.

Harold Norse
From *The Love Poems*

Harold Norse lived on Northern California's Russian River for a number of years in the 1970s. He bought a small house with a young friend and settled in, surrounded by redwoods, dark, forested hillsides, and suspicious neighbors. The poet enjoyed being out of the city for awhile. He had lived in enough of them. Born in Brooklyn in 1916, he had wandered from New York to Paris, Tangier to San Francisco. He was the metropolitan man. Time in the country could do no harm.

The Russian River region is idyllic, with small vineyards tucked into folds of hillsides and little towns like Guerneville and Monte Rio hugging the river. It didn't take him long to make contact with artists and writers who lived in the region; all of whom were pleased having the poet Harold Norse in their presence. One afternoon we sat on a sand bank at a bend in the river and talked about the writing community in North Beach. Norse said: "It's a blessing and a curse, like any such scene. You can learn from it but also waste a lot of time. The best thing is hopefully making a few loyal friends, people who will always be there for you and you for them. Ultimately, however, you have to face yourself, alone. A hard thing to do for any of us. It's you and your work. That's where you can grow. That's the arena in which true change can take place."

I visited him at the Russian River on many occasions and experienced firsthand the mood of a poet whose work had helped form my own when I was still in high school. With his ability to recall even the most trivial details of a situation, he recounted the long years of his friendship with William Carlos Williams, who helped guide Norse toward a full recognition of his own potential, and his early association with W. H. Auden, whose presence became almost palpable as Norse recounted stories from the New

York literary scene during the early 1940s. There was warmth in his voice as he told of his own long apprenticeship to the muse. He laid himself bare. "I was searching, probing, trying to build up enough confidence to strike out on my own. Having these men as friends was invaluable."

For Norse, the road itself is important. "Constantly, you will find yourself reaching a goal as a writer, and it will vanish before your eyes only to lead you to a new discovery, an entirely different challenge, and you're on the path again. At least you know that your mind is alive, you can feel a kind of electricity inside of you." As he spoke, his eyes looked directly into mine, and a kinship beyond words grew stronger. Perhaps not having known his own father made him feel fatherly toward others. I used to paint a picture in my mind of Norse as a child in Brooklyn, walking the same streets Henry Miller walked and Walt Whitman had traveled before him. His fertile, far-ranging mind constantly challenged me to begin again.

The poet's first published poem appeared in *The Brooklyn Daily Eagle*. "I was nine years old," Norse said, "when the *Eagle* published my poem. Later I discovered that Walt Whitman had been the editor of the newspaper. I believe I once said in an interview that my poem wasn't printed under his editorship. I'm not that old." Three years later they published another poem, one he had written with a storm as theme. "Four years passed before I came across *Leaves of Grass*. *Song of Myself* had a powerful effect on me, and it was at that point I knew my life would be lived as a poet." Norse would never waver from the opinion that *Song of Myself* is the greatest poem ever written. One of the things that impressed him most was Whitman's dictum: "Cross out, please, those immensely overpaid accounts." Norse understood that those words signaled a new way of perceiving, and writing about, the world. When thinking of Norse's relationship to Whitman, I recalled Norse's poem, *I'm Not a Man*, a poem that has become recognized as a major contribution to the development of gay consciousness. The poem has always seemed to me to be an extension of the kind of thinking *Leaves of Grass* promulgated. The poet gives us a long list of reasons why "I'm not a man":

I'm not a man. I cry when I'm unhappy.

I'm not a man. I do not feel superior to women.

I'm not a man. I don't wear a jockstrap.

I'm not a man. I write poetry.

Norse sensed the presence of a man in *Leaves of Grass*, not of a literary artifice. He felt as if he could almost smell the odors of Whitman's body and hear his breathing. Throughout his life, and certainly in his later years, he returned to Whitman, who remained a deep source for Norse's own poetic development, both in the context of sharing with Norse a sexual passion for men and a commitment to a new poetry.

In Hart Crane's *The Bridge*, written a few blocks from Whitman's childhood home, Norse recognized the immense appreciation of the American experience Crane had poured into that poem. Like *Song of Myself*, this work became an influential text for the maturing poet. Crane's tie to Whitman, fully acknowledged in the poem, pointed out for Norse the kinship and natural lineage between poets. It also set him on two divergent paths, one leading to the openness of Whitman and the other to Crane's formal approach to the poem. The Whitmanic impulse would eventually win out, as Norse neared a direct poetic line akin to common speech. A solid example of Norse's more structured work is this selection from *On the Steps of the Castillo*:

The sun scattered those diamonds
Like coruscations of castanets
Over the sinewy blue belly
Of the sea; while one great rock rose,
The fat fin of a whaleshaped isle . . .

In the preface to Norse's translations of *The Roman Sonnets of G. G. Belli*, published in 1960, William Carlos Williams pointed out: "The idiom into which Harold Norse has translated these sonnets was inaccessible to anyone before the present time." Of Norse's own poetry, Williams wrote in 1951, "You have breached a new lead, shown a new power over the language." In 1969 Norse appeared together with Charles Bukowski and Philip Lamantia in the Penguin Modern Poets series. One of Norse's best poems in that collection is a tribute to William Carlos Williams, in which he thanks the elder poet and mentor

for the pink locust
& the white mule
for the precise eyeglasses
& the scalpel
that sliced us memorable plums . . .

Norse's first book, *The Undersea Mountain*, was published in 1953. Soon afterward he left New York and began a long expatriate period in Europe and North Africa. Macmillan published *The Dancing Beasts* in 1962, and *Karma Circuit* appeared from Nothing Doing In London Press in 1967. When he presented me with a copy of the latter, he said, "Welcome to the Karma Circuit, which has no beginning or end." He told me that this latest collection represented a dramatic change in his style. "I've been going in a new direction the past several years, developing a freer voice." I argued that his "ear" was already free, even when the forms were stricter, as in his first collection of poems. "Well, the main point is, I am constantly in flux, just like the world around me. It's a matter of being resilient, of not becoming rigid or doctrinaire either in style or what you are hoping to express."

Early in 1987 I had come over to drive Norse to a book-signing party at City Lights Bookstore. As he readied himself, I began looking through the poems he wrote for Mohammed Rifi, a young Moroccan friend whom he knew in Tangier. Reading them, I thought that if anybody helps us break down the imaginary, yet all-too-real barriers between the gay and straight world, it is Norse.

When I talked to Norse about the AIDS crisis he said, "Things will get more oppressive. So all the more, a writer has to tell the truth. What else can a writer do? Nobody would have written any of the truly great literature if they were afraid. You have to follow your instincts. Go with what you know you have to write. I guess lots of people don't realize when you write a love poem it is simply a love poem and they ought to be happy for that."

"Well, when I first read your work it was that way," I replied. "I didn't know anything about this guy Norse except what came through in his writing. It was gritty work. Those poems made me feel as if I could smell the dust of the Greek countryside and the aroma of baking bread in the streets of Paris."

"You must have been reading pieces from when I lived in the Beat Hotel," Norse said.

"A few years later, maybe."

"I left there in 1963. Those were wild times. Like back in 1960 when I complained to William Burroughs about having a cold. He suggested I go down to the corner drugstore and buy a vial filled with little black pills made of opium and codeine. He told me they would cure my cold. I said, 'But they'll cost too much.' Bill laughed, assuring me they'd only cost about two dollars. I bought them and they worked. No more colds. No sneezing. And I could sleep well."

"Were you taking them for long?"

"For a year. I had become an addict without even knowing it. Finally I called Brion Gysin in his room at the hotel and said, 'Brion, you've got to help me get off this opium.' 'No way,' he answered, 'I've been through that already.'"

"What did you do then, Harold?"

"Cold turkey. And you know what? I immediately began having colds again. My sneezing returned, my coughing . . . all accompanied by sleepless nights."

In his introduction to *Beat Hotel*, a collection of Norse's cut-up writings, Burroughs writes, "Harold Norse was among the first to apply the cut-ups. I recall my enthusiasm and laughter when Brion and I read *Sniffing Keyholes*." The piece begins:

Z. Z. flipped, saying, "I gotta learn how to use words." She stopped thinking "What are words anyway?" She started to feel and it frightened her. She felt very lonely. Wanted to fuck. Wanted to get back into habit. Z. Z. was a lush and a nympho. Deprived of both outlets, she wandered around Tangier straight as a board wearing shades and recognizing nobody.

I mentioned to Norse that the work in *Beat Hotel* was radically different from the stories he wrote for *Hustler* and other "girlie" magazines. "For awhile, it looked as if you and Bukowski were competing for space on the porno pages."

"The guys at *Hustler* paid well," Norse said. "When you're living on poetry money, which is like living on nothing at all, you don't pass up a chance to hop on board at a place that pays well for something fun to write, not to mention titillating."

"Whenever I read those stories I wondered if the editors had any idea that they really weren't fiction. You lived them all. I must have known some of the women you wrote about. Just like I've known a lot of the men you've hopped into bed with."

"Enough reminiscing," Norse interrupted. "Let's go to North Beach."

We put on our coats and soon were drinking wine at a literary reception being held at City Lights.

The young editor of *Olé*, a mimeographed magazine published in the early 1960s, had every intention of blowing the lid off the literary establishment. Harold Norse's poetry offered him that chance. Norse's words were powerfully conversational, his attitude that of a natural outlaw, his eye like a movie camera taking snapshots of things in all their unrestricted rawness. One poem went right to the heart of the self-mockery an artist may experience while in the act of conceiving a poem, painting, or sculptural piece:

writing a poem
   & feeling absurd
about this useless
     activity
I went to the window
   & saw a scraggy nut
   beret mothy beard
     groucho moustache
       grinning

When the magazine brought out its Norse issue in the early sixties, including his poetry and tributes from William Burroughs, Anaïs Nin, James Baldwin, and others, I imagined an international literary traveler, a man who knew his way around the cities named at the bottom of his poems: Paris, Torremolinos, Athens, Rome, Naples. . . . I was caught by his words and hurtled as far as the places he described. It wasn't long before I was reading his poems aloud, intuitively responding to what I would later come to know as the colloquial tone William Carlos Williams and Walt Whitman had insisted on earlier. Norse's European poems easily lend themselves to recitation. *Carnivorous Saint* begins:

we dig up ancient shards
clicking cameras
among the dying cypresses
choked by Athenian smog.

yet cats continue basking
in the hazy sun
the chained goat sways in ecstasy
the Parthenon looks down from creamy heights
lichen and rust nibble the pediments
and tourist feet break the spell
of antiquity's vibrations.

Later in the poem, Norse adds:

bring back the carnivorous saint
whose mother is no virgin
she's Our Lady of Peace Movements
to ban the bomb and clean up the air
she'll wave her umbrella and change the world.

As with the other poems of the period from the late 1950s to mid-1960s, Norse would suddenly come through in the heat of his language, searching for, or declaring, his own identity in strong, passionate terms. That is what most attracted me. It was as if Whitman had been reborn and was now leaping through the snowfields of Northern Europe, or lazily strolling down the streets of humid Mediterranean cities. Norse seemed intent on positioning himself beyond government, beyond academia and beyond any form of ideological servitude. He had not yet written the homosexual protest poetry that would become an important part of the burgeoning gay literary movement of the 1970s. The poems in *Olé* have all the earthiness of the land he writes about:

it's Kali Yug &
the planet's exploding
like a rotten orange ready to burst
the sun hasn't long to burn
& the asteroid
earthwards with deadly aim

                      hurries to keep
its apocalyptic rendezvous . . .

   Tangible meanings reached out from the page. This, added to
a sense that purely intellectual concerns had been brushed aside
for a visceral and urgent poetry, made the work significant to me.
He had successfully created a dialogue with his environment, one
in which the reader could readily participate. He evoked scenes
that hovered between empathy and alienation, as if he stood midway between these extremes, indicating a fuller truth than mundane concerns generally allow. *greek customs* began:

you could smell the salt over the fumes
& combustion as i wheeled
the old car into the square
near the white
ships
—red eyes dripping doleful
unshakeable parts of the landscape . . .

He came down to the elemental, to what is directly at hand. Only
later would I find a different Norse, one steeped in earlier tradi-
tions who wrote a more controlled, meditative poetry.

David Moe, one of the more innovative experimental poets of San
Francisco, once read one of his poems to me that sums up how I
feel about Norse:

free of searching, hide
free of ordering, create
free of doubt, question
free of butter, sapphire,
free of breath, spin into the waves. . . .

I have spun down the streets of San Francisco with Norse, back
when we were both lonely and searching for love. In the leather
bars on Folsom Street and in the gay ghetto of the Castro District
we would companion one another, fearful of never finding a
young man with whom to share our love.
   I often said to myself, as we walked on cold and windy side-

walks, eyeing young beauties as they passed, Here I am with a man who lived in the Beat Hotel in Paris with William Burroughs, Gregory Corso, and Allen Ginsberg, and who knew W. H. Auden and Tennessee Williams intimately. Yet he appears to be as vulnerable as I am.

We walked into one darkly lit leather bar on a stormy winter evening and tried to make our way toward the bartender. We were quickly separated, Norse having been swallowed whole by a crowd of men towering over him. I tried grabbing his hand as he began to melt into the pack, but to no avail. Jesus, there goes *Hotel Nirvana*, *Carnivorous Saint*, and *Beat Hotel*. What will I say to his old friends? I went into a South of Market bar with him and he vanished. You know how short Harold is. The last thing I saw was his Greek sailor's cap bobbing up and down, and then nothing but a sea of strange faces.

There were nights when we were lucky, each meeting young men. I would joke with him, "If only Walt Whitman were with us now. He would go crazy. I bet *Leaves of Grass* would be another four hundred pages in length."

"Imagine all the love poems he could write," Harold added.

I read together with Norse, Allen Ginsberg, John Rechy, and the younger poets Dennis Cooper, Aaron Shurin, and Robert Glück at a Gay Sunshine benefit in San Francisco back in 1977. It would prove to be an exciting event held in Glide Memorial Church in the center of San Francisco's Tenderloin District. A few days earlier Norse had looked over what I was going to read, then showed me his selections, some of which came from *Hotel Nirvana*, a selection of poems City Lights published in 1974. Suddenly, Norse turned from his own concerns and stated, "Your generation is coming into its own, but it's a hard time for poetry." We agreed that prose was the way to go in terms of possibly ending up with a villa in Acapulco someday or even a small flat in Greenwich Village. Poetry just didn't bring financial reward.

Returning home to write, I thought of all those people who tell me, "I used to write poetry when I was in high school." I called Norse, hoping he would tell me where to find that secret road to glory. He is a gifted talker, and can move with rapid-fire speed from the Beat Hotel days on the rue Git-Le-Cœur to whatever comedy or tragedy might have befallen him. He knew just what to say to assuage my doubts. "I'm convinced that a lot of young writers simply lack confidence. Those who don't find it won't get anywhere. It's really the basic principle of following the lead of your own heart."

In conversation he loves describing old friends and ancient enemies with intensity. One friend seminal to his own development was William Burroughs. Norse likens him to a riverboat gambler right out of Mark Twain. He considers Burroughs to be doubly important because of the effect of his writings on younger people in the seventies and eighties. Although Norse enjoys the company of old friends and literary acquaintances, he prefers talking with young people, especially writers, and is an acute, compassionate critic of their work.

When Norse described his first meeting with William Carlos Williams, he told me, "I was afraid Williams would be unapproachable, that I wouldn't have the proper vocabulary for speaking in his presence. Remember, he had already received a lot of attention by the mid-1950s. His position as an innovator was established. I remember almost trembling before we met. But he quickly put me at ease. I've known few people who talked in such an ordinary way as Williams. There I was, a young poet, and he began asking me questions as if I knew more than he. I was also taken by the way he used small words, easy words. His vocabulary itself was not threatening."

Charles Bukowski introduced me to Norse in 1967. We were excited by the presence of a poet in Los Angeles whose work seemed so independent and stripped of excess. When I read poems like *Classic Frieze in A Garage* or *Ti Voglio Bene*, I heard a clear and uncompromising voice speaking. Finally having an opportunity to meet him resulted in a twenty-hour marathon of reading and re-reading his work. Should I be questioned by the expatriate poet who had come to live in the crumbling seaside community of Venice, with its storefront synagogues and sea smells, I wanted to appear erudite. Bukowski, as nervous as I had ever seen him, almost fled the back door of his bungalow as Norse knocked. "Jesus, he's here," Bukowski whispered. "What are we gonna do, kid?" "Open the door," I replied. He did. In marched Norse, bundled in what looked like a thousand European scarfs and faded Levi's. Bukowski, who is over six feet tall and well over two hundred pounds, looked down at Norse and said: "Jesus, is this all there is?" Smiling, Norse moved in on him and playfully punched him in the belly. Bukowski said: "Kid, I think a fly hit me." We had both expected a giant with huge, beefy arms and broad shoulders. Only when he began to speak did his real power come through. This was it. The man has brought the entire Acropolis to California. He inhabited and controlled Bukowski's living room.

Immediately I wanted to probe him about the old stones, crumbling ruins, deep blue skies, shadowy Roman ghetto voices, and cypress landscapes scattered through *The Dancing Beast*. Or, more specifically, I hoped to learn more about "the rich heiress from Tulsa, ten years of villas and male whores . . . ," and lose myself in an Italian montage of images reeling outward from Florence in an endless rapture of "light crumbling. . . ." *The Dancing Beast*, which is a transition book from an earlier, more formal style to the wilder images of *Karma Circuit* and *Hotel Nirvana*, provides a profoundly enriching onslaught of sensuous imagery. Sensuality exudes from the landscape: "the beauty—the light, frescoes catching it out of the air plentiful in the ripe Tuscan gold and blue, with saints and trees adorning creation."

But, during our first meeting, I had to remain the dutiful listener. Bukowski talked about his own career and how well things were going. He threw in a few anecdotes about life at the Terminal Annex Post Office. Norse alluded to his mountains of manuscripts waiting for publication and the need to sort out his years of traveling. Many of these poems would go into important later collections, *Carnivorous Saint* and *Love Poems*, collections of Norse's gay poetry.

A week after the meeting at Bukowski's, I took notes as I went through Norse's work again, pausing to recall his rugged body and its healthy, robust tan and probing, intelligent eyes. I wrote, "He looked like what I imagined an expatriate would look like. He talked, mostly to Bukowski, while I sat in a corner, listening. I am 'the kid,' probably a hindrance, but what could I do?" It was impossible then to imagine that twenty years later he and I would be recalling a close friendship in which we had wept in one another's arms, cruised the avenues together, laughed uncontrollably in late-night conversation, and shared the ever-evolving process of creativity.

Thinking of Norse's earlier poems, those works I discovered on my own as a college student, I remember the lines,

> but the meaning will not break
>   like light
> the message will not come thru
>
> the beast cannot follow the waterbearer
>   into the upper chamber
>   & the time
> is at hand.

Written in Delphi in 1964, a place I would visit six years later, *Addio* became a talisman in words. In my notes I wrote: "The last four lines, considered against what has come before, are so intensely mythic." Even today, when I read "the beast cannot follow the waterbearer," I remember being twenty-one, a student at a college embanked against the San Bernardino Freeway, reading *Addio* in a crowded cafeteria:

> i knelt among the hollyhocks in the olive grove
>   knowing these cliffs & chasms would once more shift
>   & tumble down
>
> i passed an enormous lizard being devoured among the shards
>   by black ants hungry & mean . . .

At Delphi I recited Norse's poem while standing on a cliffside overlooking the Gulf of Corinth. I looked back at the columns of one of the temples. I was there and here I am, noting my place amid the flow of images, wrapped up in the cosmology of Harold Norse. Here I am, and here still lives the image of Delphi, on a mountainside overlooking a dizzying view of olive orchards and placid seas, rugged outcroppings of rock and narrow, dusty roads.

From *The Undersea Mountain* to his recent *Love Poems*, Harold Norse has sought what he calls "Hotel Nirvana," and in his compact prose work *Beat Hotel* he gives us a road map for getting there. He has lived on the bohemian express, traveled its main lines between the great cities, and explored its secondary routes where the going is labored and thick with the atmosphere of adventure. He was out there, in a hundred European hotels simultaneously, weathering the vicissitudes of his own creativity, fighting to free himself from an early formalism, listening to echoes of his Brooklyn childhood, lyrically in love or weighed down with the responsibilities of a wandering poet. He has spent most of his life in poverty or on the brink of it. He knew that the life of the poet did not promise wealth, yet he continually embarked, sometimes proclaiming, "I'm sick of poetry. I want out!" only to be found the next day engrossed in some new literary venture, some ambitious new poem.

A poor boy who wanted to be a great writer, he had taken his mother's encouragement to get an education. She herself worked in factories and wanted something better for her son. He finished his M.A. in English (New York University, 1951) and was publishing in prestigious literary magazines of the day. When W. H. Auden arrived in America, shortly before the onset of World War II, Norse and Chester Kallman were there in the front row at Auden's first public reading, "flirting outrageously," as Norse once told me. Then, in 1944, while seated on a subway under the streets of Manhattan, he noticed a young man who seemed to be reciting poetry from memory. Norse could barely make out the sounds of French amid the rattle of the car, but when the train stopped at a station he turned to the poet and said, "Rimbaud." Allen Ginsberg, age eighteen at the time, answered, "You're a poet." There would be other such encounters during Norse's Manhattan days. He came to know Paul Goodman, James Baldwin, Tennessee Williams, and Dylan Thomas. He found himself well on the way to becoming a permanent and successful fixture in the New York literary scene. But he could not overcome a sense of restlessness, social, political, and sexual, and in 1953 he left New York, hungering for a freedom he couldn't find at home. With the publication of *The Undersea Mountain*, he began to think of breaking into a new style of writing, a feeling that stirred deep inside him. In leaving New York, he said farewell to the charmed encounters and literary in-fighting that had occupied his time until then. The break was final, and with it came a slow change in his literary direction. From poems that are remarkable for their formalism and varied language, the direct speech of America began to take effect. The patient muse of Walt Whitman,

William Carlos Williams, and many of the new voices in American poetry began to be heard. He turned toward a Europe that had the same almost magical effect on his writing that it had on earlier expatriates. Like the American heralded in Whitman's *Song of the Open Road*, who would be a "forth-stepper from the latent, unrealized baby days," the exhilaration of foreign cultures would open out for Norse into ever-widening circles that encompassed North Africa and the Middle East.

Today, March 1, 1987, I live ten blocks from Norse. He rents a small house nudged in between antique, wooden apartment buildings and loud, varied noises that seep into his writing. He might as well be camping out in the crowded neighborhoods of Naples or Athens for all the aromas and intrusive sounds. But what I am thinking of are his own aromas and noises: the corridors, trapdoors, fields, and seaside places of his poetry. There is enough ancient music in them, expressed in modern language, to give great scope to his work.

I remember the bus that brought me to Delphi from Thebes. It was carrying us to the oracle's ancient home. I eagerly anticipated seeing those sights recorded in *Addio*, experiencing for myself the hollyhocks and olive groves, the enormous lizards, and old columns Norse had described. My own poem, which I lost on a steamship that brought me to Haifa harbor four weeks later, had been an homage to the elements in Delphi. I realize now it was an homage to Harold Norse, whose voice kept speaking to me, not only of Greece, but of other places I would come to visit as well. Poetry can have that kind of effect. It doesn't lay imprisoned on a page. It survives in the reader's mind and can become an inexhaustible well. I was once asked if I had come to a better understanding of Samuel Taylor Coleridge's *Kubla Khan* after asserting that I read the poem aloud every day for years, and I replied, "No, but it eases the pain and makes the joy more joyful." Perhaps it is richer and less futile to *experience* a poem, rather than only to comprehend it intellectually.

What Norse has done in *The Love Poems* is analogous to Whitman with *Leaves of Grass*. For Whitman, *Leaves* became an intentional epic; *The Love Poems*—gathered from previous collections, magazines, and notebooks—is an epic by default. I wander into his book, stop and go and wait for my mind to follow. Then, in another poem, my mind has come to the end before my self. Again I must wait. Norse paints a solid, colorful portrait in *A Kind of Immortality*:

I saw a young man in my room
strangely intimate though unknown
yet loverlike and warm.
"I know this city well," he said,
"its hills and business district.
I'm a taxi-driver, 27, been thru
the big quake, the western hill
is safe," and vanished.
Was I talking to the dead,
some astral hitchhiker
between sleep and waking?
I fell back and heard:
"It is an exceptional time
and situation."

Norse and I became reacquainted in San Francisco while sitting in the Caffe Trieste. He leaned across the table to speak to me about my poems. After talking theory for awhile, he said, "You're lucky to have a supportive family. That can make quite a difference as the years go on. I never knew my father, and my mother was uneducated. She never really read my work nor understood what it meant to be a poet." When he finished, we discussed what each of us had been doing since the Los Angeles days. Neither of us had seen Bukowski recently. Both of us were putting together new books of poetry.

When I left the café with his phone number in my address book and an invitation to call anytime, I went down to City Lights Bookstore and bought a copy of *Hotel Nirvana*. Some of my early favorites were in there and many new poems. I walked up Grant Avenue, turned up the steep slope of Filbert Street, and went to my apartment in Harwood Alley. One of the poems, *We Bumped Off Your Friend the Poet*, a dramatic monologue in the person of the Fascist who killed Lorca, is memorable:

Because he was a poet
was he better than anyone else?

He was a goddamn fag
and we were sick and tired
of fags in Granada

The black assassination squads
kept busy
liquidating professors
doctors lawyers students
. . . . .
a queer communist poet!

General Franco owes me a medal
for putting 2 bullets up his ass

Always discernible in his work is a human heart. In some of the work, Norse takes an unsparing view of the human situation, lines that recall the simplicity of some of Bukowski's narratives. In *Landscape of Cruelty*, Norse writes:

Blaise Cendrars lay dying
　　　across the street from the Santé
　　　　　　the prisoners waved at us from their bars with
　　　　　　　　　sweet obscene gestures
　　　　　　　　　　　　spit drools down his chin
　　　tongue lolls in helpless mouth
　　　　　　　　　　eyes glazed & frightened

no more Trans-Siberian Blaise
no more little *poules* with a dose
it's a very long way from here to Montmartre Blaise
it's a long way
your illness a drag
your wife a real bringdown
your destination clearly the final asylum
your head weaving like a spastic . . .

The hard, harsh tone, matter-of-factly presented in terse language, is as gutsy as the subject being dealt with. The old literary hero, Blaise Cendrars, is portrayed without sentiment, exactly as the poet sees him. Pulling no punches, Norse lets the facts speak for themselves in a mini-biography of despair and ultimate ruin.

Homo is a poem filled with Norse's rage at the treatment of homosexuals throughout the ages, with its concurrent suppression of all forms of liberation. Gone is the humorous and ironic voice that fills many shorter poems critical of the treatment accorded minorities. Norse goes for broke here, reaching back into history, reasoning that oppression finally tears away at the very fabric of the society that is trying to hold itself together through acts of oppression. In opening up the history books, he reveals his own interest in historical fact and the lessons of the past. This is not the visionary Norse of *Addio* but an acutely aware social critic who finds in poetry all the means necessary to help lead men toward a greater sanity. Balancing this aspect of the poem are sections that clearly demonstrate the poet's lyrical gift, his ear for language, and his ability to sustain an image. He chooses to open the poem with a lyrical prelude. Having returned to Europe after an absence of several years, he takes time to muse on the old beauty of a European city, one he had fallen in love with years before:

Amber lamplight on the
Green canal. Leaves falling
Into the ripples. Gulls
Settle on bridges. In Amsterdam
I lean from the attic window
Under the eaves in this
16th Century brick house, the
Trap door pulls up and
Conceals the bedroom, an Anne Frank
Dutch device that saved the
Lives of many Jews. The
Bedroom also contains
A meditation room with
Fine Persian carpets and glass
Roof . . .

He has brought to the room a young man he met at a reading he had just given. The lyrical tone is maintained:

Beside me on the futon lies
The young student who followed me
After my readings and seminar
at the university. We
Made love all night. He is tall

With enormous gray luminous eyes.
Next day at the Van Gogh museum
Before the drawings of old peasants
In the Brabant he touches the glass
Frames: "This could be my grandmother. See
this old man—my grandfather!"

Soon after this poignant image, Norse ranges across the planet, pointing out that the "sex police" are prevalent everywhere. He moves from the Philippines where "blackmail attends / Each act of "affection . . . ," to "the Moslem world where the Rubaiyat / and Sufi poems extolled boy-love / The fundamentalist police / Chop noses, hands, feet, necks and dicks / Off for this universal need." But he envisions one man's oppression as everyman's tragedy:

How many Jews would Pound
Have gassed at Auschwitz and Buchenwald?
How many Otto René Castillos
Can Guatemala burn at the stake?
How many Roque Daltons
Cal El Salvador liquidate?

The poet takes us to the root of institutionalized anti-homosexuality. The historical debate is intensified, as he brings the Emperor Justinian before us and lays bare the root of gay oppression with humorous contempt:

Ever since Justinian
Who wanted more power over the Church
Passed the first law against same-sex love
With the perfectly logical excuse
That homosexuality
Caused earthquakes, we have seen
Religion and politics
Condemn gay sex as crime and sin.

I first heard parts of *Homo* as Norse read sections over the telephone. In a voice that was controlled, yet contained the pent-up rage of centuries, Norse launched into an indictment of all the oppressive forces gathered against homosexuals. Even fellow poets were not spared:

Collaged bits of reality
From various points on the planet.
Testimonials to shame. Our poets
Contribute to oppression.
Ridicule the innocent. Our
"Enlightened" poets goosestep
with swastika or hammer and sickle,
Condescending and patronizing
While praising universal love.

"What do you think of the poem?" Norse questioned me.

"I believe you've done it again . . . gone beyond yourself. I've been waiting for a poem like this. It has tenderness and a rugged quality . . . all of those things I acquaint with your poetry," I answered.

"It just came rolling out of me," he said, "and I wasn't expecting it, which is probably the best way to receive a poem."

A few days later, he handed me a copy of the poem and then began a long dialogue with himself over whether to place it at the beginning or end of *The Love Poems*, which the Crossing Press would soon be publishing. Due to its length, he finally decided to put it toward the end of the collection.

Shortly after renewing my friendship with Norse, I began attending his weekly poetry classes held at a rambling apartment in a dilapidated building half hidden under the shadow of a freeway off-ramp. In a dark-lit room, with the sound of racing cars not far off, he spent half the class talking about poetry, ranging from the works of Rimbaud to those of Artaud and from Auden to Ginsberg, and the other half looking at the poetry of his students. His excitement during these informal sessions was like that of a child discovering boxes filled with toys. A lecture on Artaud became a maze of questions, possible answers, wrong turns, and forks in the road. Dates, critical opinions from even the most stuffy literary minds, and blissful recollections of poets he had known came tumbling from his lips. Like all great teachers, he also did a lot of listening. He was eager to hear the poetry of those who had come to study.

Sometimes I am alienated by the tougher side of his later poetry. Poems from the middle period, like *Florence* and *Roman Ghetto*, for example, are hauntingly lyrical, moving in and out of history with ease. I am always asking him to find time for more florid, gentle poems written in the manner of *Roman Ghetto*. In that poem, he evokes the long history of the Diaspora with empathy, beginning at a common sight for the historical traveler, the Roman ghetto. History comes alive, never tiring or terrifying. Norse makes it a direct, immediate revelation:

We are not loud. Our women dress in black,
Their hair tight and decorous, some beautiful.
We should be ugly or presumptuous,
        if it were true
What they say of us. But our dignity
Was not bought, we never connived
        like upstart princes
for an empire, whose guests we are.

One summer afternoon Gregory Corso stopped by my apartment to visit. Out of nowhere he asked for Norse's telephone number and dialed. When Norse picked up the receiver, Corso began in utter sincerity, "Harold, this is Gregory. I lost my fame. I don't know what to do. Allen and Bill . . . they still got it. But me, I lost it. Even Kerouac still has it, dead as he is. But now you have it. You got fame through the gay scene, and I lost mine. What am I gonna do? Oh, poor Gregory." He was soon off the phone, telling me, "I bet he calls you."

Five minutes went by and then the phone rang. I picked it up to hear a serious Norse explain in almost breathless tones, "Gregory called. He told me he lost his fame. It's terrible. He said I was more famous than he. He compared himself to Ginsberg and Kerouac . . . told me they're still famous, but he isn't. I felt embarrassed. I don't know why he confessed all this to me." Gregory held in his laughter at the fulfillment of his prediction.

I am glad I met Harold Norse when I did. In Norse and Corso I find two different poets, two different worlds, and yet sharing an ability with words. I'm glad Bukowski and I were so excited back in the sixties over the expatriate coming to live in Venice. Bukowski would read Norse's work aloud as I listened. "Pretty damn good, right?" Bukowski would say.

I am approaching Delphi as I sit in my second-floor workroom overlooking San Francisco's Diamond Heights. No more will I argue over the merits of the Whitman self, flinging arms and legs over a cliff of pages, or attempt to explain the stanzas forever oozing from the fingertips of all poets. Pure man, pure language, pure water falling into the Aegean. I am with the poem. I am of it. I have given myself over to language, making my way into the poem. I call this poem *Delphi*. Trees are aflame, the sky is bright orange, and a lizard darts quickly under a rock filled with the soul of the earth.

I am the waterbearer. I am climbing that hot, dusty road from Thebes to Delphi. "Tell me, is this the way to the word?" I ask an old man who hobbles by. His eyes are ashes and his tongue is a lizard crawling under a rock.

Here is Delphi, at last, teetering on the side of a rocky mountain, as if it was going to slide right into the sea below. I wrote a long poem in a French notebook, mixing fire, water, earth, and air. Somewhere between Piraeus Harbor and the gates of Jerusalem I lost it. I would have said to Harold Norse, "I wrote this in Delphi after reading your poem *Addio*. A Canadian kid slept across from me, his legs dangling over the bed. In the morning, he was a lizard with huge Delphian eyes, glaring."

Impenetrable continents are opening. We have wings. We can fly there. The word is waiting. The word is above us and below. From Norse to me to an immense emptiness . . .

Below, on the slopes that roll inevitably to the sea, orange and olive groves, rock. Above, the Grecian sun, a pinwheel, playing on branches of the sky.

Shadows of the high peak. There is a plateful of olives and onions beside a glass of wine.

We have left the city of language. Still, in my satchel, Aleph. I take the letter out and caress its smooth edges. When I put my hands on the table there is blood.

I put my hand into a wheel of words.

I feel emboldened. My hands become pure air.

We have come from Athens. The guidebook tells us to look at the thick, dark green grass. You may still see the stones against which the runners put their feet before sprinting.

I need to see the design that we call language. This morning, I felt the remoteness of this place, despite tourist eyes and local color. Aleph. Beth. Gimel. A door to language. A house whose rafters are built from the words we seize.

I lost my dreams.

Delphi. San Francisco. A wheel.

Fire, for free, all around. Fire, at the center of the forest, in the place where poems begin.

Water, to cross over, the wing of the mind like a glint of lost words.

Earth. You are welcome. The harmony cannot be explained.

Air. "We do not change." We are charged by ancient wind. Aleph. Beth. We are handed our words. We are given the sun and immense darkness.

the beast cannot follow the waterbearer
    into the upper chamber
        & the time
is at hand

Endless Light

Away Above a Harborful . . .

Away above a harborful
                    of caulkless houses
among the charley noble chimney pots
              of a rooftop rigged with clotheslines
          a woman pastes up sails
                        upon the wind
hanging out her morning sheets
                        with wooden pins
            O lovely mammal
                      her nearly naked breasts
          throw taut shadows
                      when she stretches up
to hang at the last of her
                  so white washed sins
        but it is wetly amorous
                        and winds itself about her
          clinging to her skin
                      So caught with arms
                                  upraised
      she tosses back her head
                      in voiceless laughter
    and in choiceless gesture then
                      shakes out gold hair

while in the reachless seascape spaces

              between the blown white shrouds

      stand out the bright streamers

                      to kingdom come

Lawrence Ferlinghetti
From *Endless Life: Selected Poems*

One of the more revealing photographs I used in my biography of Lawrence Ferlinghetti (*Ferlinghetti: A Biography*, 1979) is one in which the poet sits with a bored expression in the crowded courtroom as the *Howl* obscenity trial is taking place in 1957. Since Ginsberg's *Howl and Other Poems* had been printed in England for Ferlinghetti's City Lights Books, the prosecution fell under the jurisdiction of U.S. Customs, in particular under the sharp eye of Collector of Customs Chester McPhee, who had previously shown himself a protector of public decency, having seized copies of *The Miscellaneous Man*, a poetry journal edited by William J. Margolis.

While the five hundred copies of *Howl* were being held by McPhee, City Lights released a photo-offset edition identical to the original text and placed it on sale. Meanwhile, William Hogan, book-review editor of the *San Francisco Chronicle*, offered his Sunday column to Ferlinghetti so that he might write about the seizure in defense of the poem. In his article, Ferlinghetti recommended that McPhee be awarded a medal for helping to make *Howl* famous. He wrote that he considered the title poem "the most significant long poem to be published in this country since World War II . . . ," and in a statement revelatory of his own work, "the great obscene wastes of *Howl* are the wastes of the mechanized world, lost among atom bombs and inane nationalisms. . . . Ginsberg chose to walk along with Nelson Algren, Henry Miller, Kenneth Rexroth, Kenneth Patchen, not to mention some great American dead, mostly in the tradition of philosophical anarchism."

Ten days after the article appeared, McPhee released the copies of *Howl* he had been holding. The U.S. Attorney's office in San Francisco refused to move against the book. It fell to the San

Francisco Police Department and its juvenile division, headed by Captain William Hanrahan, a well-known smut hunter, to take up the gauntlet. Hanrahan publicly announced that he hoped *Howl* would open the door for a host of book seizures.

In no time at all Ferlinghetti and his partner in the City Lights venture, Shig Murao, were arrested—Murao for selling *Howl* and Ferlinghetti for publishing it. But the charges against Murao were eventually dropped, since it could not be determined if he had read the book and knew whether or not it was obscene.

The complaint against Ferlinghetti alleged that he willfully and lewdly printed and sold obscene and indecent material: *Howl and Other Poems*. The prosecution attempted to isolate certain words and prove their obscenity. In a copy of the book the allegedly obscene words were underlined. The American Civil Liberties Union took up the defense, asserting that individual words could not make a particular book obscene. The book as a whole had to be judged.

During the trial, which stretched out over the summer of 1957, City Lights Bookstore featured a display of books that had been banned in the past. It was an impressive collection of literature that included *Ulysses*, *Lady Chatterley's Lover*, *Huckleberry Finn*, *The Odyssey*, and *Gulliver's Travels*.

The prosecution, which could only muster two so-called expert witnesses, did not stand up to the battery of distinguished scholars and writers who came to Ferlinghetti's defense. They included Mark Schorer, author and chairman of the Department of Graduate Studies at the University of California at Berkeley, and Walter Van Tilburg Clark, author and professor of language arts at San Francisco State College.

Jake Erlich, the leading attorney for the defense, cited Whitman's *Leaves of Grass* in defending *Howl*. Erlich had previously been the attorney for Caryl Chessman, the condemned kidnapper who became famous for his appeals from death row and whose execution Bob Kaufman had so powerfully lamented. Erlich picked up a copy of Ginsberg's book and said, "Is there anything about this book that indicates that there is something in it which would lead to a moral breakdown of the people of this city. . . . We are confronted with the manner in which this book is to be evaluated by the court. As I understand the law, the court must construe the book as a whole. I presume that I could take the classic *Leaves of Grass* and by cutting it to pieces find a word here or there or an idea that some people might not like. But in *Leaves of Grass* there is the intent of the poet to convey a certain idea, not lewd or lascivious or licentious or common, but a story, laying out a certain format concerning life itself."

In his decision at the end of the trial, Judge Clayton Horn, a police magistrate, stated: "I think that *Howl*, like any work of literature, attempts and intends to make a significant comment on or interpretation of human experience as the author knows it." At another point in his decision he quoted the motto: *Honi soit qui mal y pense*, "Shamed be he who thinks evil of it."

The FBI apparently never got the message that Ferlinghetti had been acquitted of obscenity. Years later, when he wrote for a copy of his FBI file under the Freedom of Information Act, Ferlinghetti discovered the rather humorous description of himself as "a beatnik rabble-rouser."

They seem to have written their profile of Ferlinghetti based on more than the mere *Howl* obscenity trial. There was the case of Anton Refrigier to consider. Battling protests from the American Legion, the Veterans of Foreign Wars, and the Society of Western Artists, Ferlinghetti took the public position against the removal of Refrigier's murals from the Rincon Annex Post Office in downtown San Francisco. Depicting the growth of the nation, and doing so with a sharply defined sense of the injustices inflicted on minorities and working people, the murals were bound to provoke controversy. Yet they had been unveiled in 1948 without a hint of trouble. As time went on, however, the long shadows of McCarthyism caught up with Refrigier, and they were attacked for their subversive nature. In 1955 the battle against the murals heated up. A congressional resolution calling for their removal cited twenty-three instances of Refrigier's association with Communist organizations or organizations of "fellow travelers." Ferlinghetti wrote that "it was all too evident then that the murals had become the latest battleground of intellectual and artistic censorship." A Committee for the Defense of the Refrigier Murals was in the process of being formed. With the passage of time, however, the furor died down as the shadow of Joe McCarthy receded into history.

The FBI might have also found out about the poet's teaching experience at the University of San Francisco in the summer of

1952. In a class on Shakespeare's work, he delivered a possible homosexual interpretation of Shakespeare's sonnets. This created an immediate outrage among students, faculty, and administration. He was allowed to complete the summer schedule but was not rehired.

There were the hundreds of poetry readings, anti-Vietnam War teach-ins, and protest marches that Ferlinghetti participated in during the 1960s and that J. Edgar Hoover's crew certainly found annoying. They might have even become familiar with his stance that an artist should not take grants from a government involved in wars of aggression. Then there is the response he gave to *Who's Who* one year: "Fuck you."

Without doubt, the FBI zealots knew intimately of Ferlinghetti's arrest in December 1967 for his participation in a demonstration at the Oakland Army Induction Center. Together with his fellow protesters, his intention was to block the entrance way to the induction center when three bus loads of prospective recruits were brought in for processing. As they blocked the entrance to the parking lot next to the center, the protesters were met by a sizeable contingent of policemen. The demonstrators tightened their ranks. They were informed that the protest was considered an unlawful assembly and were ordered to disperse. When they refused to move, they were read their rights and taken away in paddy wagons. Ferlinghetti pled no contest to a charge of disturbing the peace and received a nineteen-day sentence to be served at Alameda County's Santa Rita Prison. In a statement read to the judge he said:

The purpose of the demonstration was to stop war. Its purpose was to block the entrance to war. The motives of the demonstrators were pure and the action was totally non-violent. It was a legitimate expression of political dissent and I believe such dissent must not be suppressed and prosecuted in a society that calls itself free.

In prison Ferlinghetti worked in the laundry and kept a journal. Of his first day in jail he wrote: "Rehabilitate us, please . . . first rough impression of everybody's first time in jail: suddenly realizing what 'incarcerated' really means, paranoid fear of the unknown, fear of not knowing what's going to happen to your body . . . barbed wire fences and watchtowers . . . poor man's concentration camp?"

Nor could the FBI have been pleased with the poet's *Tentative Description of a Dinner Given to Promote the Impeachment of President Eisenhower*, written back in the mid-1950s, or the political tract *Tyrannus Nix* on President Nixon. Nor, if they studied the City Lights press book list as the years passed, would the FBI agents find anything to gladden their hearts.

Ferlinghetti, the incurable rabble-rouser, would never settle down. His own childhood had been anything but settled. Like Gregory Corso, he grew up with strangers, tossed from hand to hand, meeting his mother and older brothers for the first time when he was almost eleven years old. Born in Yonkers, New York, on March 24, 1919, Ferlinghetti is the son of an immigrant from the Lombardy region of Italy and a mother of French-Portuguese and Sephardic Jewish extraction. His father died of a heart attack several months before birth, and his mother, unable to cope with her grief and handle a newborn child, was soon placed in the state hospital in Poughkeepsie, New York, where she remained for five years. His older brothers were sent to a boardinghome in Ossining. Lawrence lived with an aunt who took him to France to stay with her relatives. There he learned to speak French, but he was soon back in New York where Aunt Emily worked as a maid for the Bislands, a wealthy family in the Bronxville suburb of New York. One day she left the sprawling mansion, never to return. A week earlier she had given her nephew a copy of *Little Lord Fauntleroy*, the story of a poor American boy who inherits a great English fortune. This was the first book Ferlinghetti ever read in its entirety.

Presley and Anna Lawrence Bisland took the young boy into their family. It wasn't long before Ferlinghetti began exploring the library filled with leather-bound volumes of Sir Walter Scott, Longfellow, James Russell Lowell, and Whittier. By the time his mother came to visit him, he had read many of the Greek and Roman classics.

Meeting his family after so many years was an emotionally demanding experience. He was given the choice of staying with the Bislands or returning to his natural mother. He chose to stay with the life he knew. In 1971, he wrote:

I lawrence ferlinghetti
wrought from the dark in my mother long ago

born in a small back bedroom—
In the next room my brother heard
the first cry,
many years later wrote me—
"Poor Mom—No husband—No Money—pop Dead—
How she went through it all—"
Someone squeezed my heart
to make it go
I cried and sprang up
Open eye Open heart where
do I wander

After high school Ferlinghetti entered the University of North Carolina at Chapel Hill, hoping to eventually become a journalist. When he graduated from college in 1941, Carl Sandburg gave the commencement address. Ferlinghetti wrote of the great populist poet: "He cast a spell. He spoke of ours as the 'bridged generation,' one foot in one war, the other in the second one."

Ferlinghetti served in the navy during World War II. He earned an M.A. at Columbia University, taking courses from some of the same professors who taught Allen Ginsberg. In 1948 he went to Paris on the GI Bill and attended the Sorbonne, from which he received a doctorate. His poetry would often reflect the years in the French capital where he saw himself as living the expatriate experience in the manner of Ernest Hemingway and Henry Miller. In his first book, *Pictures of the Gone World*, he wrote:

In Paris in a loud dark winter
              when the sun was something in
                            Provence
when I came across the poetry
              of René Char
I saw Vaucluse again
              in a summer of sauterelles
its fountain full of petals . . .

One of the most recurrent images I have of North Beach is that of Ferlinghetti walking down to the Caffe Puccini to have a morning coffee and read the *New York Times*. Often I'd be sitting in the Caffe Roma, directly across the street, and observe him at a table, engrossed in the paper. Watching him sit there, I think of how he used to tell me of the long hours he spent at the Café Mabillon in Paris, back when he lived there on the GI bill and rented a place in Montmartre for next to nothing. "I was living the expatriate myth," he would say, although it did not sound mythical at all.

After his coffee, he walks down to City Lights Bookstore, still in the same location after thirty-four years, the modern towers of the financial district a block or two closer than back in the 1950s. Once there he retreats into his office, where he spends several hours working on publishing matters with his co-editor Nancy Peters. It is, as he wrote in *One Thousand and One Fearful Words for Fidel Castro*, mostly a "quiet life."

Yet, all the years I have known him he is on the move, either to a literary colloquium in Berlin, a conference in Paris, or a reading at several Eastern universities. When we first met, back in 1975, he usually seemed to be in between trips. "I'm off to Europe," he would say, or "Greenpeace is having a protest up north. I've got to go." On other occasions his trip from North Beach merely meant a walk down to Union Square for an anti-nuclear rally. "I'm going to a Kerouac conference up in Quebec," he told me in September 1987. "I wouldn't go except that they're paying my way. And I've never been there before."

In 1959, with the Beat Generation in full bloom, he wrote in his notebook: "Beat Generation writings are vituperations—the only thing that will stand will be the narrative 'i'—whether in prose or poetry—the voice of him sounding thru the American experience, first Whitman, then Thomas Wolfe, then Kerouac. . . ." It was from Whitman, a shaper of the free man in poetry and in American life, that Ferlinghetti found his most powerful and sustaining source.

Autobiography begins:

I am leading a quiet life
in Mike's Place every day
watching the champs
of the Dante Billiard Parlor
and the French pinball addicts.
I am leading a quiet life
on Lower East Broadway.
I am an American.

I was an American boy.
I read the American Boy Magazine
and became a boy scout
in the suburbs.
I thought I was Tom Sawyer
catching crayfish in the Bronx river
and imagining the Mississippi.

The "i" dominates, and this poem of direct relationships continues on in its reflection of American life and values in the mid-
1950s. Everything flows smoothly. No jarring notes enter into the
picture. It really is "a quiet life," which slowly begins to leap out
of North Beach and the familiar surroundings of the poet's neighborhood into Whitman's America, where:

I have ridden superhighways
and believed the billboard's promises
Crossed the Jersey Flats
and seen the Cities of the Plains . . .

On the evening of the twenty-fifth anniversary of City Lights
Booksellers and Publishers in 1978, I took 250 mics of LSD with
poet Steven Schwartz. We had been at the party along with what
seemed like every other poet within five hundred miles. As the
acid took effect, we found our way up to the penthouse restaurant
in the Bank of America Building, high above North Beach. After
an hour there, in which I remained calm, I began to feel as if I was
in the waiting room of a mortuary. I ran down to the streets and
my apartment where I placed a call to my parents. My mother
said, "Go to Lawrence Ferlinghetti. You can trust him. He will
help you."
    I hung up the phone and ran to the Old Spaghetti Factory,
where the party had been held. It had ended an hour earlier.
Everyone had long since gone home. Then I began making my
way to Ferlinghetti's flat on Francisco Street. Halfway there, the
buildings on either side began to melt. As I came nearer, they
turned to what seemed like ice. This presented quite a problem.
As the sensation of sliding increased and Ferlinghetti's apartment
receded toward some ultimate ice flow, I somehow managed to
keep my composure and find my way to his flat. I knocked on the
door, holding one hand against my heart, which felt as if it were

an independent entity that wanted to jump out of my body. When the door opened, Ferlinghetti stared at me with his pale blue eyes. "What's the matter, Neeli? Why are you shaking like that?"

"I dropped some acid and I can't control myself. I don't know what to do."

"Well, come on in," he said. "Lots of people have bad trips. It's not anything to worry about. Do you remember I told you about the trip I took in Mexico when I was at Tepotzlan? I got these magic mushrooms from an old Indian woman who lived there. I rode a little Zapatista horse into the sunset. It was like a sunset that never ends. Some friends were with me. As night came we kept on riding through the valley. It was like an endless night."

His words were comforting. I walked up the stairwell and entered the hall leading to his kitchen.

"Come in back. We've got some friends over. All friends of City Lights." He put his arm around me and said, "You're one of the family . . . you can stay here tonight. My son Lorenzo is at his mother's in Bolinas."

Listening to him, I managed to regain some control. I walked into the kitchen to find his girlfriend, Paula Lillevand, sitting at the table with the printer Jack Stauffacher and his wife, Josephine. As a place was made, Ferlinghetti handed me a telegram from Allen Ginsberg congratulating City Lights on its anniversary. Halfway through the telegram, I began shaking uncontrollably. I got up from the table and went to Lorenzo's room.

At first I lay quietly on his bed with some music playing. When the music began to sound threatening, as if sending out murderous messages, I turned the radio off. Next I watched an "I Love Lucy" re-run on the small TV set next to Lorenzo's bed. This was innocent fun until Lucy and Ricky turned toward me and pointed their fingers accusingly. Lucy said, "You're nothing. Do you hear me, nothing." I flicked off the television set and ran into the hallway. By the time I got to the kitchen I realized that all the guests had left and that Ferlinghetti was asleep. I stood in the hallway for awhile and turned on a light. I decided to return to Lorenzo's room. Just then a wave of paranoia swept over me as I felt a commanding, invisible presence.

"NEELI! CAN YOU HEAR ME?"

"Who is it?" I asked.

"THIS IS THE VOICE OF LSD. THE ONLY WAY YOU

CAN RELEASE YOURSELF FROM THIS TRIP IS TO KNOCK ON FERLINGHETTI'S DOOR AND BEG HIS FORGIVENESS FOR MAKING FUN OF HIM BEHIND HIS BACK."

"But I didn't mean anything. I do imitations of everybody."

"BEG FOR HIS FORGIVENESS!"

I started for the door to his bedroom. My hand began to reach the doorknob, but I mustered the strength to pull it back.

"YOU'LL BE SORRY," the voice warned.

Struggling toward the kitchen, I fell on all fours and made my way to the telephone. I glanced at the clock: 3:00 A.M. I got information and asked for a drug-crisis line. After fourteen rings, a tired voice answered.

"I took acid and am having a bad trip. What should I do?"

"Take a warm bath and go to bed," a compassionate voice advised with only a hint of annoyance.

I did as I was told and lay peaceably in Lorenzo's room. Before falling asleep, I had an image of Ferlinghetti as captain of a ship filled with unruly writers. There were famous poets, infamous ones, unknown North Beach street people, all of whom had benefited from the stability of this man from Bronxville. My last image was of him steering the boat under the Golden Gate Bridge and out onto the open sea. Then I fell asleep. When I awoke in the morning, he and Paula were sitting at the kitchen table drinking coffee. They invited me to join them.

"That must have been some trip," Ferlinghetti said.

Typical of the way he relates to the world around him, Ferlinghetti once explained to me the impression he had when he first saw San Francisco from the ferryboat that brought him across the bay from Oakland in 1951. He came from several years in Paris and a brief stopover on the East Coast, which he found alien and depressing, even though he had grown up there. From what he had heard of San Francisco, it sounded like the kind of place he would like. It was a city of white buildings back then. There weren't many skyscrapers. He told me that San Francisco reminded him of a Mediterranean port, a place like Tunis. He said that the whiteness of the buildings reflecting the sun was something he would never forget. It looked like a place he wanted to live in.

He left the ferryboat and walked down Market Street, one of

the main thoroughfares, with trolley cars, wide sidewalks, and big department stores. It didn't take him long to find the Italian quarter of North Beach whose bakeries, Basque restaurants, and espresso cafés added up to an atmosphere that reminded Ferlinghetti of Paris. I guess the availability of cheap red wine and French bread made him want to stay in the city. Largely due to his publication of Allen Ginsberg's *Howl and Other Poems*, the neighborhood became a center for Whitman's wild children. The activity generated by those poets, artists, and bohemians of the 1950s lingers on in San Francisco and throughout the world.

In his lyrical poems, Ferlinghetti shares with e.e. cummings and William Carlos Williams a care for the way a poem lies on the page. There is a haunting, opaque quality to his poems, as if the speaker is looking at the world from a distance, over an unbridgeable gulf. The poems are direct gateways to a rare world of angelic and satanic impulses that gently merge, sometimes so subtly that it might take two or three readings before one says, "That is a damn good poem . . ." which is what happens whenever I read poems from *Pictures of the Gone World*. They are poetic telegrams from the imagination of a man who treads quietly on the great themes poets have always dealt with—those abstracts such as beauty, death, love, and happiness. When these poem/telegrams succeed, they assume an authority more readily evident in poems where a larger scope or ambition has moved the poet. Ferlinghetti deals with death in much the same disarming manner as e.e. cummings did in *Buffalo Bill's*. . . . He writes,

> The world is a beautiful place
> to be born into
> if you don't mind some people dying
> all the time
> or maybe only starving
> some of the time . . .

He ends the poem on the same straightforward note, showing us people,

> . . . and going swimming in rivers
> on picnics
> in the middle of the summer
> and just generally

<pre>
                   "living it up"
    Yes
       but then right in the middle of it
                              comes the smiling

                   mortician.
</pre>

I am tempted to find a secret opening into the heart of the language, one that would lead me into the poet's thinking processes. It is easy to ignore the originality of his muted language that looks at the world with spareness and clarity.

Ferlinghetti meets Walt Whitman in many ways. It was no accident that he published Whitman's *An American Primer*, believing it to be an important articulation of the nineteenth-century poet's ideas concerning American English. Whitman never saw it as a finished document. The philosophy in it is purely populist in nature. When confronted with a word like "spiritual" he usually ducks, but in the *Primer* we find, "Bodies are all spiritual.—All words are spiritual—nothing is more spiritual than words." Whitman did not intend to write a dogmatic, proto-religious treatise. His purpose expressed itself in the phrase, "The Americans are going to be the most fluent and melodious voiced people in the world—and the most perfect users of words.—Words follow character—nativity, independence, individuality." That is a concept that Ferlinghetti found exciting. Even more to his liking, I believe, is the last sentence in the *Primer* where Whitman called for new words "that would give that taste of identity and locality which is so dear in literature."

In the poem *Starting from San Francisco*, Ferlinghetti is consciously thinking of Whitman's *Starting from Paumonak*, the tip of land at the end of Long Island. Whitman expressed the intent of his vision and how it will manifest itself in a great American epic: "I will sing the song of companionship, / I will show what alone must finally compact these . . ." and goes on to express an optimistic vision of the awakening American land and civilization. Themes embodied in *Leaves of Grass*—the open road and the American poet as recorder of the general impulses of the land—come alive in Ferlinghetti's poem. Rather than beginning in the East, however, Ferlinghetti takes us from San Francisco back across Whitman's broad, expansive land. And, rather than seek out companionship, Ferlinghetti is alone, alienated. He will find little to celebrate on this journey and much to think about as he gathers the disparate images of American life around him.

Here I go again
crossing the country
(back to my old
lone wandering)
All night Eastward . . . Upward
over the Great Divide . . .

.   .   .   .   .

Do they have a Classified Section
as in phonebooks
as in the back of the Bibles here?

In lines that lead back to Whitman's *Out of the Cradle Endlessly Rocking*, Ferlinghetti writes:

The world is a Winter farm—
Cradle we rocked out of—
Prairie schooners into Pullmans,
their bright saloons sheeted in oblivion—. . .

Starting from San Francisco concludes with the question, "Who stole America?" followed by, "Myself I saw in the window reflected." As with Ginsberg, in much of his poetry Ferlinghetti finds that the promise of a great, visionary American civilization has been betrayed.

Beginning with *A Coney Island of the Mind*, Ferlinghetti wrote poems that have a tone reminiscent of the nineteenth-century poets, with the added touch of humor he discovered in Sandburg and through his own innate character. His poem, *I Am Waiting*, reminds me of Whitman's more rhapsodic moments:

I am waiting for my case to come up
and I am waiting
for a rebirth of wonder
and I am waiting for someone
to really discover America
and wail . . .

Late in August 1987 I joined Ferlinghetti at the Caffe Puccini, hoping he would agree to write an introduction to my forthcoming book of poems. "Be firm," my editor said, "and don't take no for an answer. Let Lawrence know that you want a good, serious discussion of your work, one that will trace your progress from a younger poet to a mature one."

I sat down at his table, directly under a portrait of the famed composer after whom the café is named, and said that my book would be published in the spring. "It's an important one for me," I said, "and will be over 135 pages. That's the kind of book I have always wanted. I would be honored if the introduction were to be written by you, one that would really probe my work."

Ferlinghetti agreed to it and asked me to give him the manuscript when I felt it was complete. Loosening up, I told him how much I had enjoyed *Over All the Obscene Boundaries*, his latest collection of poems and translations. His eyes brightened as he put aside his *New York Times*. "You know, I didn't receive any reviews for that book. I'm happy you like it."

"Why doesn't someone put together a collection of your lyrical poems?" I suggested. "Not the political ones, but those poems from *Pictures of the Gone World*, *A Coney Island of the Mind*, and your last few books that really demonstrate your ear for language."

Ferlinghetti suggested that I write to New Directions and see if they'd be interested in editing such a volume. We agreed to call the book *The Lyrical Ferlinghetti*. I went on to tell him that I thought many of his political poems, no matter how well intentioned they were, do not measure up to his shorter, lyrical works. "I like the ease with which you express emotions in some of those early poems. Many of the political works are tracts and have no sustained poetic power," I said.

Leaving him, I mentally listed the reasons why I liked his lyrical work. For one thing they convey direct, concrete images in a musical, reflective language. Also, they have a strangely pictorial quality without straining for an image. The spacing of the poems on the page gives an air of freedom to the lines and often makes the images come alive more forcibly than if they were all placed on the left-hand margin. The unique spacing serves to emphasize some of the phrases and downplay others. Then I recalled what he had told me when I was working on his biography, that he had conceived his first book as if he was putting together a gallery exhibition. "That's why I chose the title *Pictures of the Gone World*," he had said.

Ferlinghetti's lyrical poems explore an interior world, much like the surrealists he had studied while living in France. His language suggests notions of insurmountable loss, magical landscapes, and the unanswerable questions evoked by love and death. They are a sweet admixture of himself and such older writers as W. B. Yeats and Jacques Prevert. Strains of e.e. cummings can be seen in the early poems as well.

One of the first poets I met in the North Beach literary community was Jack Hirschman, whom I had known in Los Angeles as a teacher at the University of California. Tall, with a walrus mustache and long hair flowing down to his shoulders, he grew up in New York. Both scholar and accomplished poet, he greeted me with, "I'm on the street now." "And I'm right behind you," I answered.

Within a few months of our meeting, we were both involved in various literary projects, but mostly we sat around the Caffe Trieste reading our latest poems and listening to the works of fellow poets. One of the topics of discussion that occupied us all was how to get Ferlinghetti involved in our own readings and publications. When we revived *Beatitude*, a poetry journal founded by Bob Kaufman and William Margolis in 1959, Ferlinghetti submitted poetry and encouraged us to keep the magazine going, warning us not to make it too fancy. The magazine had always been mimeographed. The whole idea was to provide a real alternative to the academic journals.

Shortly after I moved to San Francisco in 1975, I sat down with Harold Norse at the Caffe Trieste. Ferlinghetti walked inside and took his place in the coffee line. He wore a faded blue work shirt and a pair of Levi's with an American-flag patch sewn sideways on the lower left leg of his trousers. He glanced over at Norse and nodded in recognition. They had known one another since their Paris days in the 1950s, and City Lights had recently published Norse's *Hotel Nirvana*.

Immediately I wanted to be introduced, thinking that the poet-publisher would say something positive concerning the huge manuscript of poems I had sent him a few days earlier. It was a collection of short poems, called *Songs for the Zen Roshi*, peppered with line drawings I had done to illustrate the text. Norse thought it entirely plausible that he would come and sit with us. I kept trying to come up with ways I might bring up the subject of my manuscript, but could think of none. I almost panicked as he picked up his cappuccino from the counter and began slowly sauntering in our direction. The closer he came, the more his round blue eyes beamed. Almost everyone in the café was aware of his presence. I felt a definite change in the mood of the European tourists sitting at the table next to us, and in the way the younger poets, who had gathered at a table near the jukebox, began to shift. No wonder, in later years, I would hear him say to admirers, "I'm not Ferlinghetti. I just look like him. He left an hour ago." By nature, he is a shy person, despite his fame. Even in his poetry he remains guarded, rarely writing confessional verse. Typical of his sense of humor is the title *Mock Confessional*. In the poem he humorously plays around with his autobiography:

. . . Anyway I hear people are wondering about me
and I've written this to clear the air
especially since
people who read my books
don't read other books . . .

But I wasn't thinking of his shyness or his confessionals as he stood near us. Norse invited him to sit down and introduced us, saying, "Lawrence, I'd like you to meet Neeli Cherry. He's just come up from Los Angeles where he was a friend of Bukowski's." He sat down and said hello in a low voice that put me somewhat at ease. "Why did you send all those poems? What am I supposed to do with them?"

"Publish them," I said.

Norse turned to Ferlinghetti: "Lawrence, you ought to get to know Neeli. He published *Laugh Literary* with Bukowski in L.A."

That got him started on Bukowski. He told us that City Lights was doing really well with Bukowski's books. Ferlinghetti wanted to handle more of them, but knew Bukowski had a good thing going with Black Sparrow.

I told him a few of my Bukowski stories, including the time Harold Norse dressed down the "dirty old man" when we were visiting Norse at his place out in Venice Beach. "It was incredible," I said. "Norse knew all the tricks of the alcoholic and chastised Bukowski for using a body bag full of them."

"We had Bukowski up here. He came to do a reading," Ferlinghetti said. "He came with his girlfriend, Linda King. They both acted wild. I think that we had a busted door and a shattered window by the time they left." He grinned and then started laughing.

I told him about the time Bukowski said he had been to a party and the host showed him a window that Robert Creeley had busted when he had gotten drunk. According to Bukowski, they asked Creeley to autograph the wall next to the window and made a big deal about how great it was. "When I shattered their goddamn window," Bukowski said, "they called the cops."

"You can sure tell funny stories," Ferlinghetti said. "But don't send any more poetry. We just can't use it."

When I returned home to a dark, cold room in the apartment of a retired service-station owner who sat in the kitchen and drank vodka all day long, I looked through a copy of my manuscript and realized that I had erred in sending it out. I had written the poems in a mad rush in response to a visit to the San Francisco Zen Center. I had gone there to learn about meditation. The Roshi, Richard Baker, looking over the crowd of one hundred assembled before him, pointed a finger at me, and said, "I know who you are, you're the great wiggler."

He was right; I could not stop fidgeting. When he asked why I had come, I said it was because I wanted to be the Roshi. He invited me to take his place on the dais, but I declined.

While having dinner with Ferlinghetti in North Beach one evening in 1976, I told him that someone should write his biography.

"Who'd want to read about me?" he replied.

"Lots of people," I said. "You could probably find a publisher easily."

On the spot we agreed that I would be his biographer. But he would not agree to an authorized biography. "I think you should be free of that," he said. "If it's authorized, then I have to be more involved. I want you to have a free hand." As it turned out, however, Ferlinghetti gave generously of his time, taking me to out-of-town readings and to his cabin in Big Sur.

I was working at the time as a staff writer for *City* magazine, edited by journalist and sometime San Francisco mayoral candidate Warren Hinckle, who made most of his editorial decisions in the bars of North Beach. My job consisted of sitting around the magazine office on Pacific Street, the old Barbary Coast, and waiting for an assignment, which usually meant a short book review. Meanwhile, I wondered who would publish the projected biography.

I sat in the Trieste going over some notes on my new enterprise when a short, curly-haired guy two tables down asked: "Are you from New York?" I told him that I came from Southern California. "That's hard to believe," he said. "You talk and move like a New Yorker." He had been observing me for the past week or so, he said. He moved to my table and introduced himself.

"I'm Jerry Rubin," he said.

"Jerry Rubin the anti-war protester?" I asked.

He nodded affirmatively and said he had heard that I was a poet. He wanted to know how I made a living. I told him I was collecting unemployment, but it would soon run out. In passing, I mentioned the Ferlinghetti project. "That's a good idea," Rubin said. "No one's ever done a book on Ferlinghetti. I think people would buy it. Do you have a publisher?"

"Not yet," I replied.

He went over to the telephone hanging by the front door of the café and dialed his agent in New York, a man named John Brockman. After talking with Brockman a few minutes, Rubin motioned me over.

"I like the idea of a Ferlinghetti biography," the agent said. "Can you tell me exactly what you have in mind?"

I explained my idea for the book, that I wanted to write it in a way that young people could read it, just as they can Ferlinghetti's poetry. Brockman said, "Yeh, I like that idea. Sounds hot." He believed he could sell the book, even though he had little experience in literary matters. "When can you send something?" he asked.

I told him that I would need two weeks to write a proposal. Ten days later, having written nothing, I stayed up all night at the *City* magazine offices and composed a seven-page justification for the biography, working on pure instinct.

The agent liked what I sent him and said he would get back to me. A few weeks later, I learned that Doubleday had accepted my proposal. Immediately, I began taping interviews with my subject, finding him either reticent or apt to give me one version of a story in the morning and an entirely different one in the afternoon. Somehow the manuscript began taking shape. I found that I worked best sitting in the St. Francis Hotel lobby, where I did much of my writing.

One of the most moving poems from *A Coney Island of the Mind* is about Beniamino Bufano's statue of Saint Francis when it sat in front of a small church in North Beach. I mentioned the poem to Bufano when he was a guest at my parents' home in 1960. He asked me to read it aloud. The poem is a lyric masterpiece of line spacing and word placing, creating a deep atmosphere of images that move in gentle unison down the page:

> They were putting up the statue
>   of Saint Francis
>   in front of the church
>   of Saint Francis
>   in the city of San Francisco
> in a little side street
>   just off the Avenue
>   where no birds sang
>   and the sun was coming up on time
>   in its usual fashion . . .

Few poets are as similar to their poems as is Ferlinghetti. Mild mannered, sometimes seeming to move and talk in slow motion, he projects the same hushed atmosphere as in his poetry. I recall a time in Big Sur when I stayed with him and his son, Lorenzo, at his Bixby Canyon cabin. I wanted to talk about poetry, North Beach, and Big Sur, but he plunged immediately into a one-on-one communication with the flora and fauna, as if I didn't exist. Only at the campfire, later in the evening, did he begin to talk at any length. I asked about his copy of *Leaves of Grass* in the cabin. Ferlinghetti told me that it was one of the few books he always kept in Big Sur for himself and his guests.

Soon after the stay in Bixby Canyon, I accompanied Ferlinghetti to a state teachers' convention in Sacramento, where he held his audience captive for more than an hour. He is the most popular modern poet among high-school teachers, precisely because of his accessibility. In my biography I referred to him as "an initiatory bridge" for younger poets. *Dog* is one poem that still remains a part of the high-school teacher's canon:

The dog trots freely in the street
and sees reality
and the things he sees
are bigger than himself
and the things he sees
are his reality
Drunks in doorways
Moons on trees
the dog trots freely thru the street
and the things he sees
are smaller than himself . . .

It is one of the "oral poems" included in *A Coney Island of the Mind,* works that Lawrence wrote specifically with public reading in mind. Ever since hearing Sandburg read in the 1930s, his commitment to oral presentation of poetry has been steadfast. In the 1950s he helped to revive the idea of public poetry events. James Broughton told me of returning to San Francisco and finding that poetry had come alive in the streets. This was a tradition handed down from Carl Sandburg and Vachel Lindsay, who became popular through their own public performances. Going back further there is Whitman, of course. The ending of Ferlinghetti's *Populist Manifesto* reads: "Whitman's wild children still sleeping there, / Awake and walk in the open air."

In 1975, not long after Harold Norse brought us together in the Caffe Trieste, I told Ferlinghetti he should do more public readings. "I can't," he said. "I'm retired."

"Seriously. We need you. I can get the Little Fox Theater anytime I want it. Francis Ford Coppola owns it now, and he will rent it out for readings. Each event will be a benefit like the one I'm planning for Bob Kaufman."

"Well, I don't know. You guys should make it on your own. You don't need me."

"Yes we do. You talk about being a populist poet. But you're always up in your office at the bookstore. You should be one of us."

It wasn't long before his name was on a poster with the new generation of poets who had landed in North Beach. His international fame made the backstage activity more exciting and our own readings more defined. When he came before the audience he wore a derby hat with a hand-penciled note on it: DIRECTOR OF ALIENATION. He then read a poem of the same title, beginning: "Looking in the mirror at Macy's / and thinking it's a subterranean plot / to make me feel like Chaplin . . ."

I felt he represented the outsider, much as Bukowski does in a different context. Bukowski had been silent about it, choosing to dive into a job for the U.S. Postal Service. Ferlinghetti, however, was at the center of poetic and cultural activity. When he first came to town, he was the San Francisco correspondent for *Art News*. He also taught at colleges. Soon he was a bookstore owner, publisher of poetry, and a famous poet in his own right. Unlike Bukowski, Ferlinghetti chose to dissociate himself from mainstream American culture through political activism and sees himself more as a gadfly to the established order than the alienated outsider.

I read quickly through Ferlinghetti's *Selected Poems* this morning and felt myself at ease with his language. It is not difficult to become absorbed by his music. He makes us feel comfortable, more at home with ourselves and the world. What intrigues me most in his writing are those poems that appear as pictures of life, or as he wrote of Jacques Prevert: he is more "see-er" than seer. I think of *The Old Italians Dying*, a poem about North Beach in the process of change, one I gave to the daughter of an eighty-year-old Italian who had lived across the hall from me and who had put a gun to his head one morning, not wanting to be a burden in his old age:

You have seen them sitting there
waiting for the bocci ball to stop rolling
waiting for the bell
                    to stop tolling & tolling
for the slow bell
                    to be finished tolling
telling the unfinished *Paradiso* story
as seen in an unfinished phrase
                    on the face of a church

as seen in a fisherman's face
in a black boat without sails
making his final haul

Soon after Ferlinghetti wrote the poem, he sent Allen Ginsberg a copy. In response, Ginsberg wrote a note praising the poem for its humor. "It's not meant to be humorous," Ferlinghetti complained. "Allen is missing the point." Nancy Peters, co-editor at City Lights, tried to explain that Ginsberg meant well. "The poem does have a lot of humor, Lawrence." She turned to me and asked what I thought. "Yeh, it does. You've made a good balance between humor and tragedy." We emphasized that there had never been such a beautiful tribute to North Beach.

One day while tacking up an announcement for a poetry reading on a utility pole in North Beach, two policemen grabbed my posters and led me into a paddy wagon. "It's against the law to be doing that," the older, red-faced cop sneered. While I sat in the paddy wagon in front of the North Beach station, Ferlinghetti and Nancy Peters walked by. "What're you doing in there?" Ferlinghetti asked. "I broke the law . . . apparently." Ferlinghetti talked of his arrest years earlier because of an outstanding warrant for handling allegedly obscene comic books at City Lights. He had come to the police station to check on a traffic citation, and the officer on duty looked up his name and found the old warrant. The matter had been settled long before, but he still spent several hours locked up. When he had told them that he was the owner of City Lights Bookstore down on Columbus Avenue, only two blocks away, they said that they had never heard of the place.

As for me, I managed to call the mayor's office when I got to the county jail and was soon released. The next day I appeared in court. The judge threw the matter out and chastised the police for the arrest. I went back to North Beach and celebrated by buying a stack of books at City Lights. Ferlinghetti was up at his desk on the balcony of the store, working. He leaned over and waved.

"Ferlinghetti's not wild," a young poet told me as we walked along Columbus Avenue.

"Maybe not," I said, "but think of all those times he either led or joined protests or walked picket lines and stood at the forefront of unpopular causes."

"Yeh, I guess you're right," she said.

"Just being a poet kind of makes you somewhat wild," I continued. "Look at us. We don't exactly live regular lives."

She nodded in agreement. We walked on and I thought of how Ferlinghetti, long before we met, had spoken to me in those early poems. I had called him "an initiatory bridge," thinking mostly of how I and my friends had experienced his poems back in 1958 and 1959.

My drama teacher had read *Thanatopsis* by William Cullen Bryant to us, and I stood up to say it was okay, but I had a modern poem on death.

Mr. Briggs grew furious. Then he issued the challenge to bring the poem before the class. "We'll see just how good it is," he said.

I came to class the next day with *A Coney Island of the Mind* and launched into a recital of *Sometime During Eternity*. It only took half a minute for Briggs to stop my reading.

"That's not a poem," he said, "and besides, it is insulting to your fellow students."

Then he called for a vote, but the class was wildly unanimous that I continue reading. That morning the entire poem was read.

In looking through *Leaves of Grass*, I wanted to find the poem that matched Ferlinghetti, not one of the loud or boisterous catalogues, nor such sweeping works as *Song of Myself* or *Out of the Cradle Endlessly Rocking*. It could be a descriptive poem, perhaps, but I finally settled on the last section of a short work, *Laws for Creation*. It reminds me both of Ferlinghetti's *Populist Manifesto* and of his life in general. Part of the strength of Ferlinghetti's poetry, from *Pictures of the Gone World* on, is his ability to deal with metaphysics in a direct manner, cutting away excess and complexity while never sacrificing his poetic instincts. Whitman does the same thing. In *Laws for Creation* he touches on the idea of the profanely divine, that sense that each of us redefines creation for ourselves:

What do you suppose creation is?
What do you suppose will satisfy the soul, except to walk free and own no superior?
What do you suppose I would intimate to you in a hundred ways, but that man or woman is as good as God?
And that there is no God any more divine than yourself?

In a few matter-of-fact lines, Whitman sums up his entire philosophy of life. They are part of the poetic workshop that one finds embedded in Whitman's epic poem, one that always remains open and accessible. Part of Ferlinghetti's attraction to Whitman was in his recognition of the nineteenth-century poet's position both as poetic innovator and as teacher. Ferlinghetti's own work fits easily into those two categories. I can picture him reciting the lines from his poem *Endless Life*:

Endless the splendid life of the world
Endless its lovely living and breathing
its lovely sentient beings
seeing and hearing Feeling and thinking . . .